ARCO
MASTER THE
PUBLIC SAFETY
DISPATCHER/
911 OPERATOR
EXAM

3rd Edition

A **nelnet** COMPANY

About Peterson's

To succeed on your lifelong educational journey, you will need accurate, dependable, and practical tools and resources. That is why Peterson's is everywhere education happens. Because whenever and however you need education content delivered, you can rely on Peterson's to provide the information, know-how, and guidance to help you reach your goals. Tools to match the right students with the right school. It's here. Personalized resources and expert guidance. It's here. Comprehensive and dependable education content—delivered whenever and however you need it. It's all here.

Petersons.com/publishing

Check out our Web site at www.petersons.com/publishing to see if there is any new information regarding the test and any revisions or corrections to the content of this book. We've made sure the information in this book is accurate and up-to-date; however, the test format or content may have changed since the time of publication.

For more information, contact Peterson's, 2000 Lenox Drive, Lawrenceville, NJ 08648; 800-338-3282; or find us on the World Wide Web at www.petersons.com/about.

Stephen Clemente, President; Bernadette Webster, Director of Publishing; Therese DeAngelis, Editor; Jill Schwartz, Production Editor; Ray Golaszewski, Manufacturing Manager; Linda M. Williams, Composition Manager

ISBN-13: 978-0-7689-2817-4
ISBN-10: 0-7689-2817-6

Printed in the United States of America

10 9 8 7 6 5 4 3 2 1   11 10 09

Third Edition

By producing this book on recycled paper (40% post consumer waste) 60 trees were saved.

Contents

Before You Begin

Congratulations! You have in your hands a powerful tool to ensure your best chances of getting a great score on the Public Safety Dispatcher/911 Operator exam. By working through this book, taking time to practice the sample exercises, and studying the various strategies and techniques for tackling various question types, you will put yourself at a significant advantage for achieving a top-notch score.

HOW TO USE THIS BOOK

This book is designed as a teach-yourself training course, complete with test-taking tips and strategies, exercises, and two full-length Practice Tests.

Part I is a review of jobs with the municipal (city), state, and federal governments and private industry. Each sector has its own requirements and tests, but as you will see, certain types of questions will appear on most civil service exams, regardless of the type of test you're taking. You'll review expert test-taking techniques and guidelines to help you prepare for your exam. You'll also find information on the various types of public safety dispatcher careers available, with descriptions of the typical dispatcher work environment, earnings potential, and the hiring process. If you are new to public safety dispatching, the number of job opportunities available in this field may surprise you. Did you know that almost 300,000 jobs in the United States are in the field of dispatching?

Part II is a review of the specific types of questions you're most likely to see on the public safety dispatcher exam. Because qualifying exams for public safety dispatchers vary greatly from state to state and from one municipality to another, we cannot predict exactly what question types you'll encounter on your exam. However, if you thoroughly review the test question types in this section of the book, you will be well prepared when you take the exam. We suggest you review this section carefully to get a good idea of where your strengths and weaknesses lie, so that you'll know where to focus your studies.

Part III provides two full-length practice tests, including detailed answer explanations for each question. These tests are closely patterned on actual public safety dispatcher exams. Time limits, level of difficulty, question styles, and scoring methods all conform to the examinations for which they are meant to prepare you.

Try to set aside the full amount of time for each exam and take it in one sitting, as you would on your actual test day. Time yourself, and stop working when time is up. Check your answers against the correct answers provided in the book. Carefully study all the answer explanations—even for questions you answered correctly. You'll develop a better understanding about how best to answer actual exam questions and the reasoning behind the correct answer choices.

Regardless of which test you think you'll be taking, try to get through all of the practice exercises and both of the full-length exams in this book. It may seem like a lot of extra work, but you never know where you may end up. You may be interested in a job with a local city government but end up working for a private company instead. Or perhaps the exam you are hoping to take will not be administered for another year, but another type of test is scheduled for next month. It's always best to be prepared.

The Appendixes at the end of the book provide information on finding and getting a job with the federal government or with a state, municipal, or local government. We also provide a glossary of definitions for some of the most important and frequently used terms you can expect to see when studying for your exam, and a list of 400 frequently misspelled words that you may encounter in the spelling section of your exam.

SPECIAL STUDY FEATURES

Master the Public Safety Dispatcher/911 Operator Exam is designed to be as user-friendly as it is complete. To this end, it includes two features to make your preparation more efficient.

Overview

Each chapter begins with a bulleted overview listing the topics covered in the chapter. This will allow you to quickly target the areas in which you are most interested.

Summing It Up

Each chapter ends with a point-by-point summary that reviews the most important items in the chapter. The summaries offer a convenient way to review key points

YOU'RE WELL ON YOUR WAY TO SUCCESS

You've made the decision to become a public safety dispatcher. *Master the Public Safety Dispatcher/911 Operator Exam* will help prepare you for the steps you'll need to take to achieve your goal—from scoring high on the exam to finding the best dispatcher or operator job for you. Good luck!

GIVE US YOUR FEEDBACK

Peterson's publishes a full line of resources to help guide you through the exam process. Peterson's publications can be found at your local bookstore or library, and you can access us online at www.petersons.com.

We welcome any comments or suggestions you may have about this publication and invite you to complete our online survey at www.petersons.com/survey. Or you can fill out the survey at the back of this book, tear it out, and mail it to us at:

Publishing Department
Peterson's, a Nelnet company
2000 Lenox Drive
Lawrenceville, NJ 08648

Your feedback will help us make your education and career dreams come true.

PART I

WORKING FOR THE GOVERNMENT

Jobs with Federal, State, and Local Governments

OVERVIEW

- Where the jobs are: Federal civilian employment
- The merit system
- Where the jobs are: State and local governments
- Where to find out about government job openings
- The format of the government job announcement
- Summing it up

Government service is one of the nation's largest sources of employment. About 1 in every 6 employed persons in the United States works in some form of civilian government service. Of those government employees, 5 out of 6 are employed by state or local governments. The remainder work for the federal government.

Government employees represent a significant portion of the nation's workforce. They are present in cities, small towns, and remote and isolated places such as lighthouses and forest ranger stations. A small number of federal employees even work overseas. In this chapter, we will outline the various types of careers available in the federal, state, and local governments of the United States.

WHERE THE JOBS ARE: FEDERAL CIVILIAN EMPLOYMENT

The federal government is the nation's largest employer, with nearly 3 million full-time civilian workers in the United States, including postal employees. Although the headquarters of most federal departments and agencies are in the Washington, D.C., area, nine out of ten federal jobs are located outside the nation's capital. Federal jobs exist throughout the United States—and throughout the world. In fact, approximately 90,000 federal employees work outside the United States, most of them in embassies or defense installations.

Many federal occupations are similar to jobs in the private sector, such as those in accounting, computer programming, and health care. Other types of employment opportunities are unique to the federal government, such as regulatory inspectors, Foreign Service officers, and Internal Revenue Service agents. More than 100 agencies and bureaus exist within the federal government, and each has specific employment needs. The numerous job opportunities with the federal government include careers in the executive, legislative, and judicial branches.

chapter 1

The executive branch employs the majority of federal workers. This includes the Office of the President, the cabinet departments, and about 100 independent agencies, commissions, and boards. The executive branch is responsible for administering federal laws, handling international relations, conserving natural resources, treating and rehabilitating disabled veterans, delivering U.S. mail, conducting scientific research, maintaining the flow of supplies to the Armed Forces, and administering other programs that promote the health and welfare of the people of the United States.

The Department of Defense, which includes the Joint Chiefs and the Departments of the Army, Navy, Air Force, and Marines, is the largest department in the executive branch of the federal government. It employs about 35 percent of all civilian government workers. Employees of the U.S. Postal Service account for another 25 percent of federal workers. Other federal jobs are distributed among other agencies in the government, including large employers such as the Department of Veterans Affairs, the Department of Homeland Security, and the Department of the Treasury.

Some agencies in the executive branch do not fall under the jurisdiction of these large departments. These independent agencies, such as the Social Security Administration, the National Aeronautics and Space Administration (NASA), and the Environmental Protection Agency (EPA), account for fewer than 200,000 federal jobs, but they should be considered when searching for government employment.

Federal civilian employment is also available in the legislative branch, which includes Congress, the Government Printing Office, the General Accounting Office, and the Library of Congress. The judicial branch, the smallest employer of the federal government, hires people for work within the courts system.

Professional Occupations

Because of its wide range of responsibilities, the federal government employs professional workers in a broad variety of occupational fields. Professional jobs account for approximately 90 percent of all federal civilian jobs. According to the Bureau of Labor Statistics, one third of all federal employees work in management, finance, or business.

Management

Upper-level managers are responsible for directing the activities of government agencies; mid-level managers supervise various government programs and projects. Senators and legislators are considered part of management because they are responsible for overseeing the executive branch of the government.

Finance and Business

Accountants and auditors with the federal government analyze financial reports and investigate government spending and inefficiencies. The General Accounting Office, the Internal Revenue Service, and the Department of the Treasury employ accounting experts and budget administrators.

Additional business experts work in purchasing, cataloging, storage, and supply distribution, which occurs on a large scale in the federal government. These include managerial and administrative positions—such as supply management officers, purchasing officers, and inventory management specialists—and a great number of specialized clerical positions. Most of these jobs are with the Department of Defense.

Professions Requiring Specialized Training

Another one third of federal workers include professionals who have earned a specialized degree, including lawyers, doctors, computer experts, scientists, and engineers. The majority of these employees work in life sciences, physical sciences, or social science.

Life Sciences

Biologists, geologists, and forest technicians determine the effectiveness of new medications, predict hurricanes, and prevent forest fires in national parks and other federally owned land. The federal government, mostly in the Departments of Agriculture and Interior, employs about 50,000 biological and agricultural science workers, many of whom work in forestry and soil conservation. Others administer farm assistance programs.

Physical Sciences

The Departments of Defense, Interior, and Commerce typically employ physical scientists such as chemists, physicists, meteorologists, and cartographers. Opportunities also exist for physical science technicians, meteorological technicians, and cartography technicians.

Approximately 80,000 federal employees are nurses, surgeons, and physicians who work in hospitals or in medical, dental, and public health services. Other occupations in this field include dieticians, technologists, and physical therapists. Technician and aide jobs include medical technicians, medical laboratory aides, and dental assistants. Health-care employees work primarily for the Veterans Administration; others work for the Department of Defense and the Department of Health and Human Services.

Social Sciences

Economists and other social science experts are employed throughout the government. Psychologists and social workers work primarily for the Veterans Administration; foreign affairs and international relations specialists typically find employment with the Department of State. Social insurance administrators are employed largely by the Department of Health and Human Services.

Engineering and Mathematics

Many government departments require the expertise of engineers to construct bridges, develop computer systems, and design spacecraft. The Department of Defense employs experts in electronics, surveying, and drafting. Computer software engineers and computer network administrators are necessary throughout the government to write computer programs, analyze data, and ensure that computer systems run smoothly.

Professional mathematicians, statisticians, mathematics technicians, and statistical clerks work in the federal government, primarily with the Departments of Defense, Agriculture, Commerce, and Health and Human Services.

Law

The federal government employs thousands of people in the legal field: attorneys, paralegals, passport examiners, and tax law specialists among many others. In addition, federal positions are available for claims examiners.

Other Professional Fields

Nearly 15 percent of all federal jobs consist of office and administrative support. Employees in this area assist management with administrative duties. All federal departments and agencies employ general clerical workers, such as information and record clerks and administrative assistants. Office machine operators, stenographers, clerk-typists, mail- and file-clerks, telephone operators, and workers in computer and related occupations are categorized as office support personnel. However, according to the Bureau of Labor Statistics, administrative support jobs are declining because of the increased use of automation and computers.

Some government workers are engaged in administrative work related to private business and industry. They arrange and monitor contracts with and purchase goods and services from companies in the private sector. Administrative occupations in this area include contract and procurement specialists, production control specialists, and Internal Revenue Service officers.

Eight percent of federal employees work in service occupations, including officers at federal prisons, criminal investigators, and health regulatory inspectors, many of whom are employed by the Departments of Justice or Agriculture. Local and state governments are the primary employers of firefighters, police officers, and prison guards.

Employment Requirements

Requirements for professional jobs with the federal government vary widely, from a postsecondary degree to a high school diploma. An undergraduate or advanced degree is usually required for occupations in physics, engineering, ecology, and law. Office clerk positions may not require a specific level of education or experience; other federal jobs may require some combination of education and experience for job consideration.

Prospective employees for administrative and managerial positions are usually not required to have knowledge of a specialized field. Instead, they must indicate a potential for future development by having obtained an undergraduate degree from a four-year college or by having responsible job experience. New employees usually begin as trainees and learn their duties on the job. Typical entry-level positions in management include budget analyst, claims examiner, purchasing specialist, administrative assistant, and personnel specialist.

Job seekers with a high school diploma or the equivalent can find entry-level government work as technicians, clerical workers, or aides/assistants. Many of these positions require no previous experience or training. Entry-level positions are usually trainee spots. Individuals with junior college or technical school training or who have specialized skills may enter these occupations at higher levels. Typical jobs include engineering technicians, supply clerks, clerk-typists, and nursing assistants.

Skilled-Labor Occupations

Skilled-labor occupations in fields such as construction, janitorship, and some service jobs provide full-time employment for nearly 300,000 federal workers. About 75 percent of these government workers are employed with the Department of Defense in naval shipyards, arsenals, Army depots, and in construction, harbor, flood control, irrigation, or reclamation projects. Others work for the Veterans Administration, the Postal Service, the General Services Administration, the Department of the Interior, and the Tennessee Valley Authority.

The largest single skilled-worker group consists of manual laborers. Many others are employed in machine tool and metalwork, motor vehicle operation, warehousing, and food preparation and service. The federal government employs workers in mainte-nance and repair work—such as electrical and electronic equipment installation and repair—and in vehicle and industrial equipment maintenance and repair. Each of these fields requires a range of skill levels and employs workers in a variety of occupations comparable to those in the private sector.

Although the federal government employs skilled workers in many different fields, about half are concentrated within a small number of occupations. The largest group consists of skilled mechanics, who work as air-conditioning, aircraft, automobile, truck, electronics, sheet metal, and general maintenance mechanics. Another large group is employed as painters, pipefitters, carpenters, electricians, and machinists. Others are warehouse workers, truck drivers, general laborers, janitors, and food service workers.

Employment Requirements

Prospective employees who have previous training in a skilled trade may apply for a position with the federal government at the journey level. Those with no previous training may apply for appointment to one of several apprenticeship programs. These programs generally last four years, during which trainees receive classroom and on-the-job training. After completing an apprenticeship, an employee is eligible for a journey-level position. A number of federal positions require little or no prior training or experience; these include janitors, maintenance workers, and messengers.

THE MERIT SYSTEM

More than 90 percent of jobs in the federal government fall under a merit system. The Civil Service Act, administered by the U.S. Office of Personnel Management (OPM), covers six out of ten federal titles. This act was passed by Congress to ensure that federal employees are hired based on individual merit and fitness. It provides for competitive examinations and the selection of new employees from among the most qualified applicants.

Some federal jobs are exempt from civil service requirements, either by law or by action of the OPM. However, most of these positions are covered by separate merit systems for other agencies, such as the Foreign Service of the U.S. Department of State, the Federal Bureau of Investigation (FBI), the Nuclear Regulatory Commission (NRC), and the Tennessee Valley Authority (TVA).

Earnings, Advancement, and Working Conditions

Several decades ago, most federal civilian employees were paid according to one of three major pay systems: the General Pay Schedule, the Federal Wage System, or the Postal Service Schedule. Today, however, new pay plans have been developed that are unique to their individual agencies. Because we are focusing specifically on public safety dispatcher positions, we will discuss only the General Pay Schedule and the Federal Wage System as they currently operate.

General Pay Schedule

Most federal workers are paid under the General Schedule (GS), a pay scale for workers in professional, administrative, technical, and clerical jobs, as well as for those working as guards and messengers. GS jobs are divided by the OPM into fifteen grades, according to the difficulty of duties and responsibilities and the knowledge, experience, and skills required of the workers in that pay grade. GS pay rates are set by Congress, and they apply to government workers nationwide. Pay rates are reviewed annually to determine whether they are comparable to salaries of equivalent workers in the private sector. They are generally subject to upward adjustment for regions where the cost of living is very high; in areas with a low cost of living, GS pay may exceed that of private-sector workers.

Most employees receive within-grade pay increases at one-, two-, or three-year intervals if their work is acceptable. Within-grade increases may also be given in recognition of high-quality service. Some managers and supervisors receive increases based on job performance rather than on time served in a specific grade level.

High school graduates with no related work experience usually start at the GS-2 level. Some who have specialized skills begin at grade GS-3. Graduates of two-year colleges and technical schools often begin at the GS-4 level; those who have a bachelor's degree and are appointed to professional and administrative jobs such as statisticians, economists, writers and editors, budget analysts, accountants, and physicists typically enter the government workforce at grades GS-5 or GS-7, depending on experience and academic record. A master's degree, Ph.D., or equivalent experience enables people to begin working for the government at the GS-9 or GS-11 level. Advancement to higher grades generally depends upon ability, work performance, and high-level job openings.

GENERAL SCHEDULE
(Range of Salaries)
Effective as of January 1, 2009

GS Rating	Low	High
1	$17,540	$21,944
2	19,721	24,815
3	21,517	27,970
4	24,156	31,401
5	27,026	35,135
6	30,125	39,161
7	33,477	43,521
8	37,075	48,199
9	40,949	53,234
10	45,095	58,622
11	49,544	64,403
12	59,383	77,194
13	70,615	91,801
14	83,445	108,483
15	98,156	127,604

The Federal Wage System

Most federal skilled laborers are paid according to the Federal Wage System. Under this system, craft, service, and manual workers earn hourly wages based on the local prevailing rates paid by private employers for similar work. As a result, the federal government wage rate for an occupation varies by locality. This commitment to meeting the local wage scale allows federal wage earners to bring home a weekly paycheck comparable to what they would earn in the private sector while receiving the benefits and security of a government job. The federal wage earner has the best of all possible worlds in this regard. Federal government employees work a standard 40-hour week. Employees who are required to work overtime may receive premium rates for the additional time or compensatory time off later. Most employees work 8 hours a day, five days a week, Monday through Friday. In some cases, the nature of the work requires a modified workweek. Annual earnings for most full-time federal workers are not affected by seasonal factors.

Federal employees earn thirteen days of vacation time each year during their first three years of service, twenty days each year until the end of their fifteenth year of service, and twenty-six days each year of service thereafter. In addition, workers who are members of military reserve organizations are granted up to fifteen days of paid military leave annually for training purposes. Although federal layoffs are uncommon, any federal worker who is laid off is entitled to unemployment compensation similar to what is available for employees in the private sector.

Other benefits available to most federal employees include a contributory retirement system, optional participation in low-cost group life and health insurance programs, which are partly supported by the government (as the employer), and training programs to develop maximum job proficiency and help workers achieve their highest potential. These training programs may be conducted in government facilities or at private educational facilities, at the government's expense.

WHERE THE JOBS ARE: STATE AND LOCAL GOVERNMENTS

State and local governments provide an enormous and expanding source of job opportunities in a wide variety of occupational fields. State and local government agencies in the United States employ about 15 million people; nearly three fourths of these employees work in units of local government, such as counties, municipalities, towns, and school districts. Job distribution varies greatly from that of federal government service. Defense, international relations and commerce, immigration, and mail delivery are virtually nonexistent in state and local governments. By contrast, state and local governments have a greater need for employees in education, health, social services, transportation, construction, and sanitation.

Educational Services

About one half of all jobs in state and local governments fall under educational services. Employees in education work in public schools, colleges, and various extension services. About 50 percent of all education workers in state and local governments are instructional personnel. School systems, colleges, and universities also employ administrative personnel, librarians, guidance counselors, nurses, dieticians, clerks, and maintenance workers.

Health Services

After educational services, the next-largest field of state and local government employment is health services. This includes physicians, nurses, medical lab technicians, dieticians, kitchen and laundry workers, and hospital attendants.

Social services make up another aspect of health and welfare. The need for workers in welfare and human services departments has increased dramatically over the past few years. As the need grows, so do the opportunities for social workers and their affiliated administrative and support staff.

Government Control/Financial Activities

Another 1 million workers in state and local governments are employed in general governmental control and financial activities. These include chief executives and their staff workers, legislative representatives, and those in justice administration, tax enforcement and other finances, and general administration. These positions require lawyers, judges, court officers, city managers, property assessors, budget analysts, stenographers, and clerks.

Streets and Highways

Road construction and maintenance are major concerns for local and state governments. Building and improving roads improves the safety and efficiency of a community. Highway workers include civil engineers, surveyors, equipment operators, truck drivers, concrete finishers, carpenters, and construction laborers. In some areas of the nation, snow removers perform essential tasks. Toll collectors are usually state or county employees (unless they are employed by private firms working on behalf of a state or county). Municipal mass transit in and between cities and outlying suburbs is also the province of local government. A large and varied workforce is required to maintain and staff the vehicles, as well as to maintain the roadbeds and signaling systems.

Police and Fire Protection Services

More than 1 million people are employed in police and fire departments throughout the United States. Along with uniformed officers, local fire and police departments require the assistance of support staff, such as administrative, clerical, maintenance, and custodial personnel.

Miscellaneous State and Local Occupations

Local utilities, parks and recreation, sanitation, corrections, libraries, sewage disposal, and housing and urban renewal employ hundreds of workers in state and local governments. These jobs may require economists, electrical engineers, electricians, pipefitters, clerks, foresters, and drivers as employees.

Clerical, Administrative, Maintenance, and Custodial Workers

A great percentage of employment in local and state government agencies consists of clerical, administrative, maintenance, and custodial jobs. These include administrative assistants, data processors, IT specialists, office managers, fiscal and budget administrators, bookkeepers, accountants, carpenters, painters, plumbers, guards, and janitors, among many others.

Residents of a state or locality typically fill most positions in state and local governments because of residency requirements within each locality, although most agencies make exceptions for persons with skills that are in special demand.

Earnings

The job conditions and earnings of state and local government employees vary widely depending upon occupation and locality. Salaries vary from state to state and within each state because of differences in the prevailing wage level and the cost of living of each locality.

As with the federal government, a majority of state and local government positions are filled through some type of formal civil service test; that is, employees are hired and promoted based on merit. State and local government workers have the same protections as federal government workers: They cannot be refused employment because of race; they cannot be denied promotion because another individual made a greater political contribution; and they cannot be let go because the boss's son or daughter needs a job. The classification level of a particular position provides the salary base. Periodic performance reviews are standard. Nearly every group of employees has access to a union or other labor organization, but the functions and powers of these units vary greatly.

Benefits packages offered to state and local government employees differ widely. These workers often participate in retirement plans or the federal social security program, and health coverage is a common benefit. Local and state employees typically work a standard 40-hour week and may earn overtime pay or compensatory time off for additional hours of work.

WHERE TO FIND OUT ABOUT GOVERNMENT JOB OPENINGS

Most federal, state, and municipal units have recruitment procedures for filling civil service positions. Agencies have developed a number of methods to publicize job opportunities. Here are some suggestions on where you can look for a government job:

1. State Employment Offices. There are almost 2,000 state employment offices in the United States, each administered by the state in which it is located, with financial assistance from the federal government. These offices provide support for job seekers and employers. Each state employment office is named and organized differently, but their essential services are the same. You can find the address of the one closest to you in your telephone book or online.

2. Your state Civil Service Commission. Address your inquiry to the capital city of your state.

3. Your city Civil Service Commission. In cities, this commission is sometimes called by another name, such as the Department of Personnel—but you will be able to identify it in your telephone directory or online under the listing of city departments.

4. Your municipal building and your local library.

5. Complete listings are carried by newspapers such as *The Chief-Leader* (published in New York City) and by other city and statewide publications devoted to civil service employees. Many local newspapers also run a section on regional civil service news.

6. State and local agencies seeking competent employees will contact schools, professional societies, veterans' organizations, unions, and trade associations.

7. Go directly to school boards and boards of education, which employ the greatest number of all state and local personnel, for job openings in education.

You will find more in-depth information about this at the end of this book.

THE FORMAT OF THE GOVERNMENT JOB ANNOUNCEMENT

When a government position is open and a civil service examination will be administered for the position, a job announcement is posted (for federal jobs, announcements are posted on http://www.usajobs.gov). This announcement explains everything an applicant needs to know about the position. The announcement begins with the job title and salary. A typical announcement then describes the work, the location of the position, the education and experience requirements, the kind of examination applicants must take, and the system of rating. It may also refer to veteran preferences and age specifications. The announcement indicates which application form you should fill out, where to get the form, and where and when to file it.

Study each job announcement carefully. It will answer most of your questions about the position and will help you decide whether you are interested in and/or qualified for the job. Sample job announcements are included in a later chapter of this book.

Don't bother applying for a position and taking the required exam if you do not want to work in the community where the job is located. If the location of a job is unappealing to you, simply continue searching. Focus on positions that will give you an opportunity to work in a place of your choice. Keep in mind that a civil service job that is close to home gives you the additional advantage of receiving preference as a local resident.

The front page of a job announcement may include the words **Optional Fields**—or sometimes just the word **Options.** This means that you have a choice of whether to apply for a particular position in which you are especially interested. It usually means that the duties of various positions are quite different even though they bear the same broad title. A public relations clerk, for example, performs different tasks than a payroll clerk, although they are in the same general area of work.

Not every announcement has options; however, in each announcement, the precise duties are described in detail, usually under the heading **Description of Work.** Make sure that these duties fall within the range of your experience and ability.

Most job requirements indicate a **deadline for filing** an application. No application mailed past a deadline date will be considered. Others may include the phrase **No Closing Date** at the top of the first page. This means that instead of adhering to a set deadline, the hiring agency will accept applications for the position until its needs are met. In some cases, a public notice is issued when a certain number of applications have been received.

Every job announcement has a detailed section on **education and experience requirements** for the particular job and for the optional fields. Make sure that in both education and experience, you meet the minimum qualifications for the position being advertised. If you do not meet the given standards for one job, other job openings may be more suitable. If you are a military veteran and the job announcement does not mention **veteran preference,** it's a good idea to inquire whether such a provision exists in your state or municipality so that you can be sure you'll receive any preference offered. In some cases, preference is given only to disabled veterans; in some jurisdictions, surviving spouses of disabled veterans are given preference as well. All such information can be obtained through the agency that issues the job announcement.

Applicants may be denied examinations and eligible candidates may be denied appointments for any of the following reasons:

- making intentional false statements
- being deceptive or fraudulent in examination or appointment

- using intoxicating beverages to the extent that ability to perform the duties of the position is impaired

- conducting oneself in a criminal, villainous, dishonest, immoral, or notoriously disgraceful manner

The announcement describes the **kind of test** given for the particular position. Pay special attention to this section, because it describes what will be included in the written test and lists the specific subjects that will be tested. Sometimes sample questions are provided—and these can be extremely helpful in preparing for your test.

Usually, a job announcement states whether the examination is to be **assembled** or **unassembled.** In an assembled examination, applicants gather in the same place at the same time to take a written or performance test. In an unassembled examination, an applicant does not take a test; instead, he or she receives a rating based on education, experience, and records of previous achievements.

In an assembled competitive examination, all applicants for a position compete with one another—meaning that the higher your score, the better your chance of being appointed. (Competitive examinations are also administered to determine an existing employee's eligibility for promotion.)

Civil service written tests are graded on a scale of 1–100, with 70 usually considered a passing score.

Filling Out the Application Form

You've studied a job announcement carefully and you've decided that you want the position and are qualified for it. Your next step is to get an application form. The job announcement indicates how to acquire the application.

Overall, civil service application forms differ little between states and localities. The questions tend to be simple and direct, and they are designed to elicit as much information as possible about the applicant. Many prospective civil service employees have failed to get the job they wanted because of slipshod, erroneous, incomplete, misleading, or untruthful answers. Give each application serious attention—it is the first and most important step to getting the job you want.

Here, along with some helpful comments, are the questions you will see on the average application form (although not necessarily in this order):

- **Name of examination or kind of position for which applying.** This information appears in large type on the first page of the job announcement.

- **Optional job** (if mentioned in the announcement). If you wish to apply for an option, simply copy the title from the announcement. If you are not interested in an option, write *None.*

- **Primary place of employment for which applying.** The location of the position is usually mentioned in the announcement. The announcement may list more than one location in which the same job is available. If you would accept employment in any of the places, list them all; otherwise, list the specific place or places where you would be willing to work.

- **Name and address.** Provide your full name, including your middle name and/or maiden name if applicable.

- **Home and office phones.** If none, write *None.*

- **Legal or voting residence.** The state in which you vote is the one you list here.

- **Height without shoes, weight, sex.** Answer accurately.

- **Date of birth.** Give the exact day, month, and year of your birth.

- **Lowest grade or pay you will accept.** Although the salary is clearly stated in the job announcement, there may be another opening in the same occupation with less responsibility and a lower entrance salary. You will not be considered for a job paying less than the amount you provide as an answer to this question.

- **Will you accept temporary employment if offered you for (a) one month or less, (b) one to four months, (c) four to twelve months?** Temporary positions arise frequently. Decide whether you want to be available should one open up.

- **Will you accept less than full-time employment?** Part-time work comes up occasionally. Consider whether you want to accept such a position while waiting for a full-time position.

- **Were you in active military service in the Armed Forces of the United States?** Veterans' preference, if given, is usually limited to active service during the following periods: 12/7/41–12/31/46; 6/27/50–1/31/55; 6/1/63–5/7/75; 6/1/83–12/1/87; 10/23/83–11/21/83; 12/20/89–1/3/90; 8/2/90 to end of Persian Gulf hostilities.

- **Do you claim disabled veterans credit?** If you do, you have to show proof of a war-incurred disability compensable by at least 10 percent. This is done via certification by the Veterans Administration.

- **Special qualifications and skills.** Even though these are not directly related to the position for which you are applying, the agency requests information about licenses and certificates obtained for teacher, pilot, registered nurse, and so on. List your experience in machinery and equipment and whatever other skills you may have acquired. Also list any published writings, public speaking experience, membership in professional societies, and honors and fellowships you may have received.

- **Education.** List your entire educational history, including all diplomas, degrees, and special courses taken in any accredited or Armed Forces school. Also provide information regarding any additional college or graduate-level course credits you have earned.

- **References.** List the names of people who can provide information about you, including their occupation, business address, and contact information.

- **Medical history.** You are expected to have the physical and psychological capacity to perform the job for which you are applying. Standards vary, of course, depending on the requirements of the position. A physical handicap usually will not bar an applicant from a job unless the safety of the public is involved.

- **Work history.** Considerable space is allotted on the form for applicants to describe previous employment experiences. Examiners check these answers closely, so don't embellish or falsify your history. If you were ever fired, say so. It is better for you to state this openly than for the examiners to find out the truth from a former employer.

On the following pages are samples of a New York City Application for Examination and a state application from Louisiana.

DEPARTMENT OF CITYWIDE ADMINISTRATIVE SERVICES
DIVISION OF CITYWIDE PERSONNEL SERVICES
1 Centre Street, 14th floor   New York, NY 10007

APPLICATION FOR EXAMINATION

(Directions for completing this application are on the *back* of this form. Additional information is on the Special Circumstances Sheet)

Download this form on-line: nyc.gov/html/dcas

FOLLOW DIRECTIONS ON BACK
Fill in all requested information clearly, accurately, and completely.

The City will only process applications with complete, correct, legible information which are accompanied by correct payment or waiver documentation.

All unprocessed applications will be returned to the applicant.

Questions 14 & 15:
Discrimination on the basis of sex, sexual orientation, race, creed, color, age, disability status, veteran status or religious observance is prohibited by law. The City of New York is an equal opportunity employer. The identifying information requested on this form is to be used to determine the representation of protected groups among applicants. This information is voluntary and will not be made available to individuals making hiring decisions.

1: EXAM #:

2. EXAM TITLE:

Check One:
☐ Open Competitive
☐ Promotion

3. SOCIAL SECURITY NUMBER:

4. LAST NAME:

5. FIRST NAME:

6. MIDDLE INITIAL:

7. MAILING ADDRESS:

8. APT. #:

9. CITY OR TOWN:

10. STATE:

11. ZIP CODE:

12. PHONE:

13. OTHER NAMES USED IN CITY SERVICE:

14. RACE/ETHNICITY (Check One):
☐ White
☐ Black
☐ Hispanic
☐ American Indian/ Alaskan Native
☐ Asian/Pacific Islander

15. SEX (Check One):
☐ Male
☐ Female

16. ARE YOU EMPLOYED BY THE HEALTH AND HOSPITALS CORPORATION? (Check One)   ☐ YES   ☐ NO

17. CHECK ALL BOXES THAT APPLY TO YOU: (Directions for this section are found on the "Special Circumstances" Sheet)
☐ I AM A SABBATH OBSERVER AND WILL REQUEST AN ALTERNATE TEST DATE (Verification required. See Item A on Special Circumstances Sheet)
☐ I HAVE A DISABILITY AND WILL REQUEST SPECIAL ACCOMMODATIONS (Verification required. See item B on Special Circumstances Sheet)
☐ I CLAIM VETERANS' CREDIT (For qualifications see item C on Special Circumstances Sheet)
☐ I CLAIM DISABLED VETERANS' CREDIT (For qualifications see item C on Special Circumstances Sheet)

18. Your Signature: Date:

SF10
(Page 1)
REV. 1/97

STATE PRE-EMPLOYMENT APPLICATION

**STATE OF LOUISIANA
DEPARTMENT OF CIVIL SERVICE**
P.O. Box 94111, Capitol Station
Baton Rouge, Louisiana 70804-9111

AN EQUAL OPPORTUNITY EMPLOYER

FOR OFFICE USE

Special _____
Promo _____
Action(s) _____
_____
Session _____
Data Entry Completed _____

1. TEST LOCATION-Check only one.

Baton Rouge (3) (Weekday) ☐	New Orleans (6) (Weekday) ☐	Lafayette (4) (Sat. only) ☐	Shreveport (7) (Sat. only) ☐
	New Orleans (12) (Saturday) ☐	Lake Charles (5) (Sat. only) ☐	West Monroe (8) (Sat. only) ☐

2. Enter Name and Complete Address below.

3. Parish of Residence

4. Are you 18 or older? ☐ Yes ☐ No

5. Other names ever used on SF-10

NAME - First   Middle   Last

Mailing Address

City   State   Zip Code

6. Social Security Number (For identification purpose)

Work Telephone No.

Home Telephone No.

L A S T → P R I N T   F I R S T   N A M E → M I D D L E

JS No.

V.P.

S.R.

7. REGISTER TITLE(S) APPLIED FOR

REGISTER TITLE(S) APPLIED FOR	FOR OFFICE USE					ADDITIONAL TITLES	FOR OFFICE USE				
	SER	CD	REJ	GRD	TR		SER	CD	REJ	GRD	TR

ALL TITLES LISTED ABOVE MUST HAVE THE SAME SERIES NO.

8. JOB LOCATION AVAILABILITY - IMPORTANT: Read Item 9 on the Instruction Page before completing this item. Mark at least one (1), but no more than twenty (20) parishes.

☐ 01 Acadia	☐ 09 Caddo	☐ 17 E. Baton Rouge	☐ 25 Jackson	☐ 33 Madison	☐ 41 Red River	☐ 49 St. Landry	☐ 57 Vermillion
☐ 02 Allen	☐ 10 Calcasieu	☐ 18 E. Carroll	☐ 26 Jefferson	☐ 34 Morehouse	☐ 42 Richland	☐ 50 St. Martin	☐ 58 Vernon
☐ 03 Ascension	☐ 11 Caldwell	☐ 19 E. Feliciana	☐ 27 Jeff Davis	☐ 35 Natchitoches	☐ 43 Sabine	☐ 51 St. Mary	☐ 59 Washington
☐ 04	☐ 12 Cameron	☐ 20 Evangeline	☐ 28 Lafayette	☐ 36 Orleans	☐ 44 St. Bernard	☐ 52 St. Tammany	☐ 60 Webster
☐ 05 Avoyelles	☐ 13 Catahoula	☐ 21 Franklin	☐ 29 Lafourche	☐ 37 Ouachita	☐ 45 St. Charles	☐ 53 Tangipahoa	☐ 61 W. Baton Rouge
☐ 06 Beauregard	☐ 14 Claiborne	☐ 22 Grant	☐ 30 LaSalle	☐ 38 Plaquemines	☐ 46 St. Helena	☐ 54 Tensas	☐ 62 W. Carroll
☐ 07 Bienville	☐ 15 Concordia	☐ 23 Iberia	☐ 31 Lincoln	☐ 39 Pte. Coupee	☐ 47 St. James	☐ 55 Terrebonne	☐ 63 W. Feliciana
☐ 08 Bossier	☐ 16 DeSoto	☐ 24 Iberville	☐ 32 Livingston	☐ 40 Rapides	☐ 48 St. John	☐ 56 Union	☐ 64 Winn

9. ☐ Permanent ☐ Temporary—Type of employment you will accept
NOTE: Most Temporary Appointments are 3 - 12 months

10. ☐ YES ☐ NO Do you possess a valid driver's license?

11. ☐ YES ☐ NO Do you possess a valid commercial driver's license?

12. ☐ YES ☐ NO Are you currently holding or running for an elective public office?

13. ☐ YES ☐ NO Have you ever been on probation or sentenced to jail/prison as a result of a felony conviction or guilty plea?

14. ☐ YES ☐ NO Have you ever been fired from a job or resigned to avoid dismissal?

NOTE: If answers to Items 13 and/or 14 are "YES", you MUST complete Item 24 on Page 2 of this application

15. ☐ YES ☐ NO Are you claiming Veteran's Preference points on this application? (If "YES", see Item 20 on Page 2.)

The following information is collected to complete Equal Opportunity Reports required by law. You ARE NOT LEGALLY OBLIGATED to provide this information.

16. RACIAL/ETHNIC GROUP **16A. DATE OF BIRTH** **17. SEX** ☐ Male ☐ Female

_____ _____

I HAVE READ THE FOLLOWING STATEMENTS CAREFULLY BEFORE SIGNING THIS APPLICATION:

18. Date | **Social Security No.** (for verification)

19. Signature of Applicant

AUTHORITY TO RELEASE INFORMATION: I consent to the release of information concerning my capacity and/or all aspects of prior job performance by employers, educational institutions, law enforcement agencies, and other individuals and agencies to duly accredited investigators, personnel technicians, and other authorized employees of the state government for the purpose of determining my eligibility and suitability for employment.

I certify that all statements made on this application and any attached papers are true and complete to the best of my knowledge. I understand that information on this application may be subject to investigation and verification and that any misrepresentation or material omission may cause my application to be rejected, my name to be removed from the eligible register and/or subject me to dismissal from state service.

20. ACTIVE MILITARY SERVICE/VETERAN'S PREFERENCE

See Item 10 on the Instruction Page to determine your eligibility for Veteran's Preference. If you are a first-time applicant or if you are claiming Veteran's Preference for the first time, required PROOF MUST BE ATTACHED to this application to have preference points added to your score.

List the dates (month and year) and branch for all ACTIVE DUTY military service. Was this service performed on an active, full-time basis with full pay and allowances? (Check YES or NO for each period of service.)

FROM	TO	BRANCH OF SERVICE	YES	NO

List all GRADES held and dates of each grade. Begin with the highest grade. IMPORTANT: Use E-, O-, or WO-grade.

FROM	TO	GRADE HELD	FROM	TO	GRADE HELD

21. TRAINING AND EDUCATION

Have you received a high school diploma or equivalency certificate?

☐ YES   Date received _____

☐ NO   Highest grade completed _____

A. LIST BUSINESS OR TECHNICAL COLLEGES ATTENDED	NAME/LOCATION OF SCHOOL	Dates Attended (Month & Year) FROM — TO	Did You Graduate? YES — NO	TITLE OF PROGRAM	CLOCK HOURS PER WEEK

List any accounting practice sets completed: _____

B. LIST COLLEGES OR UNIVERSITIES ATTENDED (Include graduate or professional schools)	NAME OF COLLEGE OR UNIVERSITY/ CITY AND STATE	Dates Attended (Month & Year) FROM — TO	Total Credit Hours Earned Semester — Quarter	Type of Degree Earned	Major Field of Study	Date Degree Received (Month & Yr.)

C. MAJOR SUBJECTS	CHIEF UNDERGRADUATE SUBJECTS (Show Major on Line 1.)	Total Credit Hours Earned Semester — Quarter	CHIEF GRADUATE SUBJECTS (Show Major on Line 1.)	Total Credit Hours Earned Semester or Qtr.
1				
2				
3				

22. LICENSES AND CERTIFICATION

List any job-related licenses or certificates that you have (CPA, lawyer, registered nurse, etc.)

	TYPE OF LICENSE OR CERTIFICATE (Specify Which One)	DATE ORIGINALLY LICENSED/ CERTIFIED	EXPIRATION DATE	NAME AND ADDRESS OF LICENSING OR CERTIFYING AGENCY
1				
2				

23. TYPING SPEED

_____ WPM

DICTATION SPEED

_____ WPM

24. Explain a "YES" answer to Items 13 and/or 14 here. A "YES" ANSWER WILL NOT NECESSARILY BAR YOU FROM STATE EMPLOYMENT. WE WILL CONSIDER THE DATE, FACTS, AND CIRCUMSTANCES OF EACH INDIVIDUAL CASE. For Item 13, give the law enforcement authority (city police, sherrif, FBI, etc.), the offense, date of offense, place, and disposition of case.

_____

_____

                     Name _____

Name _____

25. WORK EXPERIENCE — <u>IMPORTANT</u>: Read Item 11 of Instruction Page carefully before completing these items. List all jobs and activities including military service, part-time employment, self-employment, and volunteer work. BEGIN with your FIRST job in Block A; END with your MOST RECENT or PRESENT job.

A

EMPLOYER/COMPANY NAME	KIND OF BUSINESS

STREET ADDRESS	YOUR OFFICIAL JOB TITLE

CITY AND STATE	BEGINNING SALARY	ENDING SALARY

DATES OF EMPLOYMENT (MO/DA/YR)	AVERAGE HOURS WORKED PER WEEK	REASON FOR LEAVING	NO. OF EMPLOYEES YOU DIRECTLY SUPERVISED
FROM	TO		

NAME/TITLE OF YOUR SUPERVISOR)	LIST JOB TITLES OF EMPLOYEES YOU DIRECTLY SUPERVISED
NAME/TITLE OF PERSON WHO CAN VERIFY THIS EMPLOYMENT (IF OTHER THAN SUPERVISOR)	

DUTIES: List the major duties involved with job and give an approximate percentage of time spent on each duty.

% OF TIME	MAJOR DUTIES
100%	

B

EMPLOYER/COMPANY NAME	KIND OF BUSINESS

STREET ADDRESS	YOUR OFFICIAL JOB TITLE

CITY AND STATE	BEGINNING SALARY	ENDING SALARY

DATES OF EMPLOYMENT (MO/DA/YR)	AVERAGE HOURS WORKED PER WEEK	REASON FOR LEAVING	NO. OF EMPLOYEES YOU DIRECTLY SUPERVISED
FROM	TO		

NAME/TITLE OF YOUR SUPERVISOR)	LIST JOB TITLES OF EMPLOYEES YOU DIRECTLY SUPERVISED
NAME/TITLE OF PERSON WHO CAN VERIFY THIS EMPLOYMENT (IF OTHER THAN SUPERVISOR)	

DUTIES: List the major duties involved with job and give an approximate percentage of time spent on each duty.

% OF TIME	MAJOR DUTIES

100%	

USE REVERSE SIDE OF THIS PAGE IF ADDITIONAL SPACE REQUIRED FOR WORK EXPERIENCE

Name _____

25.   WORK EXPERIENCE (Continued)

C

EMPLOYER/COMPANY NAME	KIND OF BUSINESS	
STREET ADDRESS	YOUR OFFICIAL JOB TITLE	
CITY AND STATE	BEGINNING SALARY	ENDING SALARY
DATES OF EMPLOYMENT (MO/DA/YR) AVERAGE HOURS WORKED PER WEEK FROM TO	REASON FOR LEAVING	NO. OF EMPLOYEES YOU DIRECTLY SUPERVISED
NAME/TITLE OF YOUR SUPERVISOR	LIST JOB TITLES OF EMPLOYEES YOU DIRECTLY SUPERVISED	
NAME/TITLE OF PERSON WHO CAN VERIFY THIS EMPLOYMENT (IF OTHER THAN SUPERVISOR)		

DUTIES: List the major duties involved with job and give an approximate percentage of time spent on each duty.

% OF TIME	MAJOR DUTIES

100%	

D

EMPLOYER/COMPANY NAME	KIND OF BUSINESS	
STREET ADDRESS	YOUR OFFICIAL JOB TITLE	
CITY AND STATE	BEGINNING SALARY	ENDING SALARY
DATES OF EMPLOYMENT (MO/DA/YR) AVERAGE HOURS WORKED PER WEEK FROM TO	REASON FOR LEAVING	NO. OF EMPLOYEES YOU DIRECTLY SUPERVISED
NAME/TITLE OF YOUR SUPERVISOR)	LIST JOB TITLES OF EMPLOYEES YOU DIRECTLY SUPERVISED	
NAME/TITLE OF PERSON WHO CAN VERIFY THIS EMPLOYMENT (IF OTHER THAN SUPERVISOR)		

DUTIES: List the major duties involved with job and give an approximate percentage of time spent on each duty.

% OF TIME	MAJOR DUTIES

SUMMING IT UP

- The government is one of the nation's largest sources of employment, with 1 in every 6 employed people working in some type of civilian government service. Government employees work in cities, small towns, and remote and isolated places; some work overseas.

- Many federal occupations are similar to jobs in the private sector, such as those in accounting, computer programming, and health care. Others are unique to the federal government, such as regulatory inspectors, Foreign Service officers, and Internal Revenue Service agents.

- The executive branch of the federal government employs the majority of federal workers. The Department of Defense, the largest department in the executive branch, employs about 35 percent of all civilian government workers; the U.S. Postal Service accounts for another 25 percent.

- Federal civilian employment is also available in the legislative branch, which includes Congress, the Government Printing Office, the General Accounting Office, and the Library of Congress. The judicial branch, the smallest employer of the federal government, hires people for work within the courts system.

- Professional positions account for approximately 90 percent of all federal civilian jobs and include work in management, finance, business, law, medicine, computer technology, the sciences, and engineering. All federal departments and agencies employ general clerical workers, some of whom arrange and monitor contracts with and purchase goods and services from private industries.

- Requirements for professional federal jobs vary from a postsecondary degree to a high school diploma. An undergraduate or advanced degree is usually required for specialized occupations in areas such as physics, engineering, ecology, and law. Office clerk positions may not require a specific level of education or experience; other federal jobs may require some combination of education and experience.

- More than 90 percent of jobs in the federal government fall under the merit system, established by an act of Congress to ensure that federal employees are hired based on individual merit.

- Most federal workers are paid under the General Schedule (GS). GS jobs are divided into fifteen grades, according to the difficulty of duties and responsibilities and the knowledge, experience, and skills required of the workers in that pay grade. GS pay rates are set by Congress, and they apply to government workers nationwide.

- State and local government agencies in the United States employ about 15 million people, three fourths of whom work in counties, municipalities, towns, and school districts. State and local governments have a greater need than does the federal government for employees in education, health, social services, transportation, construction, and sanitation.

- Most federal, state, and municipal government units have recruitment procedures for filling civil service positions. The best places to seek a government job include state employment offices, your state's or city's Civil Service Commission, your local municipal building or public library, job newspapers such as New York City's *The Chief-Leader*, schools, professional societies, veterans' organizations, unions, trade associations, and local boards of education.

- Follow the steps outlined in this chapter to learn how to read government job announcements and apply for desired positions. The announcement will tell you whether you need to take a test to qualify for consideration and what kind of test it will be. In an assembled competitive examination, all applicants for a position compete with one another; the higher your score, the better your chance of being appointed.

What Public Safety Dispatchers and 911 Operators Do

OVERVIEW

- **The nature of the work**
- **Employment and job outlook**
- **The public safety dispatcher hiring process**
- **Summing it up**

THE NATURE OF THE WORK

Public Safety Dispatcher, 911 Operator, Police Communications Technician, E911 Call-taker/Dispatcher (in New York City), and other similar job titles refer to people who collect information about emergency situations and relay that information to the divisions that can provide emergency help. Clearly, those who manage emergency assistance control centers serve a vital public purpose. They earn good wages, and they gain the psychological reward of knowing that they are truly helping people.

Dispatchers act as a link between the public requesting assistance and the appropriate service provider. They see that each request for service is carried out quickly and accurately. Their specific duties depend on the type of service being rendered.

Police, fire, and ambulance dispatchers—called public safety dispatchers—are usually the first people contacted in an emergency. They receive reports from the public concerning crimes, fires, and medical emergencies; broadcast orders to units near the scene of the event to respond or investigate; and relay information or orders to proper officials. Public safety dispatchers manage emergency calls in a variety of settings, including police stations, fire stations, hospitals or other health care centers, and centralized city communications centers.

In many cities, the police department serves as the communications center. In such situations, all 911 calls go to the police department, where a dispatcher handles the emergency police-related calls and screens all other calls before transferring them to the appropriate service or department. Dispatchers carefully question each caller to determine the type, seriousness, and location of the emergency. The dispatcher then quickly determines the type and number of response units needed, locates the closest and most suitable ones, and sends them to the scene of the emergency.

chapter 2

Dispatchers remain in contact with response units until the emergency has been handled, in case further instructions are needed. When appropriate, they stay in close contact with other service providers as well. For example, a police dispatcher would monitor the response of the fire department during a major fire. In a medical emergency, dispatchers stay in contact not only with the responding ambulance team but also with the caller who reported the emergency. They often provide extensive first-aid instructions while the caller is waiting for the ambulance. Dispatchers give continual updates on the patient's condition to ambulance personnel and provide a link between the medical staff at the hospital where a patient will be taken and the emergency medical technicians in the ambulance.

For more helpful information about the nature of public safety dispatcher work, you may want to explore the following options:

- Do a "sit along" or "ride along" with one or more emergency agencies.
- Attend a citizen's academy and find out about any 911 courses you can complete online.
- Take one or more criminal justice courses.

The following is a typical job description for a police communications technician. Read through it for additional insight into the duties and responsibilities associated with public safety dispatchers.

Typical Job Description

Police Communications Technician Occupational Group

Police Communications Technician

GENERAL STATEMENT OF DUTIES AND RESPONSIBILITIES

In a police department, under direct supervision, serves as an emergency operator and radio dispatcher; performs all clerical, administrative, and other duties related to the provision of emergency service; performs related work.

Incumbents may be required to work varied tours—including nights, weekends, and holidays—depending upon the needs of the department.

EXAMPLES OF TASKS

- Receives calls from the public for emergency assistance.
- Evaluates each call for assistance; checks accuracy of information with caller, and checks computer for prior entries on incorrect or incomplete information that may have been entered.
- Inputs information into computer terminal.
- Operates computer terminal and other equipment in support of the request for emergency assistance.

continued

- Maintains liaison with other emergency services for the provision of appropriate assistance.

- Refers callers to other agencies for provision of nonemergency assistance.

- Operates computer, radio, telephone, FATN, and other equipment as required.

- Consults computer to ascertain pending assignments and changing situations.

- Dispatches police resources to emergencies.

- Interacts with operating personnel to provide and receive information and assistance in support of the provision of emergency response.

- Reviews priority listing of assignments for accuracy and possible reevaluation of priority codes.

- Communicates with other agencies concerning involvement in emergency situations.

- Performs responsible clerical duties and maintains statistics in support of the 911 emergency function.

- Operates office apparatus, including telephone, alarm board, and related equipment.

- Maintains logbooks, receipt books, and other records and ledgers.

- Reviews and verifies written information and writes reports and other communication documents.

- Instructs and assists other personnel in the performance of their duties.

- Attends training sessions.

QUALIFICATION REQUIREMENTS

1. High school graduation or evidence of having passed an examination for a High School Equivalency Diploma or United States Armed Forces GED certificate with a score of at least 35 on each of the five tests and an overall score of at least 225 in the examination for the certificate, plus the following:

   - one year of full-time experience performing clerical duties, **or**

   - one year of full-time paid responsible experience in public contact work requiring the obtaining of information from persons, **or**

   - the successful completion of 30 college credits in an accredited college, **or**

   - two years of active military duty.

2. Education and/or experience equivalent to "1" above. However, high school graduation or its equivalent as described above is required of all candidates. In addition, all candidates will be required to pass a qualifying fitness assessment.

Physical Requirements

A public safety dispatcher must have keen hearing. He or she must be able to filter out a message even with a great deal of background noise or interference on the phone line. In this position, a worker seldom has the luxury of asking the caller to repeat his or her message. Because good hearing is so important, many jurisdictions administer a hearing test to applicants. Poor hearing may disqualify a candidate.

A speech impairment may also lead to a candidate's disqualification. During emergencies, dispatchers must speak on the telephone to citizens who need assistance and to police officers, firefighters, and other emergency personnel. It is imperative that a dispatcher be easily understood by those he or she is assisting.

Work Environment

The work of dispatchers can be very hectic, especially when many calls come in at the same time. The job of public safety dispatchers is particularly stressful because a slow or improper response to a call may result in serious injury or further harm to another person or people. Callers who are anxious, panicky, or afraid may become too excited or upset to provide needed information; in such difficult circumstances, some may even become abusive. Despite such challenges, dispatchers must remain calm, objective, and in control of the situation.

Dispatchers sit for long periods, using telephones, computers, and two-way radios. Much of their time is spent at video display terminals, viewing monitors, and observing traffic patterns. Because they work for long stretches with computers and other electronic equipment, dispatchers may experience significant eyestrain and back discomfort.

Most dispatchers work a 40-hour week; however, rotating shifts and compressed work schedules are common in this line of work. Alternative work schedules are necessary to accommodate evening, weekend, and holiday work and 24-hour-a-day, seven-days-a-week operations.

Most public safety dispatchers are entry-level workers who are trained on the job and need no more than a high school diploma. However, many states require specialized training or certification.

Education and Training

Public safety dispatchers usually develop the necessary skills on the job. This informal training lasts from several days to a few months, depending on the complexity of the position. While working with an experienced dispatcher, new employees monitor calls and learn how to operate a variety of communications equipment, including telephones, two-way radios, and various wireless devices. As trainees gain confidence, they are permitted to handle calls themselves. Many public safety dispatchers also participate in structured training programs sponsored by an employer. Increasingly, public safety dispatchers are also trained in stress and crisis management as well as in family counseling. The skills they learn from this training helps them provide more effective services to others—and it also helps them manage the stress that comes with the work they do.

Licensure

Several states require their public safety dispatchers to undergo specific types of training or secure certification from a professional association. Certification often requires several months in a classroom for instruction in computer-assisted dispatching and other emerging technologies, in addition to courses on radio dispatching and stress management.

Other Qualifications

State or local government civil service regulations usually govern police, fire, and emergency medical dispatching job requirements. Candidates for these positions may have to pass written, oral, and performance tests. They may also be asked to attend training classes to qualify for advancement. Residency in the city or county of employment is often required for public safety dispatchers.

Communication skills and the ability to work under pressure are important personal qualities for dispatchers. Those who work in the transportation industry must also be able to deal with sudden influxes of shipments and disruptions of shipping schedules caused by bad weather, road construction, or accidents.

Certification and Advancement

Although no mandatory licensing requirements exist for public safety dispatchers, some states require them to be certified to work on a state network, such as the Police Information Network. Many dispatchers participate in these programs as a means of improving their prospects for advancement.

Dispatchers who work for private firms (usually small businesses) generally have few opportunities for advancement. By contrast, a public safety dispatcher may be promoted to shift or divisional supervisor or may be eligible to become chief of communications. Public safety dispatchers may also move to higher-paying administrative jobs. Some ultimately become police officers or firefighters.

EMPLOYMENT AND JOB OUTLOOK

Dispatchers held about 289,000 jobs in 2006. About one third of these worked as police, fire, and ambulance dispatchers in local and state governments. Dispatcher positions are also available outside the scope of law enforcement agencies. School districts, universities, and city parks require the skills of dispatchers to manage minor and major emergencies. Public safety dispatcher positions are available in national parks across the United States, where campers may become lost or sustain injuries or where traffic accidents may occur, especially during peak travel seasons. Similar positions are available at local and long-distance trucking companies and with bus lines, telephone, electric, and gas utility companies, and wholesale and retail establishments. Although dispatchers work throughout the United States, most positions are in metropolitan areas. Large communications centers and private businesses that require dispatching services are often based in urban areas.

Employment of dispatchers is expected to increase 6 percent between 2006 and 2016, according to the Bureau of Labor Statistics. Population growth and economic factors are expected to stimulate employment growth for all types of dispatchers. In addition, an aging general population will require greater need for emergency services and is expected to spur job growth for police, fire, and ambulance dispatchers. Job openings will also increase as more workers transfer to other occupations or retire. Successful public safety dispatchers are promoted into supervisory positions or other roles with greater responsibility—and as they move up, their former positions become available. Once you have served successfully as a public safety operator or dispatcher, you, too, can look forward to promotion, or perhaps a move into private industry.

Current competition for public safety dispatcher jobs is intense. The job security of public safety dispatchers is unlikely to be affected by a sluggish economy. By contrast, employment opportunities for dispatchers who work in transportation industries may decrease with an economic downturn. To be considered for a public safety dispatcher position, you must earn a high score on a competitive exam and rank near the top of the list of eligible candidates. You must also demonstrate good typing and computer skills. And perhaps most important, you must impress interviewers with your communication skills, good judgment, patience, and tact.

Information about job opportunities for police, fire, and public safety dispatchers is available from state and local civil service commissions and police departments. This information is generally distributed in the form of Official Job Announcements. On the next few pages, you'll see sample job announcements from two cities in different parts of the United States. As you read the announcements, note the similarities—and significant differences—among job descriptions and the qualifying exams. Keep these in mind as you search actual job postings in and around your locality.

Earnings

The profession of public safety dispatching is exciting and challenging—but it can be tedious and stressful as well. Being a public safety dispatcher is a difficult job that takes time and patience to learn. However, successful dispatchers can earn a comfortable living and serve their communities at the same time. When reviewing the requirements and salaries for public safety dispatching jobs, remember that both aspects of the profession vary greatly by agency and location.

According to the Bureau of Labor Statistics, median annual wage-and-salary earnings of dispatchers (except police, fire, and ambulance dispatchers) as of May 2006 were $32,190. The middle 50 percent earned between $24,860 and $42,030 annually. The lowest-paid dispatchers earned $19,780; the highest-paid 10 percent earned $53,250 annually.

Median annual wage-and-salary earnings of police, fire, and ambulance dispatchers as of 2006 were $31,470. The middle 50 percent earned between $25,200 and $39,040. The lowest-paid public safety dispatchers earned less than $20,010; the highest-paid 10 percent earned more than $47,190 annually.

THE PUBLIC SAFETY DISPATCHER HIRING PROCESS

As with any government job, state and federal laws regulate the hiring process. A candidate should know which questions a potential employer is legally allowed to ask and which topics are forbidden. Applicants should understand their rights during each step of the process. The Fair Inquiry Guidelines established by the Equal Employment Opportunity Commission (EEOC) help clarify what an employer can ask during an interview. Browsing the EEOC Web Site (www.eeoc.gov) may provide useful information regarding interview questions.

The process of applying, testing, and screening for a public safety dispatcher position involves a number of steps. Most of them are designed to determine whether a candidate can perform the specific tasks required of a public safety dispatcher. A candidate who meets the initial requirements is typically given a "conditional job offer." This candidate may then take an additional series of tests to determine whether he or she meets the necessary qualifications to be an employee of the city, county, or state.

The typical employment process for a government job involves the following steps. Not every government agency follows all these steps to fill job openings; for example, many agencies do not require candidates to undergo a polygraph exam.

1. application
2. written test
3. practical test
4. interview
5. conditional job offer
6. full job offer
7. medical exam
8. psychological test
9. polygraph test
10. background check

Since the events of September 11, 2001, and the establishment of the Department of Homeland Security (DHS), numerous new rules and regulations have gone into effect. Stringent hiring policies and procedures may affect the hiring process for a federal, state, regional, or local job in which you're interested. These rules and regulations generally fall under the jurisdiction of the DHS, and they should be set forth in writing at every level of the application process.

NOTE: Federal labor law requires that a medical, psychological, or polygraph exam be administered only *after* a conditional job offer—not before. The Employee Polygraph Protection Act of 1988 prohibits private firms from subjecting job candidates or employees to lie detector tests in most circumstances. However, the law does not cover federal, state, and local governments. Therefore, an applicant for a public safety dispatcher position may be required to take a polygraph test as part of the screening process.

Sample Dispatcher Qualifications

Many government agencies set minimum standards for skills, abilities, related experience, or education before an applicant is accepted for a position as a public safety dispatcher. The following samples come from actual job announcements for public safety dispatcher positions. Each describes the typical qualifications a public safety dispatcher must meet to be considered for employment.

Sample 1

Knowledge of standard radio and telephone communications receiving and transmitting equipment, standard broadcasting procedures and rules, operation of common radio dispatch equipment, public safety classification codes, basic provisions of the vehicle and penal code.

Sample 2

Ability to interpret and give both verbal and written instructions. Excellent verbal and written communication skills. Bilingual skills strongly desired. Ability to speak clearly and concisely over the radio and telephone. Have prioritization skills and ability to multi-task. Ability to make sound decisions using all available information. Knowledge of FCC laws, regulations, procedures, and practices applicable to basic radio-telephone operation. Skill to accomplish tasks in a controlled, effective manner while working under stress. Ability to read maps. Ability to develop and maintain cooperative working relationships with coworkers and customers. Keyboard skills.

Sample 3

Knowledge of operational procedures and methods used in operation of a public safety communications center, general functions of public safety agencies, use and proper care of computer and radio-telephone equipment, geography of the county/city. Working knowledge of FCC regulations applicable to the operation of public safety radio-telephone communications equipment, all computer assisted dispatch (CAD) files, commonly used law violations. Some knowledge of supervision and training practices. Skill to accurately type a minimum of 25 wpm, operate a CAD computer, keep accurate records of information received via computer, operate a variety of communications equipment. Ability to remain calm, think clearly, quickly assess and evaluate situations, organize thoughts, and respond quickly in emergency and stressful situations; effectively coordinate emergency dispatch of public safety equipment and personnel; prepare work schedules for all shifts for routine assignments and emergency situations. Prepare written reports and trainee evaluations; recommend training methods; interpret and apply rules and regulations; establish and maintain cooperative working relationships; communicate clearly and effectively with the general public, safety officials, and other governmental and private staff persons. Take and transmit clear and complete directions and information. Perform a variety of tasks simultaneously.

Sample 4

Knowledge of modern office practices and procedures; CAD equipment operation; proper English usage, diction, grammar, spelling, and punctuation; demonstrated proficiency in alphabetic, chronological, and numeric filing systems; techniques, procedures, and methods used on the operation of a highly technical communications center; community resources; emergency response procedures; department procedures and activities; effective communication techniques; specialized police network computer operations; the law enforcement culture and its nuances; the rank structure within a police agency; automated systems dedicated to law enforcement; maintenance of standard operating procedure (SOP) integrity while working under emotional conditions; various penal, vehicle, health and safety codes as well as alpha mnemonics; map reading, listening and interrogation techniques to control direction and length of telephone calls; personal computer operating systems and software applications.

Ability and skills that accompany speaking and hearing clearly; demonstrate excellent interpersonal skills including communicating effectively with those contacted in the course of work; analyze situations quickly and make sound decisions in emergency and routine situations; perform two or more tasks concurrently; input and retrieve computer data quickly; learn the techniques, procedures, and methods used in the operation of a highly technical communications center; quickly read and retain information; quickly interpret maps and floor layouts; relate effectively to coworkers; recognize and discern various emotional states when dealing with citizens in person and while on 911, emergency, and business lines; recognize the voices of field units; use patience and tact in dealing with the public; quickly operate electronic data processing equipment and radio consoles; perform a number of tasks simultaneously; listen and interrogate callers to control the direction and length of telephone calls; read and disseminate court orders and warrant information; use personal computers and computer software to perform word processing and spreadsheet functions. The ability to understand and speak Spanish is preferred.

Sample 5

Knowledge of public safety dispatching methods using various communications equipment, including CAD or similar equipment. Ability to operate CAD equipment under stress; type at a corrected speed of 30 words per minute. Skill in establishing and maintaining effective working relationships with a variety of individuals, including police and fire personnel, other city employees, and the public. Skill in reading, writing, and communicating in English at an appropriate level.

Certain features of public safety dispatcher work are common throughout all agencies. Here are sample descriptions of some of these features.

Stationary work: Dispatchers are required to sit at telephone/radio consoles for extended periods.

Most work is verbal: Dispatchers must receive, evaluate, and produce verbal information.

Work is random and reactive: Dispatchers do not choose calls/situations to be handled; they do not know ahead of time what the situation will be.

Must be able to multi-task: Dispatchers are required to perform multiple activities simultaneously and work with frequent interruptions.

Dispatchers are required to **interact with many different people** on a daily basis, often at the same time.

Work structure is rigid: Dispatchers must work within a framework of many rules, procedures, and regulations.

Dispatchers have a **high visibility** for their actions and decisions—performance is taped.

Dispatchers have a high level of responsibility, and there will be **serious consequences if an error** is made.

Dispatchers must deal with **unpleasant situations.**

Work is often repetitive and alternates between periods of high activity and low activity.

Dispatchers have access to **sensitive information.**

A dispatcher must, with little time to spare, **provide information, make decisions, and perform duties** that may be critical to the safety of the public and field officers.

Dispatchers are often the only contact citizens have with the police department. They are in a **public relations role.** The dispatcher's demeanor and competence in handling calls from the public combine to form what is often the first impression that people have about law enforcement agencies.

SAMPLE JOB ANNOUNCEMENTS

POLICE COMMUNICATIONS TECHNICIAN

Application Period: March 7 through March 27, 2010

Application Fee: $30.00. *Payable by money order only to D.C.A.S. (EXAMS).*

Salary: The current minimum salary as of 6/1/10 is $35,642 per annum. This rate is subject to change.

Notice of Examination (NOE) is for this title and is therefore subject to change. Please consult the NOE for this title during the application period.

What the Job Involves: Police Communications Technicians, working under direct supervision in the Police Department Communications Section,

- serve as 911 emergency operators.
- obtain necessary information from callers to initiate emergency assistance.
- perform clerical, administrative, and other duties related to the provision of emergency service.
- serve as radio dispatchers of police resources.
- perform related work.

Examples of Typical Tasks: Some of the physical activities performed by Police Communications Technicians are

- sitting for extended periods of time while wearing a headset and monitoring a computer screen.
- coordinating hand-eye movements while handling emergency calls for the efficient use of console and computer.
- speaking calmly and clearly in order to elicit information and offer instructions to a continuous flow of callers under stress.
- listening carefully to understand emergency information clearly.
- making response judgments where timing is critical.
- sitting within hearing distance of other operators working under similar conditions.

continued

This is a brief description of what you might do in this position, as well as the environmental conditions you are likely to encounter. It does not include all the duties of this position.

Other Job Factors: You may be required to work rotating tours for shifts around the clock, including Saturdays, Sundays, and holidays, and you may be required on occasion to work overtime tours, depending on the needs of the department.

Education and Experience Requirements: By the last day of the application period, you must have a four-year high school diploma or its educational equivalent, plus the following:

1. One year of satisfactory full-time responsible experience performing clerical or typing or secretarial work, **or**

2. One year of satisfactory full-time responsible experience dealing with the public, including the obtaining of information from persons, **or**

3. The successful completion of 30 college credits at an accredited college or university, **or**

4. Two years of active U.S. military duty with honorable discharge, **or**

5. A satisfactory combination of education and/or experience that is equivalent to requirements 1, 2, 3, or 4 above. However, all candidates must have a four-year high school diploma or its educational equivalent.

Applicants may be summoned for the test prior to a review of their qualifications.

Medical and Psychological Requirement: You are required to undergo a medical examination and a psychological examination.

Drug/Alcohol Screening Requirement: You must pass a drug/alcohol screening in order to be appointed.

Residency Requirement: You must be a city resident within 90 days of the date you are appointed to this position. If you begin city service as a result of this examination, or you are currently a city employee and you began city service on or after September 1, 2010, you must maintain city residency as a condition of employment.

English Requirement: All candidates must be able to understand and be understood in English.

Proof of Identity: Under the Immigration Reform and Control Act of 1986, you must be able to prove your identity and your right to obtain employment in the United States prior to employment with the City of New York.

Selective Certification for Foreign Language: If you can speak a foreign language, you may be considered for appointment to positions requiring this ability through a process called "Selective Certification." If you pass a qualifying test, you may be given preferred consideration for positions requiring this ability. Follow the instructions given to you in the multiple-choice test booklet on the day of the test to indicate your interest in such Selective Certification.

continued

Probationary Period: The probationary period for Police Communications Technician is 18 months. You will be required to pass an eight-week 911 operator-training course and a four-week radio dispatcher-training course. In accordance with the Personnel Rules and Regulations of the City of New York, probationers who fail to successfully complete such training courses may be terminated.

List Termination: The eligible list will be terminated one year from the date it is established.

Test Description: You will be given a multiple-choice test. Your score on this test will be used to determine your place on an eligibility list. You must achieve a score of at least 70% to pass the test. The multiple-choice test may include questions about understanding written information; communicating written information to another person; remembering new information; recognizing the existence of a problem; combining separate pieces of information to form a general conclusion; applying general rules to a specific situation; understanding the order in which things should be done; quickly combining information into a meaningful pattern; identifying an object in its surroundings; recognizing your position relative to a given space; using a map or diagram to get from one position to another; and other related skills.

Test Date: The multiple-choice test will be held on Saturday, June 26, 2010.

POLICE SERVICE REPRESENTATIVE

Job Description: Police Service Representatives are civilian employees of the Police Department assigned to the Communications Division or to a geographic area police station. They receive and analyze telephone and in-person requests for service from citizens, field officers, and other agencies; take crime and other reports; handle referral calls and dispatch patrol units using radio, digital terminal, and other methods; and perform related station duties.

Notes:

1. Police Service Representatives' initial assignments will be to the Communications Division in positions that have been designated as temporary training positions by the Civil Service Commission. Employment in such positions will be limited to six months, during which time employees must successfully complete a comprehensive training program for Police Service Representatives. Upon completion of the training program, employees will receive regular appointments to the class of Police Service Representative and begin a six-month probationary period in the Communications Division.

2. Police Service Representatives must be available to work weekend, holiday, day, night, and early-morning shifts on a rotating basis. You will not necessarily be assigned to the permanent shift of your choice.

Distinguishing Features: A Police Service Representative is a civilian employee of the police department who may wear a uniform but carries no weapon. An employee of this class, when assigned to a public counter of a geographic police station, is usually the first person to assist visitors and receive most telephone calls. A Police Service Representative also prepares crime and traffic reports based on information provided by citizens and other agencies and must be able to deal effectively with emergency situations that arise.

When assigned to the Communications Division, a Police Service Representative receives citizens' requests, responds to the citizens' concerns, and, if necessary, dispatches patrol units using radio, digital terminal, and other methods. An employee of this class must make independent decisions that affect the safety of police officers, citizens, and property—such as those involved in determining the urgency of requests received—and the appropriate action to take. A Police Service Representative receives extensive training in police communications procedures, arrest and report follow-up, search procedures, and interview techniques.

Examples of Duties:

- Takes both telephone and in-person reports of crimes from citizens and other agencies.

- Dispatches urgent calls to the proper unit or section.

- Assists persons who enter the station in need of police assistance or general information.

- Screens individuals who enter the station.

continued

- Receives, reviews, and routes messages.

- Updates the station supervisor's message board.

- Directs station record clerks to send messages; answers questions from field officers.

- Maintains police department logs.

- Reviews daily field activity reports for accuracy and completeness.

- Ensures that reports are submitted in a timely and accurate manner.

- Monitors police department radio transmissions to keep informed of field situations requiring station personnel action.

- May verify and resolve discrepancies on bail monies received; deposits bail money; completes and authorizes bank checks; forwards checks, security bonds, and other necessary documents to appropriate court; maintains the divisional bail file, schedule, and instructional booklet; may, at an area station, interview persons (in person or by telephone) who have previously reported crime incidents or who were alleged witnesses to reported incidents, and prepare and forward appropriate reports to concerned department entities; and, if required in connection with such interviews, search and retrieve information from the department's Automated Information System.

- Forwards subpoenas to the proper supervisors or units for service; accepts the returned, served, or unserved subpoenas and forwards them to the concerned court; maintains liaison with concerned courts to ensure station personnel appear as scheduled; may maintain a subpoena control log; and may pick up and deliver evidential or other documents to police stations using an automobile.

- May act as a communications dispatch center operator responsible for receiving calls from the public requesting services and taking crime and other reports; analyzes the caller's request for service to determine if any emergency exists and if the call should result in a dispatch of a police unit, or if the call should be transferred to another department or person; uses radio, digital terminal, and other methods to dispatch field units to the scene, if necessary; handles referral calls and uses appropriate computer systems.

- May assist with other departmental duties as necessary.

Requirements: Experience that includes assisting and referring telephone or two-way radio callers and entering and retrieving computer data using video display terminals is desired but not required.

Notes:

1. Prior to appointment, eligible candidates will be given two opportunities to pass a typing test with a speed requirement of 32 net words per minute.

continued

2. Some of the positions to be filled by this examination may require the ability to speak or write a language other than English. Only persons who have the necessary language skills may be posted on the eligible list to fill such positions. If you have the ability to speak or write a language other than English, indicate this language in the appropriate box on the application. Proficiency in Spanish is especially desired.

Application Information: Application may be made by mail or in person. Filing may close without prior notice any time after a sufficient number of applications have been received. Immediate vacancies will be filled from among those who apply first. Candidates will be scheduled for the next available written test. The written test will be given approximately every two months.

The Examination: The multiple-choice written test will cover the following: speed and accuracy in matching numerical and alphabetical sequences; spelling and vocabulary; reading comprehension; the ability to learn, apply, and make decisions based on rules; and the ability to follow verbal and written directions. Also included will be a test of approximately 30 minutes in length, which measures personal characteristics required for the position of Police Service Representative.

The interview will consist of an evaluation of your oral communication skills and the extent to which your work experience and training demonstrate the abilities to deal tactfully and effectively with the public, officials, and city employees; make decisions under various situations; perform multiple tasks with frequent interruptions; retrieve and provide information; and perform other necessary tasks.

Examination Weights:

Written Test	50%
Interview	50%

You may take the written test and interview only once in a calendar year. Your name may be removed from the open competitive eligible list after 180 calendar days.

SUMMING IT UP

- Public safety dispatchers go by many titles, including 911 Operator, Police Communications Technician, and E911 Call-taker/Dispatcher. All of these titles refer to people who collect information in emergency situations and relay that information to those who can provide immediate assistance. Dispatchers are the link between citizens requesting help and the appropriate service provider.

- Police, fire, and ambulance dispatchers are usually the first people contacted in an emergency. They receive reports from the public concerning crimes, fires, and medical emergencies; broadcast orders to units near the scene of the event to respond or investigate; and relay information or orders to proper officials.

- Dispatchers remain in contact with response units until the emergency has been handled, in case further instructions are needed. When appropriate, they stay in close contact with other service providers as well.

- Dispatcher work can be extremely busy, but it can also be monotonous and repetitive. It's particularly stressful because a slow or improper response to a call may result in serious injury or further harm to another person or people, and callers may be fearful, anxious, upset, or even abusive. Dispatchers must remain calm, objective, and in control in all situations.

- Dispatchers sit for long periods and use telephones, computers, and two-way radios almost constantly. The job often requires evening, weekend, and holiday shifts.

- Public safety dispatchers are often trained on the job. Many also attend structured training programs sponsored by an employer, and they are increasingly being trained in stress and crisis management and in family counseling.

- Some states require public safety dispatchers to undergo specific types of training or secure certification from a professional association. Candidates for police, fire, and emergency medical dispatching positions may have to pass written, oral, and performance tests. They may also be asked to attend training classes to qualify for advancement.

- Although dispatchers who work for private firms often have few opportunities for advancement, public safety dispatchers may be promoted to shift or divisional supervisors or may be eligible to become chief of communications. Public safety dispatchers may also move to higher-paying administrative jobs, and some become police officers or firefighters.

- Employment of dispatchers is expected to increase 6 percent between 2006-2016, according to the Bureau of Labor Statistics. Population growth and economic factors are expected to stimulate employment growth for all types of dispatchers.

- Current competition for public safety dispatcher jobs is intense. To be considered for a position, you must earn a high score on a competitive exam and rank near the top of the list of eligible candidates.

- State and federal laws regulate the public safety dispatcher hiring process. The steps involved in the hiring process include the application, a written test, a practical test, an interview, a conditional job offer, a full job offer, a medical exam, a psychological test, a polygraph test, and a background check. Not every government agency follows all these steps to fill job openings; for example, many agencies do not require candidates to undergo a polygraph exam.

PART II

ALL ABOUT CIVIL SERVICE EXAMS

CHAPTER 3   Civil Service Exams Explained

Civil Service Exams Explained

OVERVIEW

- Taking a civil service exam
- Manage your test time
- Should you guess?
- How your exam is scored
- 12 tips to raise your score
- Summing it up

TAKING A CIVIL SERVICE EXAM

Many factors contribute to a civil service test score—but the most important factor, of course, is the ability to answer the questions correctly, which in turn indicates the ability to learn and perform the duties of the job for which you are being evaluated. Assuming that you have this ability, knowing what to expect on the exam and becoming familiar with the techniques of effective test taking should give you the confidence you need to do your best on your public safety dispatcher exam.

There is no quick substitute for long-term study and development of your skills and abilities to prepare you for doing well on such tests. However, you can take some steps to help you gain an edge over others who will be taking the exam. These steps fall into four major categories:

1. Being prepared
2. Avoiding careless errors
3. Managing your test time wisely
4. Taking educated guesses

Be Prepared

Do not make your exam more difficult than it has to be by not preparing yourself. You are taking a very important step in preparing for a public safety dispatcher career by reading this book and taking the sample tests we've included. This will help you to become familiar with the tests and the kinds of questions you will have to answer—and therefore more comfortable taking the actual test on exam day.

As you use this book, carefully and thoroughly read the sample questions and directions for taking the test. Read every word, even if you think you know what the question is asking. When you're ready to take the full-length Practice Tests, find a quiet place where you're not likely to be interrupted and time yourself, to simulate as closely as possible the atmosphere you'll experience on exam day.

As you work through the sample questions in this book, avoid checking the answer keys and explanations before you've attempted to answer them correctly on your own. Doing otherwise might fool you into believing that you fully understand a question. Once you've completed the question or the exam, then compare your answers with the one provided. This will help you determine where you might need additional practice and which question types are most difficult for you. Remember, in a sample test, you are your own grader; you gain nothing by pretending to understand something that you don't.

What to Expect on Exam Day

On exam day (a test date will be assigned to you), allow the exam itself to be the main attraction of the day. Avoid fitting it in between other activities. The night before the exam, lay out all the materials you'll need to bring with you—your admission card, identification, sharpened pencils, directions to the test center—and place them where you're unlikely to forget them in the rush to get out the door. Get a good night's sleep and leave your house in plenty of time to get to the test center before the exam begins (in fact, it's a good idea to leave a bit early, to account for traffic tie-ups or other unforeseen situations). Arriving rested, relaxed, and on time for your exam will go a long way toward making you feel confident and in control.

At the testing center, the administrator will hand out forms for you to complete. Next, he or she will give you the exam instructions and explain how to fill in the answer sheet. He or she will explain time limits and timing signals. Don't hesitate to ask questions if you don't understand something the administrator is telling you. Remember, complete understanding is one key to scoring high, so it makes no sense not to be sure you're completely clear on what you have to do.

You must follow instructions *exactly*. Fill in the grids on the forms carefully and accurately. Mis-gridding may lead to a loss of veteran's credits to which you may be entitled, or a misaddressing of your test results. Don't begin the exam until you are told to do so, and stop as soon as the administrator tells you to. Don't turn pages unless you're told to do so, and don't return to parts of the exam that you've already completed unless you are instructed that you may do so. Any infraction of the rules is considered cheating—and that disqualifies you from eligibility for the job you're seeking.

Avoid Careless Errors

Don't reduce your score by making careless mistakes. Be very careful when marking your answer sheet that you're filling in the correct space for the question you're answering. Always read the directions for each test section carefully—even when you think you already know what the directions are. It is why we stress throughout this book that it is important to understand the directions for the different question types before you go into the actual exam. Following these two pieces of advice will not only help you reduce errors, but it will also save you time—time you will need for answering exam questions.

Marking Your Answer Sheet

Keep in mind that the answer sheets for most multiple-choice exams are scored by machine. Be sure to fill out your answer sheet clearly and correctly. After all, you can't "explain" your answers to a scoring machine.

1. Blacken your answer space firmly and completely. ● is the only correct way to mark the answer sheet. ◑ , ⊗ , ⊘ , and ⊘ are unacceptable. The machine might not read them at all, or might read them incorrectly.

2. Mark only one answer for each question; otherwise your answer is read as incorrect.

3. If you change your mind about an answer, erase your mark completely; don't cross it out. An incomplete erasure might be read as a second answer, and you will end up being marked incorrect for that question.

4. All of your answers should be in the form of blackened spaces. The machine cannot "read" English, so avoid making notes in the margins of the answer sheet.

5. Answer each question in the right place. This is one of the most frequent reasons why test takers' questions are scored as incorrect. Question 1 must be answered in space 1; question 2 in space 2, and so on. If you should skip an answer space and mark a series of answers in the wrong places, you'll need to erase all your answers and mark your answer sheet all over again, with answers in the proper spaces. Remember, however, that you're being timed—you cannot afford to use your limited test time doing this. Instead, keep rechecking as you go along that you're filling in the correct answer space for the question you're answering. Look at the question number, check that you are marking your answer in the proper space, and then move on.

6. If your exam includes a typing test, type steadily and carefully. Avoid rushing through the test—that's when you're most likely to make errors. Keep in mind that each error subtracts 1 word per minute (wpm) from your final typing score.

Reading and Following Directions

What if you don't understand the directions on the exam? You risk answering incorrectly for an entire test section. For example, vocabulary questions sometimes ask about synonyms (words that are similar in meaning) but sometimes ask about antonyms (words with opposite meanings). You can easily see how misunderstanding directions in this case could make a whole set of answers incorrect.

If you have time, reread any complicated instructions after you complete the first few questions to check that you really do understand them. If you're still stumped, do not hesitate to ask the examiner to clarify anything you find confusing.

Other mistakes may affect only the response to particular questions—but you still want to avoid them. For instance, some test takers are prone to making what are called "response errors." A response error usually stems from a momentary lapse of concentration.

Example

The question states, "The capital of Massachusetts is …." The correct answer is **(D)** Boston, but you mark **(B)** because "B" is the first letter of the word "Boston."

Example

The question states, "8 − 5 = …." The correct answer is **(A)** 3, but you mark **(C)** thinking "third letter of the alphabet."

A common error in reading comprehension questions is inadvertently bringing your own knowledge into the question. This usually happens when you encounter a passage that discusses a subject you know something about. In exam questions like this, you are instructed to rely *solely* on information within the passage to answer correctly. Although knowing a bit about the subject of the passage can make it easier for you to read and understand, it can also tempt you to rely on your own knowledge rather than on the information provided in the passage. In fact, sometimes an "incorrect" answer to a question is actually based on true information about the subject—but that information is not given in the passage. Keep in mind that test makers are assessing your reading ability, not your general knowledge of a subject, and be sure to answer based on information in the passage—whether or not it is accurate in real life.

MANAGE YOUR TEST TIME

Before you begin the exam, take a moment to plan your progress. In most timed exams, you are not expected to get to all of the questions on a test, but you should at least form an idea of how much time you can spend on each question in order to answer them all. For example, if your exam contains 60 questions and you have 30 minutes to complete the exam, you have about one-half minute to spend on each question. Making a quick calculation like this will help you stay on track and avoid getting bogged down on any one question.

Keep track of the time using your watch or a clock in the exam room—but try not to fixate on how much time you have left. Your task is to answer questions. Avoid spending too much time on any one question: If you feel stuck on a particular question, avoid taking it as a personal challenge. Make an educated guess (we'll discuss this in a moment) or skip the question and move on. Then, if you have time at the end of the exam or section, you can return to the question and give it another try. If you do skip the question, remember to skip the appropriate answer space on your answer sheet as well.

Answering Multiple-Choice Questions

Almost all of the questions on most civil service exams are multiple-choice format. You'll usually have four or five answer choices per question—but remember that there is only one correct answer for each multiple-choice question. Because the exam you're taking has been administered repeatedly, the test developers have a good sense of which types of questions work well and which do not—so it's rare to see ambiguous answer choices. The questions may be complex or somewhat confusing at first, but you will always have only one correct answer choice. Let's review a basic technique for answering this question type that may help you feel less stressed when taking your exam.

First, look at the question and read it thoroughly without reviewing the answer choices. Try to come up with the correct answer *without* reading any of the answer choices.

Now, with a tentative answer in mind, review all the answer choices provided. If your answer is among the choices provided, chances are pretty good that the one it's most similar to is the correct answer choice for that question.

This may work especially well with questions involving math or other calculations. Try to solve the problem without reading the answer choices. If your answer is among the choices, that answer choice is probably the correct one. Pay careful attention to function signs (addition, subtraction, multiplication, division) and to whether numbers are negative or positive to avoid being tripped up when choosing from among the answer choices provided. Some will *appear* to be the correct answer because they result from a common error in calculation.

SHOULD YOU GUESS?

What if you don't know the correct answer? You could use what is called the process of elimination. First, take a moment to eliminate answers that you know are incorrect. Then quickly consider and guess from the remaining choices. Having fewer viable choices is likely to increase your odds of choosing the correct answer. Once you've decided to make a guess—whether it's an educated guess or a wild stab, do it right away and move on. Don't dwell on a particular question; you will be wasting valuable time. A good idea is to use your scratch paper to keep track of questions for which you've guessed the answer. If you have time at the end of the exam or the section, you can quickly return to them and try again.

You may be wondering whether it is wise to guess when you're not sure of an answer (even if you have reduced the odds to 50 percent) or whether it is better to skip a question you're unsure of. Whether you should guess depends for the most part on the method used to score your exam. Civil service exams generally are scored in one of three ways:

1. rights only

2. rights minus wrongs

3. rights minus a fraction of wrongs

If the score is *rights only*, that means it's based only on correct answers. In other words, you are given one point for each correct answer and do not lose points or fractions of points for incorrect ones. In such a case, it's smart to make a guess, even if it isn't an educated one. Of course, you should still read the question and all of the answer choices carefully and try to eliminate choices you believe are wrong before you guess—but if you are not penalized for incorrect answers, even a "lucky" guess might help you gain a point.

In fact, on exams for which you receive no penalty for incorrect answers, you should try to fill in all the answer spaces. If it appears that you will run out of time before completing such an exam, fill in all the remaining answer spaces with the same letter. According to the law of averages, you should get some portion of those questions right and gain points toward your final score.

On the other hand, if the scoring method for your exam is *rights minus wrongs*, meaning that you receive a point for each question answered correctly but have a point subtracted for each incorrect answer, your best bet is to *avoid* guessing. In this type of exam, a wrong answer counts heavily against you. Never fill answer spaces randomly at the end of such an exam. Instead, work as quickly as possible and concentrate on accuracy. Keep working carefully until time is up; then stop and leave the remaining answer spaces blank.

On some exams, you are given a point for questions you answer correctly and have a fraction of a point subtracted from your score for each question you answer incorrectly. In this type of exam, taking educated guesses is acceptable, but you may want to avoid making wild guesses.

Consider: A correct answer gives you one point. A skipped answer gives you nothing, but it also costs you nothing except the chance of getting a correct answer. An incorrect answer costs you 1/4 point. If you're uncomfortable with guessing on this type of exam, you should skip the question—but of course, remember to skip the corresponding answer space as well. However, the risk of losing your place if you skip many questions is so great that you may want to try and guess, even if you are not sure of the answer. If you find that you are spending too much time on any one question for fear of answering incorrectly, you may decide to take a guess, simply to avoid becoming bogged down. If you run short of time, *avoid* filling in answer spaces for uncompleted questions. Work steadily and accurately until time is up.

Finding out which of these scoring methods will be used to grade your exam will go a long way toward helping you establish a test-taking strategy that will help you raise your score.

HOW YOUR EXAM IS SCORED

We mentioned that most civil service exams are machine scored and consist of multiple-choice questions. If your exam is a short-answer written exam, however, such as those often used by companies in the private sector, your answers may be scored by a personnel officer trained in grading test questions. If you blackened spaces on the separate answer sheet accompanying a multiple-choice exam, your answer sheet will be machine scanned or hand scored using a punched card stencil. Then a raw score will be calculated using the scoring formula that applies to that test or test portion—rights only, rights minus wrongs, or rights minus a fraction of wrongs. The raw scores of test sections are then added together for a total raw score.

A raw score is neither a final score nor the score that finds its way onto an eligibility list. The civil service testing authority, U.S. Postal Service, or other testing body converts raw scores to a scaled score, according to an unpublicized formula. The scaling formula allows for slight differences in difficulty of questions from one form of the exam to another and allows for equating the scores of all candidates. The entire process of conversion from raw to scaled score is confidential. The score you receive for your exam does not tell you the number of correct responses you had or a percentage of those responses, even though it is a 1–100 grade.

If you are entitled to veterans' service points, these points are added to your *passing* scaled score to boost your rank on the eligibility list. Veterans' points are added only to passing scores. A failing score cannot be brought to passing level by adding veterans' points. The score earned, plus any veterans' service points, is the score that will be on the eligibility list rankings. Highest scores go to the top of the list.

12 TIPS TO RAISE YOUR SCORE

1. Get to the test center early. Give yourself plenty of time to get there, park your car, and even grab a cup of coffee before the test.

2. Listen to the test administrator and follow his or her instructions carefully.

3. Read *every word* of the instructions. Read *every word of every question.*

4. Mark your answers by completely darkening the answer space of your choice. Do not use the test paper to work out your answers or make notes.

5. Mark *only one* answer for each question, even if you think that more than one answer is correct. You *must* choose only one. If you mark more than one answer, you will be marked incorrect for that question.

6. If you change your mind about an answer, erase your previous answer mark completely. Leave no doubt as to which answer you choose.

7. If your test administrator permits you to use scratch paper or the margins of the test booklet for figuring, don't forget to mark your final answer on the answer sheet as well. Only the answer sheet is scored.

8. As you work, check often to be sure that the question number matches the answer space and that you haven't skipped a space accidentally.

9. Guess according to the suggestions described in this chapter (see "Should You Guess?"). Find out before or on exam day what method of scoring is used to grade your exam.

10. Stay alert. Be careful not to mark a wrong answer because you had a momentary lapse of concentration.

11. If you run out of time to finish any part of the exam before time is called, don't panic. If your responses are accurate, you can do well even without finishing a section. It is even possible to earn a scaled score of 100 without entirely finishing an exam section if you are very accurate. At any rate, do not let your performance on any one section of an exam affect your performance on any other section.

12. Check and recheck your answers as time permits. If you finish any section of your exam before time is called, use the remaining time to be sure you've answered each question in the right space and that you've chosen only one answer for each question. If time still remains, return to the most difficult questions and take another shot at them.

SUMMING IT UP

- Knowing what to expect on a civil service exam and becoming familiar with the techniques of effective test taking will help you do your best on your public safety dispatcher exam. Follow the steps outlined in this chapter to help you gain an edge over others who will be taking the exam: be prepared, avoid careless errors, manage your test time wisely, and know when and how to make educated guesses.

- Don't make your exam more difficult by not preparing for it. Read this book and take the sample tests to become familiar with the kinds of questions you are likely to encounter on your public safety dispatcher exam. When taking the Practice Tests—and especially on your exam day—carefully and thoroughly read every word of directions, even if you think you know what the question is asking. Find a quiet place where you're not likely to be interrupted and time yourself to simulate as closely as possible the test conditions on exam day.

- While practicing for your exam, avoid checking the answer keys and explanations before you've attempted to answer questions correctly on your own. Once you've completed the exam, compare your answers with those provided to determine where you might need additional practice and which question types are most difficult for you.

- Careless mistakes from momentary inattention can lower your test score. Be very careful when marking your answer sheet that you're filling in the correct space for the question you're answering, and read all directions carefully. Following these two pieces of advice will help you reduce errors and save you valuable time on exam day.

- Before you begin the exam, take a moment to plan your progress. Form an idea of how much time you can spend on each question in order to answer them all. This will help you stay on track and avoid getting bogged down on any one question. During the exam, keep track of the time, but try not to fixate on how much time you have left. If you feel stuck on a particular question, make an educated guess or skip the question and move on. If you have extra time, you can give it another try.

- Whether you should guess at answers depends on the method by which your exam is scored. Civil service exams generally are scored as rights only, rights minus wrongs, or rights minus a fraction of wrongs. Follow the tips in this chapter to make the best of whatever scoring method is used for your exam.

PART III

PREPARING FOR THE PUBLIC SAFETY DISPATCHER EXAM

Reading
Comprehension

OVERVIEW

- Reading comprehension on the Public Safety Dispatcher
  Exam
- Practice reading comprehension questions
- Police-related practice reading comprehension questions
- More practice questions
- Summing it up

In Chapter 3, we explained what you can expect when taking a civil service exam and reviewed a few basic strategies for answering multiple-choice questions. In this chapter, we'll take a closer look at the types of questions you'll see on the public safety dispatcher exam.

READING COMPREHENSION ON THE PUBLIC SAFETY DISPATCHER EXAM

A recent survey of dispatcher exams administered nationwide indicates that the subject matter of these exams varies widely. The single common question type, however, is reading comprehension. Some exams include classic reading comprehension questions, in which you are presented with a passage and then asked to answer questions about what you've read. Other exams require candidates to determine a dispatcher or other public safety officer's appropriate response based on a reading of printed procedures and regulations. A third type of reading comprehension question requires the test taker to predict the next step in a process or procedure based on the information presented in a passage. Of course, questions of judgment in emergency and non-emergency situations rely heavily on reading as well.

Before you begin studying strategies for answering reading-based questions, think about your present reading habits and skills. Of course, you already know how to read. But how *well* do you read? Do you concentrate on reading? Do you get the point on your first reading? Do you notice details?

If you answered negatively to any of those last three questions, you'll probably need to improve your reading concentration and comprehension before exam day. It's not as difficult as you might think. Your daily newspaper provides an excellent source to help improve your reading. Begin by making a point of reading all the way through any article that you begin. Don't be satisfied with skimming the first paragraph or two. Read with a pen in hand and underline details and ideas that seem crucial to the meaning of the article. Notice points of view, arguments, and supporting information. When you finish the article, summarize it for yourself. Do you know the purpose of the article? The main idea presented? The attitude of the writer? Any points of controversy? Did you find certain information lacking? As you answer these questions, review your underlined text. Did you focus on important words and ideas? Did you read with comprehension?

Try to repeat this process each day. Before long, you'll find that you'll become more efficient in and glean more information from your reading.

Changing Your Reading Habits

You can't simply sit down the night before a test containing reading comprehension questions and cram for it. The only way to strengthen your reading skill is to practice systematically. The gains you make will show, not only in an increased score on the test but also when you read for study or pleasure.

Trying to change reading habits you've probably had your whole life can be difficult and discouraging. Don't attempt to employ every reading comprehension suggestion presented here all at once. Take it a little at a time, as the program here suggests.

1. Set aside 15 minutes a day to practice new reading techniques.

2. Start with a short, easy-to-read article from a magazine or newspaper. Note the amount of time you take to read and understand the article. At the end of this practice session, time yourself on another short article, and record both times.

3. Read an editorial or a review of a book, movie, or performance in a literary magazine or newspaper. This type of article always expresses the author's (or the paper's) point of view, so it's good practice for seeking the main idea of a reading passage. After you've finished, see whether you can come up with a good title for the article, and jot down in one sentence the author's main idea.

4. Find one new word and write the sentence in which it appears. Try to determine its meaning from the context in which it's used. Then look up the definition in a dictionary. Form your own sentence using the word; then try to use the word in conversation at least twice the next day.

If you follow this program daily, you'll find that your test score will show the improvements you have made in reading comprehension.

Reading Includes Vocabulary

Building your vocabulary is one of the most effective ways to strengthen your reading comprehension. The most effective readers have a rich, extensive vocabulary. As you read, make a list of words you come across that are unfamiliar. Include in the list any words that you understand within the context of the article, but that you cannot readily define. Also include words that you do not understand at all. When you put aside your article, refer to a dictionary and look up every new and unfamiliar word you encountered. In a special notebook, write down each word and its definition: Writing helps seal the information in your memory far better than simply reading, and the notebook will be a handy reference. Being sensitive to the meaning of words and trying to understand each word you encounter will make reading easier and more enjoyable—even if none of the words you learn in this process crops up on your exam. In fact, the practice of vocabulary building is a good lifetime habit to develop.

5 Steps to Answering Reading Comprehension Questions

Success with reading-based questions on the public safety dispatcher exam depends on more than simply understanding what you read; you must also know how to draw the correct answers to the questions from the reading selection and how to distinguish the best answer from a number of answers that seem correct—or from several answers that all seem incorrect. Follow the following five steps to help you score your highest on the reading comprehension section of your exam:

1. **Read the questions first.** Strange as it may seem, it's a good idea to approach reading comprehension questions by reading the questions—not the answer choices, just the questions—before you read the passage. Doing so alerts you to specific details, ideas, and points of view that you'll need to know to answer correctly. Use a pencil to underline key words in the questions; it will help you focus your attention as you read.

2. **Scan the reading passage quickly.** This gives you an idea of the passage's subject matter and organization before you read it more thoroughly. If key words or ideas pop out at you, underline them, but try not to search for details in this preliminary skim.

3. **Read for detail.** Next, read the passage carefully, with comprehension as your main goal. Underline the most significant words, just as you have been doing in your newspaper readings.

4. **Return to the questions.** Read each question carefully. Be sure you understand what it asks: Misreading questions is a major cause of errors on reading comprehension questions. Then, read *all* the answer choices and eliminate the obviously incorrect answers. You may be left with only one possible answer. If you have more than one possible answer left, reread the question, focusing on catching words that might destroy the validity of a seemingly acceptable answer. These include expressions like *under all circumstances, at all times, never, always, under no condition, absolutely, entirely,* and *except when.*

5. **Scan the passage again.** Finally, skim the passage once more, focusing on the underlined segments. By now, you should be able to conclude which answer is best.

Quick Tips

After you follow the five steps listed above, keep in mind these tips for answering reading comprehension questions.

- If the author quotes material from another source, make sure that you understand the purpose of the quote. Does the author agree or disagree with the substance of the quote?

- Avoid inserting your own judgments into your answers. Even if you disagree with the author or spot a factual error in the selection, remember that you are being asked to answer based only on what is stated or implied in the selection.

- Don't spend too much time on any one question. If reviewing the passage doesn't help you determine the correct answer, try to make an educated guess from among the answers remaining after you eliminate the obviously incorrect choices. Then mark your answer in the test booklet or answer sheet and move on. If you have time at the end of the section or the exam, you can return to the passage and take another shot at the question. Often, a fresh look provides new insights.

Types of Reading-Based Questions

Reading-based questions are presented in a number of forms. Here's a look at the most commonly used types:

1. **Question of fact or detail.** You may have to mentally rephrase or rearrange the words of a passage to answer this type of question, but the answer can always be found in the body of the passage.

2. **Best title or main idea.** The answer may be obvious, but the incorrect answer choices for the "main idea" question are often half-truths that you might easily confuse with the main idea. They may misstate the idea, omit part of the idea, or even offer a supporting idea quoted directly from the text. The correct answer is the one that deals with the largest portion of the selection.

3. **Interpretation.** You will be asked what the selection means rather than what it states outright.

4. **Inference.** This is the most difficult type of reading-based question. It asks you to go beyond what the selection says and predict what might happen next. You may have to choose the best course of action to take based on given procedures and a factual situation, or you may have to judge the actions of others. In any case, your answer must be based on the information in the selection and on your own common sense—but not on any other information outside of the passage that you may have or know. A variation of the inference question might begin with the phrase, "The author would expect that. . . ." To answer this question type, you must first determine the author's viewpoint and then make an inference from that viewpoint based on the information in the selection.

5. **Vocabulary.** Some reading questions directly or indirectly ask for the meanings of certain words that appear in the selection.

PRACTICE READING COMPREHENSION QUESTIONS

Let's take a look at some typical reading comprehension passages and questions.

QUESTIONS 1–4 ARE BASED ON THE FOLLOWING PASSAGE.

The recipient gains an impression of a typewritten letter before beginning to read the message. Factors that give a good first impression include margins and spacing that are visually pleasing, formal parts of the letter that are correctly placed according to the style of the letter, copy that is free of obvious erasures and overstrikes, and transcript that is even and clear. The problem for the typist is how to produce that first positive impression of his or her work.

There are several general rules that a typist can follow when he or she wishes to prepare a properly spaced letter on a sheet of letterhead. The width of a letter ordinarily should not be less than four inches nor more than six inches. The side margins should also have a proportionate relation to the bottom margin, as should the space between the letterhead and the body of the letter. Usually the most appealing arrangement is when the side margins are even and the bottom margin is slightly wider than the side margins. In some offices, however, a standard line length is used for all business letters, and the typist then varies the spacing between the date line and the inside address according to the length of the letter.

1. The best title for the preceding passage is
   (A) Writing Office Letters.
   (B) Making Good First Impressions.
   (C) Judging Well-Typed Letters.
   (D) Good Placing and Spacing for Office Letters.

2. According to the passage, which of the following might be considered the way that people quickly judge the quality of work that has been typed?
   (A) By measuring the margins to see whether they are correct
   (B) By looking at the spacing and cleanliness of the typescript
   (C) By scanning the body of the letter for meaning
   (D) By reading the date line and address for errors

3. According to the passage, what would be definitely undesirable as the average line length of a typed letter?
   (A) 4 inches
   (B) 5 inches
   (C) 6 inches
   (D) 7 inches

4. According to the preceding paragraphs, when the line length is kept standard, the typist
   (A) does not have to vary the spacing at all because this also is standard.
   (B) adjusts the spacing between the date line and inside address for different lengths of letters.
   (C) uses the longest line as a guideline for spacing between the date line and inside address.
   (D) varies the number of spaces between the lines.

Helpful Hints

Begin by skimming the questions and underlining key words. Your underlined questions should look more or less like this:

1. The <u>best title</u> for the preceding passage is. . . .

2. According to the passage, which of the following might be considered the way that people <u>quickly judge the quality</u> of work that has been typed?

3. According to the passage, what would be definitely <u>undesirable</u> as the <u>average line length</u> of a typed letter?

4. According to the preceding paragraphs, <u>when the line length is kept standard</u>, the typist. . . .

Now skim the selection. A quick reading should give you an idea of the structure of the selection and of its overall meaning.

Next, read the selection carefully and underline words that seem important or that you think hold keys to the answers. Your underlined selection should look something like this:

The recipient gains an impression of a typewritten letter before beginning to read the message. <u>Factors that give a good first impression</u> include <u>margins and spacing that are visually pleasing</u>, formal parts of the letter that are <u>correctly placed</u> according to the style of the letter, copy that is <u>free of obvious erasures and overstrikes</u>, and transcript that is <u>even and clear</u>. The problem for the typist is how to produce that first, positive impression of his or her work.

There are several general rules that a typist can follow when he or she wishes to prepare a properly spaced letter on a sheet of letterhead. The width of a letter ordinarily <u>should not be less than four inches nor more than six inches</u>. The side margins should also have a proportionate relation to the bottom margin, as well as the space between the letterhead and the body of the letter. Usually the most appealing arrangement is when the <u>side margins are even</u> and the <u>bottom margin is slightly wider</u> than the side margins. In some offices, however, a <u>standard line length is used for all business letters</u>, and the clerk then <u>varies the spacing between the date line and the inside address</u> according to the length of the letter.

Now go back and read the questions and answer choices again, and try to choose the correct answer for each question. The answers and explanations can be found on page 66.

QUESTIONS 5–9 ARE BASED ON THE FOLLOWING PASSAGE.

Cotton fabrics treated with the XYZ Process have features that make them far superior to any previously known flame-retardant-treated cotton fabrics. XYZ Process-treated fabrics endure repeated laundering and dry cleaning; are glow resistant as well as flame resistant; form tough, pliable, and protective chars when exposed to flames or intense heat; are inert physiologically to persons handling or exposed to the fabric; are only slightly heavier than untreated fabrics; and are susceptible to further wet and dry finishing treatments. In addition, the treated fabrics exhibit little or no adverse change in feel, texture, and appearance, and are shrink-, rot-, and mildew-resistant. The treatment reduces strength only slightly. Finished fabrics have "easy care" properties in that they are wrinkle resistant and dry rapidly.

5. It is most accurate to state that the author of the preceding selection presents
   (A) facts but reaches no conclusion concerning the value of the process.
   (B) a conclusion concerning the value of the process and facts to support that conclusion.
   (C) a conclusion, unsupported by facts, concerning the value of the process.
   (D) neither facts nor conclusions, but merely describes the process.

6. Of the following articles, for which is the XYZ Process most suitable?
   (A) nylon stockings
   (B) woolen shirts
   (C) silk ties
   (D) cotton bedsheets

7. Of the following aspects of the XYZ Process, which is NOT discussed in the preceding selection?
   (A) costs
   (B) washability
   (C) wearability
   (D) the human body

8. The main reason for treating a fabric with the XYZ Process is to
   (A) prepare the fabric for other wet and dry finishing treatments.
   (B) render it shrink-, rot-, and mildew-resistant.
   (C) increase its weight and strength.
   (D) reduce the chance that it will catch fire.

9. Which of the following would be considered a minor drawback of the XYZ Process?
   (A) It forms chars when exposed to flame.
   (B) It makes fabrics mildew-resistant.
   (C) It adds to the weight of fabrics.
   (D) It is compatible with other finishing treatments.

Helpful Hints

Skim the questions and underline the words or phrases that you consider important. The questions should look something like this:

5. It is most accurate to state that the author of the preceding selection <u>presents</u>. . . .

6. Of the following articles, for which is the <u>XYZ Process most suitable</u>?

7. Of the following aspects of the XYZ Process, which is <u>NOT discussed</u> in the preceding selection?

8. The <u>main reason for treating</u> a fabric with the XYZ Process is to. . . .

9. Which of the following would be considered a <u>minor drawback</u> of the XYZ Process?

Skim the reading selection. Get an idea of the subject matter of the selection and of how it is organized. Now read the selection carefully and underline the words that you think are especially important. The passage might be underlined like this:

> <u>Cotton fabrics treated</u> with the <u>XYZ Process</u> have <u>features</u> that make them far superior to any previously known <u>flame-retardant-treated cotton fabrics</u>. XYZ Process treated fabrics <u>endure repeated laundering</u> and <u>dry cleaning</u>; are <u>glow resistant</u> as well as <u>flame resistant</u>; <u>form tough, pliable</u>, and <u>protective chars</u> when exposed to flames or intense heat; are <u>inert physiologically to persons handling</u> or exposed to the fabric; are only <u>slightly heavier than untreated fabrics</u>; and are <u>susceptible to further wet</u> and <u>dry finishing</u> treatments. In addition, the treated fabrics exhibit <u>little</u> or <u>no adverse change in feel, texture</u>, and <u>appearance</u>, and are <u>shrink-, rot-, and mildew-resistant</u>. The treatment <u>reduces strength only slightly</u>. Finished fabrics have "easy care" properties in that they are <u>wrinkle resistant</u> and <u>dry rapidly</u>.

Now go back and read these questions and answer choices again, and try to choose the correct answer for each question. The answers and explanations are on pages 66–67.

You should be getting better at reading and answering questions. Try the next questions on your own. The answers and explanations are given on pages 67–68.

QUESTIONS 10–12 ARE BASED ON THE FOLLOWING PASSAGE.

> Language performs an essentially social function: It helps us get along together, communicate, and achieve a great measure of concerted action. Words are signs that have significance by convention, and those people who do not adopt the conventions simply fail to communicate. They do not "get along," and a social force arises that encourages them to achieve the correct associations. By "correct," we mean as used by other members of the social group. Some of the vital points about language are brought home to an English visitor to America, and vice-versa, because our vocabularies are nearly the same—but not quite.

10. As defined in the preceding selection, usage of a word is "correct" when it is

(A) defined in standard dictionaries.

(B) used by the majority of persons throughout the world who speak the same language.

(C) used by the majority of educated persons who speak the same language.

(D) used by other persons with whom we are associating.

11. In the preceding selection, the author is concerned primarily with the

(A) meaning of words.

(B) pronunciation of words.

(C) structure of sentences.

(D) origin and development of language.

12. According to the preceding selection, the main language problem of an English visitor to America stems from the fact that an English person

(A) uses some words that have different meanings for Americans.

(B) has different social values than the Americans.

(C) has had more exposure to non-English speaking persons than Americans.

(D) pronounces words differently than Americans.

QUESTIONS 13–18 ARE BASED ON THE FOLLOWING PASSAGE.

Because almost every office once had some contact with data-processed records, a senior stenographer had to have some understanding of the basic operations of data processing. Data processing systems once handled about one-third of all office paperwork. On punched cards, magnetic tape, or other media, data were recorded before being fed into the computer for processing. A machine such as the keypunch was used to convert the data written on the source document into the coded symbols on punched cards or tapes. After data was converted, it had to be verified to guarantee absolute accuracy of conversion. In this manner, data became a permanent record that could be read by computers that compared, stored, computed, and otherwise processed data at high speeds. One key person in a computer installation was a programmer, the man or woman who put business and scientific problems into special symbolic languages that could be read by the computer. Jobs done by the computer ranged from payroll operations to chemical process control, but most computer applications were directed toward management data. About half of the programmers employed by business came to their positions with college degrees; the remaining half were promoted to their positions, without regard to education, from within the organization on the basis of demonstrated ability.

13. Of the following, the best title for the preceding selection is

(A) The Stenographer as Data Processor.

(B) The Relation of Key Punching to Stenography.

(C) Understanding Data Processing.

(D) Permanent Office Records.

14. According to the passage, a senior stenographer had to understand the basic operations of data processing because

(A) almost every office had contact with data-processed records.

(B) any office worker might have been asked to verify the accuracy of data.

(C) most offices were involved in the production of permanent records.

(D) data may have been converted into computer language by typing on a keypunch.

15. According to the passage, the data that the computer understands were most often expressed as
    (A) a scientific programming language.
    (B) records or symbols punched on tape, cards, or other media.
    (C) records on cards.
    (D) records on tape.

16. According to the passage, computers were used most often to handle
    (A) management data.
    (B) problems of higher education.
    (C) the control of chemical processes.
    (D) payroll operations.

17. Computer programming was taught in many colleges and business schools. The passage implies that programmers in industry
    (A) had to have professional training.
    (B) needed professional training to advance.
    (C) had to have at least a college education to do adequate programming tasks.
    (D) did not need college education to do programming work.

18. According to the passage, data to be processed by computer should have been
    (A) recent.
    (B) complete.
    (C) basic.
    (D) verified.

POLICE-RELATED PRACTICE READING COMPREHENSION QUESTIONS

On exams that are written specifically for dispatchers in the police department, many reading passages will relate to legal definitions, laws, and police procedures. When reading these passages, you must pay special attention to details relating to exceptions, special pre-conditions, combinations of activities, choices of actions, and prescribed time sequences. Sometimes the printed procedure specifies that certain actions are to be taken only when there is a combination of factors, such as that a person actually breaks a window *and* has a gun. At other times, the procedures give choices of action under specific circumstances. You must read carefully to determine whether the passage requires a combination of factors or gives a choice, then make the appropriate judgment. When a time sequence is specified, be certain to follow that sequence in the prescribed order.

The following passages are based on police-specific questions. Beyond requiring reading comprehension skills, they require the special police exam emphasis we have just discussed.

QUESTIONS 19–23 ARE BASED ON THE FOLLOWING PASSAGE.

If we are to study crime in its widest social setting, we will find a variety of conduct that, although criminal in the legal sense, is not offensive to the moral conscience of a considerable number of persons. Traffic violations, for example, do not brand the offender as guilty of moral offense. In fact, the recipient of a traffic ticket is usually simply the subject of some good-natured joking by friends. Although there may be indignation among certain groups of citizens against gambling and liquor law violations, these activities are often tolerated, if not openly supported, by the more numerous residents of the community. Indeed, certain social and service clubs regularly conduct gambling games and lotteries for the purpose of raising funds. Some communities regard violations involving the sale of liquor with little concern to profit from increased license fees and taxes paid by dealers. The thousand and one forms of political graft and corruption that infest our urban centers only occasionally arouse public condemnation and official action.

19. According to the passage, all types of illegal conduct are
    (A) condemned by all elements of the community.
    (B) considered a moral offense, although some are tolerated by a few citizens.
    (C) violations of the law, but some are acceptable to certain elements of the community.
    (D) found in a social setting and therefore not punishable by law.

20. According to the passage, traffic violations are generally considered by society to be
    (A) crimes requiring the maximum penalty set by the law.
    (B) more serious than violations of the liquor laws.
    (C) offenses against the morals of the community.
    (D) relatively minor offenses requiring minimal punishment.

21. According to the passage, a lottery conducted for the purpose of raising funds for a church
    (A) is considered a serious violation of the law.
    (B) may be tolerated by a community that has laws against gambling.
    (C) may be conducted under special laws demanded by the more numerous residents of a community.
    (D) arouses indignation in most communities.

22. On the basis of the passage, the most likely reaction in the community to a police raid on a gambling casino would be
    (A) more an attitude of indifference than interest in the raid.
    (B) general approval of the raid.
    (C) condemnation of the raid by most people.
    (D) demand for further action, since this raid is not sufficient to end gambling activities.

23. Of the following, which best describes the central thought behind this passage and would be most suitable as a title?
    (A) Crime and the Police
    (B) Public Condemnation of Graft and Corruption
    (C) Gambling Is Not Always a Vicious Business
    (D) Public Attitudes Toward Law Violations

QUESTIONS 24–26 ARE BASED ON THE FOLLOWING PASSAGE.

The law enforcement agency is one of the most important agencies in the field of juvenile delinquency prevention. This is so, however, not because of the social work connected with this problem—for this is not a police matter—but because the officers are usually the first to come in contact with the delinquent. The manner of arrest and detention makes a deep impression on the delinquent and affects his or her lifelong attitude toward society and toward the law. The juvenile court is perhaps the most important agency in this work. Contrary to general opinion, however, it is not primarily concerned with putting children into correctional schools. The main purpose of the juvenile court is to save the child and to develop his or her emotional makeup so that he or she can grow up to be a decent and well-balanced citizen. The system of probation is the means by which the court seeks to accomplish these goals.

24. According to the passage, police work is an important part of a program to prevent juvenile delinquency because
    (A) social work is no longer considered important in juvenile delinquency prevention.
    (B) police officers are the first to have contact with the delinquent.
    (C) police officers jail the offender so that they can change his or her attitude toward society and the law.
    (D) it is the first step in placing the delinquent in jail.

25. According to the passage, the chief purpose of the juvenile court is to
    (A) punish the child for the offense.
    (B) select a suitable correctional school for the delinquent.
    (C) use available means to help the delinquent become a better person.
    (D) provide psychiatric care for the delinquent.

26. According to the passage, the juvenile court directs the development of delinquents under its care chiefly by
    (A) placing the child under probation.
    (B) sending the child to a correctional school.
    (C) keeping the delinquent in prison.
    (D) returning the child to his or her home.

QUESTION 27 IS BASED ON THE FOLLOWING PASSAGE.

When a person commits a traffic infraction, a police officer should

1. inform the violator of the offense committed.

2. request the violator to show his or her driver's license, vehicle registration, and insurance identification card. Failure to produce this required material may result in additional tickets. (Taxis, buses, and other rented vehicles do not require insurance identification cards.)

3. enter only one infraction on each ticket.

4. use a separate ticket for each additional infraction.

27. Police Officer Herrmann has been assigned to curb traffic violations at the intersection of Main Street and Central Avenue. Officer Herrmann observes a taxicab going through a red light at this intersection and signals the driver to pull over. The officer informs the cab driver of his violation and asks for the required material. The driver surrenders his license and registration to the officer. Police Officer Herrmann should

(A) issue the cab driver a ticket for the red light violation and issue him a separate ticket for not surrendering his insurance card.

(B) issue the cab driver one ticket including both the red light violation and the absence of the insurance card.

(C) issue the cab driver a ticket only for the red light violation.

(D) issue the cab driver a ticket only for not having an insurance card.

ANSWER KEY AND EXPLANATIONS

1. D	7. A	13. C	18. D	23. D
2. B	8. D	14. A	19. C	24. B
3. D	9. C	15. B	20. D	25. C
4. B	10. D	16. A	21. B	26. A
5. B	11. A	17. D	22. A	27. C
6. D	12. A			

1. **The correct answer is (D).** The best title for any reading passage is one that takes in all of the ideas presented without being too broad or too narrow. Choice (D) provides the most inclusive title for this passage. A look at the other choices shows you why. Choice (A) can be eliminated because the passage discusses typing a letter, not writing one. Although the first paragraph states that a letter should make a good first impression, the passage is clearly devoted to the letter, not the first impression, so choice (B) also can be eliminated. Choice (C) puts the emphasis on the wrong aspect of the typewritten letter. The passage concerns how to type a properly spaced letter, not how to judge one.

2. **The correct answer is (B).** Both spacing and cleanliness are mentioned in the first paragraph as ways to judge the quality of a typed letter. The first paragraph states that the margins should be "visually pleasing" in relation to the body of the letter, but that does not imply margins of a particular measure, so choice (A) is incorrect. Meaning is not discussed in the passage, only the look of the finished letter, so choice (C) is incorrect. The passage makes no mention of uncorrected errors, only the avoidance of erasures and overstrikes, so choice (D) is incorrect.

3. **The correct answer is (D).** The second sentence in the second paragraph states that the width of a letter "should not be less than four inches nor more than six inches." According to this rule, seven inches is an undesirable length.

4. **The correct answer is (B).** The answer to this question is stated in the last sentence of the reading passage. When a standard line length is used, the clerk "varies the spacing between the date line and the inside address according to the length of the letter." The passage offers no support for any other choice.

5. **The correct answer is (B).** This is a combination main idea and interpretation question. If you cannot answer this question readily, reread the selection. The author clearly thinks that the XYZ Process is terrific and says so in the first sentence. The rest of the selection presents a wealth of facts to support the initial claim.

6. **The correct answer is (D).** At first glance, you might think that this is an inference question requiring you to make a judgment based upon the few drawbacks of the process. Closer reading, however, shows that there is no contest for a correct answer here. This is a simple question of fact. The XYZ Process is a treatment for cotton fabrics.

7. **The correct answer is (A).** The text you chose to underline should help you with this question of fact. Cost is not mentioned; all other aspects of the XYZ Process are. If you are having trouble finding mention of the effect of the XYZ Process on the human body, add to your vocabulary list "inert" and "physiologically."

8. **The correct answer is (D).** This is a main-idea question. You must distinguish between the main idea and the supporting and incidental facts.

9. **The correct answer is (C).** A drawback is a negative feature. The selection mentions only two negative features. The treatment reduces strength slightly, and it makes fabrics slightly heavier than untreated fabrics: Only one of these negative features is offered among the answer choices.

10. **The correct answer is (D).** The answer to this question is stated in the next-to-last sentence of the selection.

11. **The correct answer is (A).** This is a main-idea question. From reading the passage you should have gleaned that the reading was primarily about the meaning of words.

12. **The correct answer is (A).** This is a question of fact. The phrasing of the question is different from the phrasing of the last sentence, but the meaning is the same.

13. **The correct answer is (C).** Choosing the best title for this selection is not easy. Although the senior stenographer is mentioned in the first sentence, the selection is really not concerned with stenographers or with their relationship to key punching. Thus, choices (A) and (B) can be eliminated. Permanent office records are mentioned in the selection, but only along with other equally important uses for data processing. This fact eliminates choice (D). When in doubt, the most general title is usually correct.

14. **The correct answer is (A).** This is a question of fact. Any one of the answer choices could be correct, but the answer is given almost verbatim in the first sentence. Take advantage of answers that are handed to you in this way.

15. **The correct answer is (B).** This is a question of fact, but it is a tricky one. The program language is a symbolic language, not a scientific one. Reread carefully and eliminate choice (A). Choice (B) includes more of the information in the selection than either choice (C) or (D), and so is the best answer.

16. **The correct answer is (A).** This is a question of fact. The answer is stated in the next-to-last sentence.

17. **The correct answer is (D).** Remember that you are answering the questions on the basis of the information given in the selection. In spite of any information you may have to the contrary, the last sentence of the selection states that half the programmers employed in business achieved their positions by moving up from the ranks without regard to education.

18. **The correct answer is (D).** The answer appears in the second-to-last sentence in the first paragraph: "After data has been converted, it must be verified to guarantee absolute accuracy of conversion."

19. **The correct answer is (C).** The words "although" and "occasionally," which pop up in this passage, are the clues to the answer. Although illegal conduct is, by definition, violation of law, much illegal conduct is not repulsive to many elements of the

community. Choice (A) is a direct contradiction of the meaning of the passage, as is choice (B). Choice (D) is unsupported by the passage.

20. **The correct answer is (D).** The third sentence supports this answer. The fourth sentence directly contradicts choice (B) in its statement that gambling and liquor law violations may raise some indignation.

21. **The correct answer is (B).** The clear implication is that law-abiding citizens readily engage in gambling and lotteries for fund-raising purposes. Nothing is said about special laws enabling this activity, so (C) is not a correct choice.

22. **The correct answer is (A).** Since gambling is not considered a serious criminal activity by the bulk of the populace, a raid on a gambling establishment would meet with indifference rather than approval or disapproval.

23. **The correct answer is (D).** Choice (A) is too broad; the passage deals specifically with certain kinds of crime. Choice (B) is opposite in thought to the content of the passage. Choice (C) is too narrow since other crimes are discussed in addition to gambling.

24. **The correct answer is (B).** The correct answer is stated in the second sentence: "… officers are usually the first to come in contact with the delinquent." The point with reference to social work is not that social work is unimportant, but that it is not a police matter. Choices **(C)** and **(D)** are in direct contradiction to the passage.

25. **The correct answer is (C).** The purpose of the juvenile court is to choose the best possible method to "save the child." The passage implies that punishment and reform school are not the methods of choice—that probation is preferred. While psychiatric care may be the correct method in some cases, it is not mentioned in the passage and is not the best answer choice.

26. **The correct answer is (A).** The last sentence in the passage clearly states that probation is the method that the juvenile courts use to direct the development of delinquents.

27. **The correct answer is (C).** The taxi driver violated the law by going through a red light. Officer Herrmann correctly informed the driver of this infraction and must issue a ticket. If the violator had been driving a private automobile, Officer Herrmann would have had to issue a separate ticket for his not producing an insurance card. (See rules 3 and 4.) However, in this case, an exception applies. The exception is that taxis, along with buses and rented vehicles, do not need to have insurance identification cards.

MORE PRACTICE QUESTIONS

Just as all exams for similar positions are not alike, and all reading-based questions are not alike, so all traditional-style reading questions are not alike. Some traditional reading comprehension questions introduce novel situations and totally unfamiliar information. Others construct reading passages that use vocabulary and situations immediately relevant to the position for which the exam is testing. Some base each question upon a single reading passage, others use a series of questions based upon one passage. In the two exercises that follow, you will have an opportunity to review a variety of reading comprehension styles. In each exercise, circle the letter of the correct answer to each question. You will find correct answers and answer explanations at the end of each exercise.

Exercise 1

Directions: Read the passages below, then answer the questions that follow.

In a pole-vaulting competition, the judge decides on the minimum height to be jumped. The vaulter may attempt to jump any height above the minimum. Using flexible fiberglass poles, vaulters have jumped as high as 18 feet, 8¼ inches.

1. The passage best supports the statement that pole vaulters
   (A) may attempt to jump any height in competition.
   (B) must jump higher than 18 feet, 8¼ inches to win.
   (C) must jump higher than the height set by the judge.
   (D) must use fiberglass poles.

Only about one tenth of an iceberg is visible above the water. Eight to nine times as much ice is hidden below the water line. In the Antarctic Ocean, near the South Pole, some icebergs rise as high as 300 feet above the water line.

2. The passage best supports the statement that icebergs in the Antarctic Ocean
   (A) are usually 300 feet high.
   (B) can be as much as 3,000 feet high.
   (C) are difficult to spot.
   (D) are hazards to navigation.

You can tell a frog from a toad by its skin. In general, a frog's skin is moist, smooth, and shiny, while a toad's skin is dry, dull, and rough or covered with warts. Frogs are also better at jumping than toads are.

3. The passage best supports the statement that you can recognize a toad by its
   (A) great jumping ability.
   (B) smooth, shiny skin.
   (C) lack of warts.
   (D) dry, rough skin.

Thomas Edison was responsible for more than 1,000 inventions in his 84-year lifespan. Among the most famous of his inventions are the phonograph, the electric light bulb, motion picture film, the electric generator, and the battery.

4. The passage best supports the statement that Thomas Edison
   (A) was the most famous inventor.
   (B) was responsible for 84 inventions.
   (C) invented many things in his short life.
   (D) was responsible for the phonograph and motion picture film.

Amateur sportsmen or sportswomen are those who take part in sports purely for enjoyment, not for financial reward. Professionals are people who are paid to participate in sports. Most athletes who compete in the Olympic Games are amateurs.

5. The passage best supports the statement that one example of an amateur in sports might be
   (A) an Olympic champion.
   (B) a member of the Philadelphia Eagles.
   (C) the holder of the heavyweight boxing crown.
   (D) a participant in the World Series.

A year—the time it takes the Earth to go exactly once around the sun—is not 365 days. It is actually 365 days, 6 hours, 9 minutes, 9½ seconds—or 365¼ days. Leap years make up for this discrepancy by adding an extra day once every four years.

6. The passage best supports the statement that the purpose of leap years is to
   (A) adjust for the fact it takes 365¼ days for the Earth to circle the sun.
   (B) make up for time lost in the work year.
   (C) occur every four years.
   (D) allow for differences in the length of a year in each time zone.

Scientists are taking a closer look at the recent boom in the use of wood for heating. Wood burning, it seems, releases high-level pollutants. It is believed that burning wood produces a thousand times more CO—carbon monoxide—than natural gas does when it burns.

7. The passage best supports the statement that CO is
   (A) natural gas.
   (B) wood.
   (C) carbon monoxide.
   (D) heat.

The average American family makes a major move every ten years. This means that family history becomes scattered. In some cases, a person searching for his or her family's past must hire a professional researcher to track down his or her ancestors.

8. The passage best supports the statement that every few years
   (A) somebody tries to trace his or her family's history.
   (B) the average American family moves.
   (C) family history becomes scattered.
   (D) professional researchers are hired to track down ancestors.

When gas is leaking, any spark or sudden flame can ignite it. This can create a "flashback," which burns off the gas in a quick puff of smoke and flame. But the real danger is in a large leak, which can cause an explosion.

9. The passage best supports the statement that the real danger from leaking gas is a(n)
   (A) flashback.
   (B) puff of smoke and flame.
   (C) explosion.
   (D) spark.

With the exception of Earth, all of the planets in our solar system are named for gods and goddesses in Greek or Roman legends. This is because the other planets were thought to be in heaven, like the gods, and our planet lay beneath, like the earth.

10. The passage best supports the statement that all the planets except Earth
    (A) were part of Greek and Roman legends.
    (B) were thought to be in heaven.
    (C) are part of the same solar system.
    (D) were worshipped as gods.

The Supreme Court was established by Article 3 of the Constitution. Since 1869 it has been made up of nine members—the Chief Justice and eight associate justices—who are appointed for life. Supreme Court justices are named by the President and must be confirmed by the Senate.

11. The passage best supports the statement that the Supreme Court
    (A) was established in 1869.
    (B) consists of nine judges.
    (C) consists of justices appointed by the Senate.
    (D) changes with each presidential election.

The sport of automobile racing originated in France in 1894. There are five basic types of competition: (1) the Grand Prix, a series of races that leads to a world championship; (2) stock car racing, which uses specially equipped standard cars; (3) midget car racing; (4) sports car racing; and (5) drag racing. The best-known U.S. race is the Indianapolis 500, first held in 1911.

12. The passage best supports the statement that the sport of auto racing
   (A) started with the Indianapolis 500 in 1911.
   (B) uses only standard cars, which are specially equipped.
   (C) holds its championship race in France.
   (D) includes five different types of competition.

The brain controls both voluntary behavior, such as walking and talking, and most involuntary behavior, such as the beating of the heart and breathing. In higher animals, the brain is also the site of emotions, memory, self-awareness, and thought.

13. The passage best supports the statement that in higher animals, the brain controls
   (A) emotions, memory, and thought.
   (B) voluntary behavior.
   (C) most involuntary behavior.
   (D) all of the above.

The speed of a boat is measured in knots. One knot is equal to a speed of one nautical mile per hour. A nautical mile is equal to 6,080 feet, while an ordinary mile is 5,280 feet.

14. The passage best supports the statement that
   (A) a nautical mile is longer than an ordinary mile.
   (B) a speed of 2 knots is the same as 2 miles per hour.
   (C) a knot is the same as a mile.
   (D) the distance a boat travels is measured in knots.

There are only two grooves on an LP—one on each side. The groove is cut in a spiral on the surface of the record. For stereo sound, a different sound is recorded in each wall of the groove. The pick-up produces two signals, one of which goes to the left speaker and one to the right speaker.

15. The passage best supports the statement that stereo sound is produced by
   (A) cutting extra grooves in an LP.
   (B) recording different sounds in each wall of the groove.
   (C) sending the sound to two speakers.
   (D) having left and right speakers.

The overuse of antibiotics today represents a growing danger, according to many medical authorities. Patients everywhere, stimulated by reports of new wonder drugs, continue to ask their doctors for antibiotics to relieve a cold, flu, or any other viral infections that occur during the course of a bad winter. But, for the common cold and many other viral infections, antibiotics have no effect.

16. The passage best supports the statement that

   (A) the use of antibiotics is becoming a health hazard.

   (B) antibiotics are of no value in the treatment of many viral infections.

   (C) patients should ask their doctors for a shot of one of the new wonder drugs to relieve the symptoms of the flu.

   (D) the treatment of colds and other viral infections by antibiotics will lessen their severity.

A prompt report of every unusual occurrence on a train will be made by telephone to the Station Supervisor's office, whether or not a written report is used. The telephone report should include the time and place and a concise statement of the circumstances and actions taken, including the names and addresses of passengers and the names and badge numbers of all employees and police officers involved. Details will be confirmed in a written report when requested. No unusual occurrence is too trivial to report.

17. The passage best supports the statement that when reporting an unusual occurrence, a railroad clerk need not say

   (A) where it happened.

   (B) what was done about it.

   (C) when it occurred.

   (D) why it happened.

Alertness and attentiveness are essential qualities for success as a telephone operator. The work the operator performs often requires careful attention under conditions of stress.

18. The passage best supports the statement that a telephone operator

   (A) always works under great strain.

   (B) cannot be successful unless he or she memorizes many telephone numbers.

   (C) must be trained before he or she can render good service.

   (D) must be able to work under difficulties.

To prevent accidents, safety devices must be used to guard exposed machinery, the light in the plant must be adequate, and mechanics should be instructed in safety rules that they must follow for their own protection.

19. The passage best supports the statement that industrial accidents

(A) are always avoidable.

(B) may be due to ignorance.

(C) usually result from inadequate machinery.

(D) cannot be entirely overcome.

The leader of an industrial enterprise has two principal functions. He or she must manufacture and distribute a product at a profit, and he or she must keep individuals and groups of individuals working effectively together.

20. The passage best supports the statement that an industrial leader should be able to

(A) increase the distribution of his or her plant's products.

(B) introduce large-scale production methods.

(C) coordinate the activities of employees.

(D) profit by the experience of other leaders.

ANSWER KEY AND EXPLANATIONS

1. C	5. A	9. C	13. D	17. D
2. B	6. A	10. B	14. A	18. D
3. D	7. C	11. B	15. B	19. B
4. D	8. B	12. D	16. B	20. C

1. **The correct answer is (C).** The judge decides on the minimum height to be jumped, so pole vaulters must jump higher than the height set by the judge.

2. **The correct answer is (B).** Since some icebergs in the Antarctic Ocean rise as high as 300 feet above the water, and since only one tenth of an iceberg is visible above the water, there are icebergs in the Antarctic Ocean that are as much as 3,000 feet long altogether.

3. **The correct answer is (D).** A toad's skin is dry, dull, and rough or covered with warts.

4. **The correct answer is (D).** The phonograph and motion picture film are listed among Thomas Edison's inventions. Since Edison lived 84 years, his was not a short life. While Edison may well be in the running for designation as the most famous inventor, such a statement is not supported by the paragraph.

5. **The correct answer is (A).** Since the other three options involve monetary gain for the athlete, the correct answer is (A).

6. **The correct answer is (A).** This is a restatement of the paragraph. The other choices have no relevance whatsoever to the paragraph.

7. **The correct answer is (C).** The answer is stated in the last sentence.

8. **The correct answer is (B).** While all four statements are somewhat supported by the paragraph, the *best* support is from the statement that the average American family moves every few years.

9. **The correct answer is (C).** See the last sentence.

10. **The correct answer is (B).** Choice (B) is a restatement of the last sentence.

11. **The correct answer is (B).** The other three choices are incorrect statements. The date 1869 refers to the establishment of the current nine-member court. Justices are appointed by the President, are confirmed by the Senate, and serve for life.

12. **The correct answer is (D).** Most of the paragraph is devoted to describing the five different types of competition.

13. **The correct answer is (D).** The word *also* in the last sentence is the key to the fact that in higher animals the brain controls voluntary behavior, involuntary behavior, emotions, memory, and thought.

14. **The correct answer is (A).** Because 6,080 feet is longer than 5,280 feet, the correct answer is choice (A).

15. **The correct answer is (B).** Stereophonic sound is *transmitted* by sending the sound to two speakers and is received by having left- and right-hand speakers, but it is *produced* by recording different sounds in each wall of the groove.

16. **The correct answer is (B).** The paragraph may open by mentioning that there is a growing danger in the overuse of antibiotics; however, the paragraph does not expand on this theme. The quote mainly focuses on the ineffectiveness of antibiotics against viral infections. Because more than twice as much of the paragraph is devoted to the second theme, choice (B) is the best answer.

17. **The correct answer is (D).** The report must include place (A), action taken (B), and time (C). The cause of the unusual occurrence need not be part of the report.

18. **The correct answer is (D).** The paragraph states that the work of the operator often requires careful attention under conditions of stress. This means that the operator must be able to work under difficulties. The paragraph does not state that the work must always be performed under stress.

19. **The correct answer is (B).** The answer to this question is implied in the statement that "mechanics be instructed in safety rules that they must follow for their own protection." If the mechanics must be instructed, then accidents may occur if they have not been instructed (that is, if they are ignorant).

20. **The correct answer is (C).** Keeping individuals and groups of individuals working together effectively is coordinating the activities of employees. This answer is stated. The other choices require more interpretation and more stretching than necessary to choose the correct answer. Introduction of large-scale production methods and increasing distribution of products may very well increase profits, but not necessarily.

Exercise 2

Directions: Read the passages below, then answer the questions that follow.

The force reconciling and coordinating all human conflicts and directing people in the harmonious accomplishment of their work is the supervisor. To deal with people successfully, the first person a supervisor must learn to work with is himself or herself.

1. According to the passage, the most accurate of the following conclusions is
   (A) human conflicts are the result of harmonious accomplishment.
   (B) a supervisor should attempt to reconcile all the different views subordinates may have.
   (C) a supervisor who understands himself or herself is in a good position to deal with others successfully.
   (D) the reconciling force in human conflicts is the ability to deal with people successfully.

Law must be stable and yet it cannot stand still.

2. This sentence means most nearly that
   (A) law is a fixed body of subject matter.
   (B) law must adapt itself to changing conditions.
   (C) law is a poor substitute for justice.
   (D) the true administration of justice is the firmest pillar of good government.

The treatment to be given to the offender cannot alter the fact of the offense, but we can take measures to reduce the chance of similar acts occurring in the future. We should banish the criminal, not to exact revenge nor directly to encourage reform, but to deter that person and others from further illegal attacks on society.

3. According to the passage, prisoners should be punished to
   (A) alter the nature of their offenses.
   (B) banish them from society.
   (C) deter them and others from similar illegal attacks on society.
   (D) directly encourage reform.

On the other hand, the treatment of prisoners on a basis of direct reform is doomed to failure. Neither honest persons nor criminals will tolerate a bald proposition from anyone to alter their characters or habits, least of all if we attempt to gain such a change by a system of coercion.

4. According to this passage, criminals
   (A) are incorrigible.
   (B) are incapable of being coerced.
   (C) are not likely to turn into law-abiding citizens.
   (D) possess very firm characters.

While much thought has been devoted to the question of how to build walls high enough to keep persons temporarily in prison, we have devoted very little attention to the treatment necessary to enable them to come out permanently cured—inclined to be friends rather than enemies of their law-abiding fellow citizens.

5. According to this passage, much thought has been devoted to the problem of prisons as
   (A) vengeful agencies.
   (B) efficient custodial agencies.
   (C) efficient sanatoriums.
   (D) places from which society's friends might issue.

Community organization most often includes persons whose behavior is unconventional in relation to generally accepted social definition, if such persons wield substantial influence with the residents.

6. The inference one can most validly draw from this statement is that
   (A) influential persons are often likely to be unconventional.
   (B) the success of a community organization depends largely on the democratic processes employed by it.
   (C) a gang leader may sometimes be an acceptable recruit for a community organization.
   (D) the unconventional behavior of a local barkeeper may often become acceptable to the community.

The safeguard of democracy is education. The education of youth during a limited period of more or less compulsory attendance at school does not suffice. The educative process is a lifelong one.

7. The statement most consistent with this passage is:
   (A) The school is not the only institution that can contribute to the education of the population.
   (B) All democratic people are educated.
   (C) The entire population should be required to go to school throughout life.
   (D) If compulsory education were not required, the educative process would be more effective.

The police officer's art consists in applying and enforcing a multitude of laws and ordinances in such degree or proportion and in such manner that the greatest degree of social protection will be secured. The degree of enforcement and the method of application will vary with each neighborhood and community.

8. According to this statement,
   (A) each neighborhood or community must judge for itself to what extent the law is to be enforced.
   (B) a police officer should only enforce those laws that are designed to give the greatest degree of social protection.
   (C) the manner and intensity of law enforcement is not necessarily the same in all communities.
   (D) all laws and ordinances must be enforced in a community with the same degree of intensity.

As a rule, police officers, through service and experience, are familiar with the duties and the methods and means required to perform them. Yet, left to themselves, their aggregate effort would disintegrate and the vital work of preserving the peace would never be accomplished.

9. According to this statement, the most accurate of the following conclusions is:
   (A) Police officers are sufficiently familiar with their duties as to need no supervision.
   (B) Working together for a common purpose is not efficient without supervision.
   (C) Police officers are familiar with the methods of performing their duties because of rules.
   (D) Preserving the peace is so vital that it can never be said to be completed.

ANSWER QUESTIONS 10–12 ON THE BASIS OF THE INFORMATION GIVEN IN THE FOLLOWING PASSAGE.

Criminal science is largely the science of identification. Progress in this field has been marked and sometimes spectacular because new techniques, instruments, and facts flow continuously from the scientific community. But the crime laboratories are understaffed, trade secrets still prevail, and inaccurate conclusions are often the result. However, modern gadgets cannot substitute for the skilled, intelligent investigator; he or she must be their master.

10. According to this passage, criminal science
    (A) excludes the field of investigation.
    (B) is primarily interested in establishing identity.
    (C) is based on the equipment used in crime laboratories.
    (D) uses techniques different from those used in other sciences.

11. According to the passage, advances in criminal science have been
    (A) extremely limited.
    (B) slow but steady.
    (C) unusually reliable.
    (D) outstanding.

12. According to the passage, a problem that has not been overcome completely in crime work is
    (A) unskilled investigators.
    (B) the expense of new equipment and techniques.
    (C) an insufficient number of personnel in crime laboratories.
    (D) inaccurate equipment used in laboratories.

ANSWER QUESTION 13 USING THE INFORMATION PRESENTED IN THE FOLLOWING PASSAGE.

While the safe burglar can ply his or her trade the year round, the loft burglar has more seasonal activities, since only at certain periods of the year is a substantial amount of valuable merchandise stored in lofts.

13. The generalization that this statement best illustrates is

(A) nothing is ever completely safe from a thief.

(B) there are safe burglars and loft burglars.

(C) some types of burglary are seasonal.

(D) the safe burglar considers safe-cracking a trade.

ANSWER QUESTIONS 14–17 ON THE BASIS OF THE INFORMATION GIVEN IN THE FOLLOWING PASSAGE.

When a vehicle has been disabled in a tunnel, the officer on patrol in this zone shall press the emergency truck light button. In the fast lane, red lights will go on throughout the tunnel; in the slow lane, amber lights will go on throughout the tunnel. The yellow zone light will go on at each signal control station throughout the tunnel and will flash the number of the zone in which the stoppage has occurred. A red flashing pilot light will appear only at the signal control station at which the emergency truck button was pressed. The emergency garage will receive an audible and visual signal indicating the signal control station at which the emergency truck button was pressed. The garage officer shall acknowledge receipt of the signal by pressing the acknowledgment button. This

will cause the pilot light at the operated signal control station in the tunnel to cease flashing and to remain steady. It is an answer to the officer at the operated signal control station that the emergency truck is responding to the call.

14. According to this passage, when the emergency truck light button is pressed,

(A) amber lights will go on in every lane throughout the tunnel.

(B) emergency signal lights will go on only in the lane in which the disabled vehicle is located.

(C) red lights will go on in the fast lane throughout the tunnel.

(D) pilot lights at all signal control stations will turn amber.

15. According to this passage, the number of the zone in which the stoppage has occurred is flashed

(A) immediately after all the lights in the tunnel turn red.

(B) by the yellow zone light at each signal control station.

(C) by the emergency truck at the point of stoppage.

(D) by the emergency garage.

16. According to the passage, an officer near the disabled vehicle will know that the emergency tow truck is coming when

(A) the pilot light at the operated signal control station appears and flashes red.

(B) an audible signal is heard in the tunnel.

(C) the zone light at the operated signal control station turns red.

(D) the pilot light at the operated signal control station becomes steady.

17. Under the system described in the passage, it would be correct to conclude that
    (A) officers at all signal control stations are expected to acknowledge that they have received the stoppage signal.
    (B) officers at all signal control stations will know where the stoppage has occurred.
    (C) all traffic in both lanes of that side of the tunnel in which the stoppage has occurred must stop until the emergency truck has arrived.
    (D) there are two emergency garages, each able to respond to stoppages in traffic going in one particular direction.

ANSWER QUESTIONS 18–20 USING THE INFORMATION PRESENTED IN THE FOLLOWING PASSAGE.

The use of a roadblock is simply an adaptation of the military practice of encirclement by the police. Successful operation of a roadblock plan depends almost entirely on the amount of advance study and planning given to such operations. A thorough and detailed examination of the roads and terrain under the jurisdiction of a given police agency should be made in advance, and the locations of potential roadblocks pinpointed. The first principle to be borne in mind in the location of each roadblock is the time element. The roadblock's location must be at a point beyond which the fugitive could not have possibly traveled in the time elapsed from the commission of the crime to the arrival of the officers at the roadblock.

18. According to the passage,
    (A) military operations have made extensive use of roadblocks.
    (B) the military practice of encirclement is an adaptation of police use of roadblocks.
    (C) the technique of encirclement has been widely used by military forces.
    (D) a roadblock is generally more effective than encirclement.

19. According to the passage,
    (A) advance study and planning are of minor importance in the success of roadblock operations.
    (B) a thorough and detailed examination of all roads within a radius of fifty miles should precede the determination of a roadblock location.
    (C) consideration of terrain features is important in planning the location of roadblocks.
    (D) a roadblock operation can seldom be successfully undertaken by a single police agency.

20. According to the passage,
    (A) the factor of time is the sole consideration in the location of a roadblock.
    (B) the maximum speed possible in the method of escape is of major importance in roadblock location.
    (C) the time the officers arrive at the site of a proposed roadblock is of little importance.
    (D) a roadblock should be situated as close to the scene of the crime as the terrain will permit.

ANSWER QUESTIONS 21 AND 22 USING THE INFORMATION PRESENTED IN THE FOLLOWING PASSAGE.

A number of crimes, such as robbery, assault, rape, certain forms of theft, and burglary are high visibility crimes in that it is apparent to all concerned that they are criminal acts prior to or at the time they are committed. In contrast to these, check forgeries, especially those committed by first offenders, have low visibility. There is little in the criminal act or in the interaction between the check passer and the person cashing the check to identify it as a crime. Closely related to this special quality of the forgery crime is the fact that, while it is formally defined and treated as a felonious or "infamous" crime, it is informally held by the legally untrained public to be a relatively harmless form of crime.

21. According to the passage, crimes of "high visibility"

    (A) are immediately recognized as crimes by the victims.

    (B) take place in public view.

    (C) always involve violence or the threat of violence.

    (D) are usually committed after dark.

22. According to the passage,

    (A) the public regards check forgery as a minor crime.

    (B) the law regards check forgery as a minor crime.

    (C) the law distinguishes between check forgery and other forgery.

    (D) it is easier to spot inexperienced check forgers than other criminals.

ANSWER QUESTIONS 23 AND 24 USING THE INFORMATION PRESENTED IN THE FOLLOWING PASSAGE.

The racketeer is primarily concerned with business affairs—legitimate or otherwise—and preferably those that are close to the margin of legitimacy. The racketeer gets the best opportunities from business organizations that meet the need of large sections of the public for goods or services that are defined as illegitimate by the same public, such as prostitution, gambling, illicit drugs, or liquor. In contrast to the thief, the racketeer and the establishments controlled deliver goods and services for money received.

23. It can be deduced from the passage that suppression of racketeers is difficult because

    (A) victims of racketeers are not guilty of violating the law.

    (B) racketeers are generally engaged in fully legitimate enterprises.

    (C) many people want services that are not obtainable through legitimate sources.

    (D) laws prohibiting gambling and prostitution are unenforceable.

24. According to the passage, racketeering, unlike theft, involves

    (A) objects of value.

    (B) payment for goods received.

    (C) organized gangs.

    (D) unlawful activities.

ANSWER QUESTION 25 USING THE INFORMATION PRESENTED IN THE FOLLOWING PASSAGE.

In examining the scene of a homicide, one should not only look for the usual, standard traces—fingerprints, footprints, and so on—but also have eyes open for details that at first glance may not seem to have any connection with the crime.

25. The most logical inference to be drawn from this statement is that

(A) in general, standard traces are not important.

(B) sometimes one should not look for footprints.

(C) usually only the standard traces are important.

(D) one cannot tell in advance what will be important.

ANSWER QUESTIONS 26 AND 27 USING THE INFORMATION PRESENTED IN THE FOLLOWING PASSAGE.

If a motor vehicle fails to pass inspection, the owner will be given a rejection notice by the inspection station. Repairs must be made within ten days after this notice is issued. It is not necessary to have the required adjustment or repairs made at the station where the inspection occurred. The vehicle may be taken to any garage. Reinspection after repairs may be made at any official inspection station, not necessarily the same station that made the initial inspection. The registration of any motor vehicle for which an inspection sticker has not been obtained as required, or that is not repaired and inspected within ten days after inspection indicates defects, is subject to suspension. A vehicle cannot be used on public highways while its registration is under suspension.

26. According to the passage, the owner of a car that does not pass inspection must

(A) have repairs made at the same station that rejected the car.

(B) take the car to another station and have it reinspected.

(C) have repairs made anywhere and then have the car reinspected.

(D) not use the car on a public highway until the necessary repairs have been made.

27. According to the passage, which of the following situations may be cause for suspension of the registration of a vehicle?

(A) An inspection sticker was issued before the rejection notice had been in force for ten days.

(B) The vehicle was not reinspected by the station that rejected it originally.

(C) The vehicle was not reinspected either by the station that rejected it originally or by the garage that made the repairs.

(D) The vehicle has not had defective parts repaired within ten days after inspection.

ANSWER QUESTION 28 USING THE INFORMATION PRESENTED IN THE FOLLOWING PASSAGE.

A statute states: "A person who steals an article worth less than $100 where no aggravating circumstances accompany the act is guilty of petty larceny. If the article is worth $100 or more, it may be larceny second degree."

28. If all you know is that Edward Smith stole an article worth $100, it may reasonably be said that
    (A) Smith is guilty of petty larceny.
    (B) Smith is guilty of larceny second degree.
    (C) Smith is guilty of neither petty larceny nor larceny second degree.
    (D) precisely what charge will be placed against Smith is uncertain.

ANSWER QUESTIONS 29 AND 30 USING THE INFORMATION PRESENTED IN THE FOLLOWING PASSAGE.

The city police department will accept for investigation no report of a person missing from his or her residence if such residence is located outside of the city. The person reporting same will be advised to report such fact to the police department of the locality where the missing person lives, which will, if necessary, communicate officially with the city police department. However, a report will be accepted of a person who is missing from a temporary residence in the city, but the person making the report will be instructed to make a report also to the police department of the locality where the missing person lives.

29. According to the passage, a report to the city police department of a missing person whose permanent residence is outside of the city will
    (A) always be investigated, provided that a report is also made to local police authorities.
    (B) never be investigated, unless requested officially by local police authorities.
    (C) be investigated in cases of temporary residence in the city, but a report should always be made to local police authorities.
    (D) always be investigated, and a report will be made to the local police authorities by the city police department.

30. Mr. Smith of Oldtown and Mr. Jones of Newtown have an appointment in the city, but Mr. Jones doesn't appear. Mr. Smith, after trying repeatedly to phone Mr. Jones the next day, believes that something has happened to him. According to the passage, Mr. Smith should apply to the police of
    (A) Oldtown.
    (B) Newtown.
    (C) Newtown and the city.
    (D) Oldtown and the city.

ANSWER QUESTION 31 USING THE
INFORMATION PRESENTED IN THE
FOLLOWING PASSAGE.

A police department rule reads as follows: "A Deputy Commissioner acting as Police Commissioner shall carry out the orders of the Police Commissioner, previously given, and such orders shall not, except in cases of extreme emergency, be countermanded."

31. This rule means most nearly that, except in cases of extreme emergency,
    (A) the orders given by a Deputy Commissioner acting as Police Commissioner may not be revoked.
    (B) a Deputy Commissioner acting as Police Commissioner should not revoke orders previously given by the Police Commissioner.
    (C) a Deputy Commissioner acting as Police Commissioner is vested with the same authority to issue orders as the Police Commissioner.
    (D) only a Deputy Commissioner acting as Police Commissioner may issue orders in the absence of the Police Commissioner.

ANSWER QUESTION 32 USING THE
INFORMATION PRESENTED IN THE
FOLLOWING STATEMENT.

A crime is an act committed or omitted in violation of a public law either forbidding or commanding it.

32. This statement implies most nearly that
    (A) crimes can be omitted.
    (B) a forbidding act, if omitted, is a crime.
    (C) an act of omission may be criminal.
    (D) to commit an act not commanded is criminal.

ANSWER QUESTION 33 USING THE
INFORMATION PRESENTED IN THE
FOLLOWING STATEMENT.

"He who by command, counsel, or assistance procures another to commit a crime is, in morals and in law, as culpable as the visible actor himself; for the reason that the criminal act, whichever it may be, is imputable to the person who conceived it and set the forces in motion for its actual accomplishment."

33. Of the following, the most accurate inference from this statement is that
    (A) a criminal act does not have to be committed for a crime to be committed.
    (B) acting as counselor for a criminal is a crime.
    (C) the mere counseling of a criminal act can never be a crime if no criminal act is committed.
    (D) a person acting only as an adviser may be guilty of committing a criminal act.

ANSWER QUESTION 34 USING THE
INFORMATION PRESENTED IN THE
FOLLOWING STATEMENT.

A felony is a crime punishable by death or imprisonment in a state prison, and a misdemeanor is a crime punishable by fine or imprisonment in a municipal or county jail.

34. According to this passage, the decisive distinction between "felony" and "misdemeanor" is the
    (A) degree of criminality.
    (B) type of crime.
    (C) manner of punishment.
    (D) judicial jurisdiction.

ANSWER QUESTION 35 USING THE INFORMATION PRESENTED IN THE FOLLOWING PASSAGE.

If the second or third felony is such that, upon a first conviction, the offender would be imprisoned for any term less than his or her natural life, then such person must be sentenced to imprisonment for an indeterminate term. The minimum of this term shall not be less than one half of the longest term prescribed upon a first conviction, and the maximum shall not be longer than twice such longest term. However, the minimum sentence imposed upon the second or third felony offender shall in no case be less than five years; except that where the maximum punishment for a second or third felony offender hereunder is five years or less, the minimum sentence must be not less than two years.

35. According to this passage, a person who has a second felony conviction shall receive as a sentence for that second felony an indeterminate term

(A) not less than twice the minimum term prescribed upon a first conviction as a maximum.

(B) not less than one half the minimum term of the first conviction as a maximum.

(C) not more than twice the minimum term prescribed upon a first conviction as a minimum.

(D) with a maximum of not more than twice the longest term prescribed for a first conviction for this crime.

ANSWER KEY AND EXPLANATIONS

1. C	8. C	15. B	22. A	29. C
2. B	9. B	16. D	23. C	30. B
3. C	10. B	17. B	24. B	31. B
4. C	11. D	18. C	25. D	32. C
5. B	12. C	19. C	26. C	33. D
6. C	13. C	20. B	27. D	34. C
7. A	14. C	21. A	28. D	35. D

1. **The correct answer is (C).** Before understanding and working with others, one must first understand one's own motivation and working habits. The supervisor with good self-understanding is an effective supervisor.

2. **The correct answer is (B).** To adapt means to change in response to changing conditions without a total change of substance.

3. **The correct answer is (C).** This passage expresses the philosophy that the purpose of punishment is neither to make the offender "pay for his/her crime" nor to reform the offender, but rather to protect society from the specific criminal and to serve, by example, as a deterrent to others.

4. **The correct answer is (C).** The philosophy expressed here is "Once a criminal, always a criminal." Attempts at reform and rehabilitation are futile. (Remember: Answer questions based on the information in the passages. You may disagree; you may even know that the information is incorrect. However, your answer must be based on the passage, not upon your opinions or your knowledge.)

5. **The correct answer is (B).** This question deals with a philosophy contrary to those expressed in the previous two questions. It states that we have devoted attention to the means of making prisons secure places in which to keep offenders, but have not given much thought to rehabilitation.

6. **The correct answer is (C).** You may find this principle difficult to accept, but it represents accepted practice in many quarters. The concept is that if the person with leadership qualities—even if combined with antisocial behaviors—is drawn into the mainstream, that person can learn to accept certain norms of the majority and transmit these more acceptable attitudes and behaviors to the group that respects him or her. The term used to describe the drawing into the inner circle of the unconventional leader is "co-opting."

7. **The correct answer is (A).** Since education continues throughout life, yet schooling is of limited duration, obviously education occurs in places other than schools.

8. **The correct answer is (C).** The needs and desires of communities vary; therefore, degree and manner of enforcement of different laws in different communities will also vary.

9. **The correct answer is (B).** The meaning of this passage is that good intentions and thorough knowledge of duties are not sufficient. Organization

and supervision are vital to efficient operation of the police function.

10. The correct answer is (B). The science of identification is primarily interested in establishing identity.

11. The correct answer is (D). Marked and spectacular progress is outstanding.

12. The correct answer is (C). Understaffed laboratories have insufficient personnel.

13. The correct answer is (C). The concept may be novel to you, but the question itself is an easy one. The answer is stated directly in the paragraph.

14. The correct answer is (C). See the second sentence. When a reading passage is crammed with details, most of the questions will be strictly factual.

15. The correct answer is (B). See the third sentence.

16. The correct answer is (D). See the last two sentences.

17. The correct answer is (B). The yellow zone light goes on at each signal control station and flashes the number of the zone in which the stoppage has occurred, so all officers receive this information.

18. The correct answer is (C). If the military practice of encirclement was adapted for use by the police, we may assume that it was widely and successfully used. Choice (B) reverses the order of the adaptation.

19. The correct answer is (C). This is the clear implication of the third sentence.

20. The correct answer is (B). The roadblock must be placed beyond the point that the fugitive could have possibly reached, so maximum speed of escape is vitally important in the establishment of a roadblock.

21. The correct answer is (A). See the first sentence.

22. The correct answer is (A). See the last sentence.

23. The correct answer is (C). The racketeer provides goods and services that are officially illegal, but that are desired by otherwise respectable members of the general public. Since the public wants these services, active effort to suppress the providers is unlikely.

24. The correct answer is (B). See the last sentence.

25. The correct answer is (D). The police officer must always be observant and alert to both abnormalities and routine details in the environment. This useful quality in a police officer is the reason many police officer exams include a section testing powers of observation and memory.

26. The correct answer is (C). The state is not concerned with who makes repairs or with who does the inspection, only that these be accomplished.

27. The correct answer is (D). See the next-to-last sentence.

28. The correct answer is (D). Beware of qualifying words and definite statements. If the article is worth $100 or more, it *may* be larceny second degree, but not necessarily.

29. The correct answer is (C). See the last sentence.

30. The correct answer is (B). Mr. Jones is a resident of Newtown, so the missing person report must be filed with the Newtown police. The meeting of Smith and Jones was to have taken place in the city, but Jones was not a temporary resident of the city, so the city police are not involved in this case.

31. **The correct answer is (B).** The word "countermand" means "revoke." The Deputy Commissioner carries out the orders of the Police Commissioner and revokes them only in cases of extreme emergency.

32. **The correct answer is (C).** An act of omission, if it is in violation of a public law commanding said act, is a crime. The act of omission is not a crime if it is not in violation of a public law.

33. **The correct answer is (D).** The person who conceives and sets in motion the forces for the accomplishment of a crime—in other words, the adviser who convinced another to commit a criminal act—may well be deemed guilty of committing the criminal act.

34. **The correct answer is (C).** Crimes are defined by the level and manner of punishment the offender receives.

35. **The correct answer is (D).** You may have to do some very careful reading and rereading to find the answer to this question. You will find it in the last clause before the first semicolon.

SUMMING IT UP

- The single most common question type in dispatcher exams is reading comprehension. Before you begin studying strategies for answering reading-based questions, think about whether you need to sharpen your present reading habits and skills. If so, try to work on that task before exam day. Read articles in your daily newspaper all the way through rather than skimming the first paragraph or two. Underline details and ideas that seem crucial to the meaning of the article. Notice points of view, arguments, and supporting information. If you do this every day, you're bound to become more efficient in your reading comprehension.

- Don't try to tackle every reading comprehension suggestion in this chapter all at once. Take on a little at a time and work systematically for best results. You may need just 15 minutes a day—even this small amount of time will be helpful.

- Remember that reading includes building your vocabulary—one of the most effective ways to strengthen your comprehension. Make a point of listing words with which you're unfamiliar as you read. Then look up those words and write them in a separate notebook with their definitions. This will help you "lock" the information into your memory and will provide a handy reference.

- Follow the five steps to answering reading comprehension questions outlined in this chapter: read the questions first; scan the reading passage quickly; read the passage for detail; return to the questions; and scan the passage again.

- Carefully review the five most common types of reading comprehension questions (question of fact or detail, best title or main idea, interpretation, inference, and vocabulary) and practice answering each type using the sample questions in this chapter and in the Practice Tests in this book. This will help you be at your best on exam day.

- Exams written specifically for dispatchers in the police department will contain reading passages related to legal definitions, laws, and police procedures. If you encounter these on your exam, pay special attention to details relating to exceptions, special pre-conditions, combinations of activities, choices of actions, and prescribed time sequences. You'll need to determine whether the passage requires a combination of factors or gives a choice, then make the appropriate judgment. When a time sequence is specified, be certain to follow that sequence in the prescribed order.

Vocabulary and Spelling

OVERVIEW

- **Vocabulary on the Public Safety Dispatcher Exam**
- **Practice vocabulary questions**
- **More practice questions**
- **Spelling on the Public Safety Dispatcher Exam**
- **Practice spelling questions**
- **Summing it up**

VOCABULARY ON THE PUBLIC SAFETY DISPATCHER EXAM

A public safety dispatcher must be readily understood by everyone with whom he or she speaks. Aside from having clear pronunciation and diction, dispatchers must have a strong command of the language. Perhaps even more important, public safety dispatchers must clearly understand others and must be able to draw the meaning from an excited, garbled message.

The words that appear on employment tests may not be those that an employee will need on the job. Generally, the vocabulary used in exams is more complex than what is required for a civil service position. The theory behind testing with words that are more difficult than what one uses in everyday life is that if you know the meaning of more obscure words, you will most certainly be fluent and proficient with simpler words. Test makers also use more difficult words in exams to tap into the test taker's logical thinking and reasoning powers.

Synonym questions are the most commonly used measure of vocabulary on the exam.

Synonyms

Synonyms are two words with similar meanings. A synonym can replace another word or phrase in a sentence without significantly changing the meaning of the sentence. Most exams make use of two types of synonym questions:

1. **A key word followed by a number of answer choices.** In this type of question, you must select the word or phrase that is exactly the same as, or closest in meaning to, the key word. If you are not sure about the meaning of the word, try to eliminate one or more choices. Perhaps you recognize a

...rd from your study of word stems, for example, or you might try to
... a sentence.

... **containing one word in UPPERCASE.** In this type of question,
... to choose the answer choice that is the best synonym for the uppercased
... Sentence questions offer more clues than key word questions. The overall
... meaning of the sentence may provide clues to the word's definition, and the way
in which the word is used in the sentence will tell you whether it is a noun, a verb,
or a modifier.

9 Steps to Answering Synonym Questions

1. Read each question carefully.

2. Eliminate answer choices that you know are wrong.

3. Use all of the clues provided in the question stem. If the question is a sentence, consider the part of speech and the context of the word. For both sentence and non-sentence items, see whether any word parts are familiar to you. Recall where you have seen or heard the word used. Create your own sentence using the word.

4. From the answer choices that seem possible, select the one that most nearly means the same as the given word, even if this choice is not part of your normal vocabulary. The correct answer may not be a perfect synonym, but it is closest in meaning to the given word.

5. Test your answer by putting it in place of the given word in the question sentence or the sentence you have created. Is the meaning of the new sentence the same or similar to that of the original? If so, you probably have the correct answer.

6. If the word is not part of a sentence or the sentence does not help you to define the word, you must rely on other clues. Perhaps you have seen or heard the word but were never sure of its meaning. Now look at the word carefully. Is there any part of the word whose meaning you know?

7. If the word is not used in a sentence, try creating your own sentence using the given word. Then try substituting the answer choices in your sentence.

8. If you're stumped by a question, move on to the next question and answer the least difficult ones first. Then go back to work on the questions with answers you did not immediately recognize.

9. When all else fails, take an educated guess.

PRACTICE VOCABULARY QUESTIONS

Directions: Choose the answer that means most nearly the same as the word that appears in UPPERCASE letters.

1. REMEDIAL measures need to be taken to clean up air pollution in the area.
   (A) reading
   (B) slow
   (C) corrective
   (D) graceful

2. The increased use of computers has greatly REDUCED the need for type-writers.
   (A) enlarged
   (B) canceled
   (C) lessened
   (D) expanded

3. Although a complex response was required to the difficult question, she answered with EQUANIMITY.
   (A) composure
   (B) anger
   (C) pauses
   (D) doubts

4. The UNIFORMITY of the students' answers suggested they had not considered the many possible responses.
   (A) military appearance
   (B) slowness
   (C) great variety
   (D) sameness

5. The surface of the TRANQUIL lake was as smooth as glass.
   (A) cold
   (B) muddy
   (C) deep
   (D) calm

6. The manager ordered a GROSS of pencils from the office supplies store.
   (A) disgusting
   (B) all-inclusive
   (C) twelve dozen
   (D) monster

7. To send a note of apology is the only DECENT thing to do in these circumstances.
   (A) proper
   (B) going down
   (C) children
   (D) inclination

8. The speaker had an ABRASIVE voice.
   (A) tuneful
   (B) high-pitched
   (C) loud
   (D) harsh

9. Her DOMICILE was very well maintained.
   (A) clothing
   (B) residence
   (C) appearance
   (D) office

10. DISINTERESTED
    (A) sympathetic
    (B) young
    (C) objective
    (D) poor

11. TEMPORIZE
    (A) increase
    (B) consider
    (C) flatter
    (D) stall

12. ABOMINATE
    (A) adore
    (B) help
    (C) abide
    (D) hate

13. SALIENT
    (A) prominent
    (B) true
    (C) meaningful
    (D) respectable

14. The President nominates candidates for JUDICIAL positions in the federal courts.
    (A) engineering
    (B) philosophical
    (C) technician
    (D) judge

15. When hula hoops were a fad, these toys were UBIQUITOUS in school playgrounds.
    (A) rare
    (B) enjoyed
    (C) abundant
    (D) broken

16. An efficient manager knows how to DELEGATE responsibilities.
    (A) representative
    (B) give to a subordinate
    (C) hire
    (D) elect to office

17. TRANSCRIPT
    (A) journey
    (B) videotape
    (C) correction
    (D) written copy

18. The city purchased a SITE for the new public library building.
    (A) reference
    (B) location
    (C) job
    (D) book

19. INSUFFICIENT
    (A) excessive
    (B) having enough
    (C) lacking
    (D) nonexistent

20. DETRIMENTAL
    (A) favorable
    (B) lasting
    (C) harmful
    (D) temporary

ANSWER KEY AND EXPLANATIONS

1. C	5. D	9. B	13. A	17. D
2. C	6. C	10. C	14. D	18. B
3. A	7. A	11. D	15. C	19. C
4. D	8. D	12. D	16. B	20. C

1. **The correct answer is (C).** First eliminate *reading*. Its use in this sentence does not make sense, although you may associate *remedial* with remedial reading. Because pollution is a serious problem, *slow* would not be a good choice. Why would one delay solving such a problem? *Graceful* describes a physical trait, so it is not appropriate in this sentence. After you eliminate these choices, even if you are not sure of exactly what *remedial* means, you should be able to choose (C) as the best synonym in this context.

2. **The correct answer is (C).** The meaning of the sentence should cause you to immediately rule out choice (A), *enlarged,* and (D), *expanded.* Choice (B), *canceled,* implies that there is no need at all for typewriters. If this were the case, then the modifier *greatly* would be unnecessary. Therefore, choice (C), *lessened,* is the best synonym for *reduced.*

3. **The correct answer is (A).** Even if you are not sure what *equanimity* means, you can eliminate choices (C) and (D) because the word *although* in the first part of the sentence tells you that the response was not affected by the difficulty of the question. Choice (B) is not a good choice because the emotion of the person answering is not related to difficulty of the question.

4. **The correct answer is (D).** Although *uniform* may make you think of the armed forces, clothing has nothing to do with the meaning of this sentence,

so (A) is not a possible choice. Choice (C) is an incorrect choice because the sentence says that *not* many were considered. Choice (B) makes sense in the sentence, but *slowness* changes the meaning of the sentence. Thus, the best choice based on the meaning of the sentence is choice (D), *sameness.*

5. **The correct answer is (D).** Any of these choices might substitute for the word *tranquil,* and the sentence would still make sense. However, if the surface of the lake was as smooth as glass, the water would have to be very *calm.* Thus, while a *cold, muddy,* or *deep* lake could have a smooth surface, it is most reasonable to assume, on the basis of the sentence, that *tranquil* means *calm* and that (D) is the correct answer.

6. **The correct answer is (C).** In this example, the sentence is absolutely necessary to the definition of the word. Without the sentence, you could not know if the word *gross* is the noun, which means "twelve dozen," or the adjective, which can mean "crude and disgusting" or "total" depending on the context. The sentence tells you *gross* is a noun. Choices (A) and (B) are adjectives, so they cannot be correct. Choice (D) is tricky. *Monster* is sometimes used as slang for many or a large amount, but this is an incorrect use of the word. *Monster* does not appear in dictionaries as an adjective. As a noun, a *monster* could also be a beast, but that would not fit in a sen-

tence about pencils. Therefore, choice (C), *twelve dozen,* is the only possible correct answer.

7. **The correct answer is (A).** As in the previous example, the sentence helps you to decide on the best synonym because *decent* is an adjective describing what someone will do. Thus, you will know not to confuse *decent* with a noun that sounds nearly the same, although spelled differently, *descent,* which means a downward path, or another similar-sounding noun, *descendants*—one's children. Choice (A) is the only adjective and therefore the correct answer.

8. **The correct answer is (D).** Sometimes a sentence may be of little or no use in helping you to choose the best synonym. The sentences may help you to determine the part of speech of the indicated word, but not its meaning, This sentences shows that *abrasive* is used to describe a voice, but it gives you no clue that *abrasive* means *harsh.* In this instance, you simply need to understand the meaning of *abrasive.*

9. **The correct answer is (B).** In this example, it is clear that a *domicile* is something that belongs to someone, but there is no information in the sentence to help you decide what that is. Although any of the choices could be substituted for *domicile,* the correct answer is (B), *residence.*

10. **The correct answer is (C).** When you see the word *disinterested,* you will recognize the word part "interested," which means concerned. Since the prefix *dis-* often means "not," you can eliminate choice (A). A *sympathetic* person is interested in a person or situation. You cannot immediately eliminate choice (D), *poor,* but before selecting an answer, consider all the possibilities. Since *dis-* is a negative

prefix, look for a negative word as the meaning of *disinterested.* There is no choice meaning "not interested," so you should look for a negative kind of interest. To be objective is to have no interest in the outcome of a situation. An objective person is one who makes decisions without considering personal consequences; thus to be *objective* means to be *disinterested,* and choice (C) is therefore the correct answer.

11. **The correct answer is (D).** When you see *temporize,* you will recognize the word part *tempo,* which means time. You may think of a word like "temporary," which means for a short period of time. Thus, you should look for an answer that involves the concept of time. To *stall* is to hesitate or delay before responding, so it involves time. Therefore, (D) is the correct choice.

12. **The correct answer is (D).** *Abominate* means to loathe or hate. If you think of other variations of the word, such as abominable, you might think of the abominable snowman, which you know to be a despicable monster. The word "hate" would be the only word to which you could then relate the word "abominate."

13. **The correct answer is (A).** *Salient* means prominent.

14. **The correct answer is (D).** Because the sentence tells you that these positions are in courts, you need to find a synonym for someone who works in a court. While *engineers* or *technicians* might be important witnesses to a case, they're not court employees. Some people who work in courts may have a *philosophical* character or change of mind, but that is not a description of a job. Thus you can decide that choice (D), *judge,* is the best answer.

15. **The correct answer is (C).** The word in the sentence that most helps in choosing the correct answer is *fad*. A *fad* is something that is enjoyed by many people. Thus choice (C), *abundant,* is the best choice. While choice (B), *enjoyed,* makes sense in the sentence, there are many toys that children may enjoy that do not become *ubiquitous.* Choice (A), *rare,* contradicts the idea of a fad. And while toys may get broken while they are being played with, so that the second part of the sentence would make sense, choice (D), *broken,* changes the meaning of the sentence.

16. **The correct answer is (B).** Looking at the sentence, it is clear that *delegate* is a verb. Therefore, although you may have heard of a delegate as a person who attends a convention, choice (A), *representative,* is incorrect. While choice (C), *hiring,* may be one of a manager's duties, responsibilities are duties, not something that can be hired. Similarly, responsibilities can not be *elected to office,* so choice (D) is also incorrect. To *delegate* means to authorize someone to act in one's place or take over one's responsibilities. Therefore, choice (B), *give to a subordinate,* is the best answer.

17. **The correct answer is (D).** When you see the word *transcript,* you will probably recognize the word part *script,* which means writing. You may think of a script for a movie. Since the word includes writing, choice (B), *videotape,* which is not a writing, could be eliminated. Although *tran-* may make you think of trains or transportation, there is no choice that means anything like moving writing, so choice (A), *journey,* can be eliminated. This leaves you with choices (C) and (D). Think about where you have heard or seen the word. Newspapers often print *transcripts* of speeches, which give a complete text of what a speaker said. Thus, a *transcript* is a written copy, and choice (D) is the correct answer.

18. **The correct answer is (B).** When you read the sentence, you may confuse the word *site* and *cite.* Although they may sound the same, their meanings are different. *Cite* is a verb that means to summon or quote. Because *reference* does not fit the meaning of the sentence, you can eliminate choice (A). Choice (C), *job,* is a synonym for a *situation,* which sounds like *site,* but a building cannot hold a job. Although you would find a book in a library, it does not make sense to buy a book to create a new building. Since these choices can be eliminated, choice (B), *location,* should be the answer you select.

19. **The correct answer is (C).** The word *sufficient* means enough, and the prefix *in-* often means not. So *insufficient* means not enough. Choices (A) and (B) are opposites of not enough. Choice (D) means *having none at all,* which does not mean the same thing as *not enough.* A choice meaning *not enough* is the best answer, and (C), *lacking,* means not enough, so (C) is the correct choice.

20. **The correct answer is (C).** Detrimental means harmful.

MORE PRACTICE QUESTIONS

Now try some synonym questions for yourself.

Directions: Choose the answer that means most nearly the same as the word that appears in UPPERCASE letters.

1. CARDIGAN means most nearly
   (A) storm coat.
   (B) sleeveless sweater.
   (C) turtleneck.
   (D) buttoned sweater.

2. GRAPHIC means most nearly
   (A) vivid.
   (B) unclear.
   (C) repetitious.
   (D) sickening.

3. REFRAIN means most nearly
   (A) join in.
   (B) sing along.
   (C) abstain.
   (D) retire.

4. PUNCTUAL means most nearly
   (A) polite.
   (B) prompt.
   (C) thoughtful.
   (D) neat.

5. INFRACTION means most nearly
   (A) violation.
   (B) whole.
   (C) interpretation.
   (D) part.

6. IMPASSE means most nearly
   (A) agreement.
   (B) compromise.
   (C) signed contract.
   (D) deadlock.

7. TEMERITY means most nearly
   (A) shyness.
   (B) enthusiasm.
   (C) rashness.
   (D) self-control.

8. ALLEGIANCE means most nearly
   (A) freedom.
   (B) loyalty.
   (C) defense.
   (D) protection.

9. RESCINDED means most nearly
   (A) revised.
   (B) implemented.
   (C) canceled.
   (D) confirmed.

10. VINDICTIVE means most nearly
   (A) prejudiced.
   (B) petty.
   (C) revengeful.
   (D) crude.

11. INNOCUOUS means most nearly
   (A) forceful.
   (B) harmless.
   (C) offensive.
   (D) important.

12. STRINGENT means most nearly
   (A) lengthy.
   (B) rigid.
   (C) vague.
   (D) ridiculous.

13. ORTHODOX means most nearly
    (A) pious.
    (B) godly.
    (C) traditional.
    (D) heretical.

14. ELICITED means most nearly
    (A) eliminated.
    (B) drawn out.
    (C) illegal.
    (D) confirmed.

15. REPRISAL means most nearly
    (A) retaliation.
    (B) warning.
    (C) denial.
    (D) losing.

16. IMPAIR means most nearly
    (A) improve.
    (B) conceal.
    (C) inflate.
    (D) weaken.

17. ABHOR means most nearly
    (A) tolerate.
    (B) try to change.
    (C) avoid.
    (D) hate.

18. INANE means most nearly
    (A) incessant.
    (B) argumentative.
    (C) polished.
    (D) foolish.

19. DECAY means most nearly
    (A) burning.
    (B) disposal.
    (C) rotting.
    (D) piling.

20. PROXIMITY means most nearly
    (A) nearness.
    (B) worldliness.
    (C) charisma.
    (D) fame.

ANSWER KEY AND EXPLANATIONS

1. D	5. A	9. C	13. C	17. D
2. A	6. D	10. C	14. B	18. D
3. C	7. C	11. B	15. A	19. C
4. B	8. B	12. B	16. D	20. A

1. **The correct answer is (D).** A cardigan is a collarless sweater that opens the full length of the center front and ordinarily is closed with buttons. A cardigan could be sleeveless, but the sleeves do not enter into the definition of a cardigan.

2. **The correct answer is (A).** Graphic means *vivid* or *picturesque*. A graphic description may well be false or sickening, but what makes it graphic is its vividness.

3. **The correct answer is (C).** To refrain from an act is to *keep oneself from doing it* or to *abstain*.

4. **The correct answer is (B).** Punctual means *on time* or *prompt*.

5. **The correct answer is (A).** An infraction is a *breaking of the rules* or a *violation*. You have probably heard of punishments for infractions of traffic regulations, so you know what this word means. If you did not know the word, you might well pull it apart into "not a fraction" and choose whole. Sometimes trying to figure out a meaning does not work.

6. **The correct answer is (D).** An impasse is a predicament offering no obvious escape, hence a *deadlock*. The etymology here is quite simple. The negative prefix *im-* appears before pass. If you can't pass, you are stuck.

7. **The correct answer is (C).** If you do not know the word *temerity*, you are likely to get this wrong. Temerity is in no way related to *timidity* or *shyness* except as an opposite. *Enthusiasm* might be a reasonable synonym, but *rashness, boldness, recklessness,* and *nerve* are better.

8. **The correct answer is (B).** Allegiance means *devotion* or *loyalty*.

9. **The correct answer is (C).** The prefix should help you narrow your choices. The prefix *re-*, meaning *back*, narrows the choices to (A) or (C). To rescind is to *take back* or to *cancel*.

10. **The correct answer is (C).** Vindictive means *spiteful* or *seeking revenge*.

11. **The correct answer is (B).** The prefix *in-*, meaning *not*, is your chief clue. Innocuous means *inoffensive* or *harmless*.

12. **The correct answer is (B).** Stringent means *tight* or *rigid*. Perhaps you can see the basis of "strict" in the word. If you did not know this word and guessed on the basis of its looks, you would probably choose (A) or (B). This would be a sensible way to guess, and it would give you a 50 percent chance of being right.

13. **The correct answer is (C).** One who is orthodox is *conventional, conservative,* and *traditional*. Although an Orthodox Jew may indeed be pious (Choice A), pious is not the meaning of the word *orthodox*.

14. **The correct answer is (B).** To elicit is to *draw out*, to *evoke*, or to *extract*.

15. **The correct answer is (A).** Reprisal literally means *taking back*. Stretch that meaning and you arrive at *getting back at* or *retaliation*.

16. **The correct answer is (D).** To impair is to *make worse*, to *injure*, or to *weaken*.

17. **The correct answer is (D).** To abhor is to *loathe*, to *reject*, or to *hate*.

18. **The correct answer is (D).** Inane means *empty, insubstantial, silly,* or *foolish*.

19. **The correct answer is (C).** Decay is *deterioration, decomposition,* or just plain *rotting*.

20. **The correct answer is (A).** You should be able to look at the word, see "approximate," and choose *nearness* as the meaning of proximity.

SPELLING ON THE PUBLIC SAFETY DISPATCHER EXAM

Spelling is not a major component of the public safety dispatcher position. When speed is of the essence, perfect spelling, punctuation, and even grammar are clearly secondary. On the other hand, spelling cannot be so bizarre that words will be misread. Grammar must be sufficiently accurate so that there is no doubt about who is the victim and who the suspect, and there must be no doubt about the sequence of events.

Most public safety dispatchers keep records. Some dispatchers prepare full-fledged daily reports. Reports must be correct in content and in form. In positions in which keeping logs or preparing reports is a regular part of the job description, spelling questions may appear on the exam. As in vocabulary testing, spelling words on the exam may be more challenging than the words you need to use in everyday work situations. Again, the theory is that if you can spell difficult words, you can spell easier ones.

Some fortunate individuals seem to be "natural" spellers. They are able to picture a word and instinctively spell it correctly. Most of us must memorize rules and rely on a dictionary. It is *not* a sign of weakness to consult a dictionary when you are in doubt about the spelling of a word. On the other hand, constant use of the dictionary does slow your work. Under the pressure of emergency communications, referring to a dictionary may be impossible.

Here are a few rules you can learn to help you improve your spelling:

1. The letter *i* comes before *e* except after *c*, or when sounded like *ay*, as in *neighbor* or *weigh*.

   Exceptions: Neither, leisure, seize, weird, height.

   NOTE: This rule does not apply when the *ie* combination is pronounced *eh* (as in *foreigner*), even if *ie* immediately follows the letter *c*.

   Examples: ancient, conscience, deficient, efficient, foreigner, proficient.

2. If a word ends in a *y* that is preceded by a vowel, keep the *y* when adding a suffix.

   Examples: day, days; attorney, attorneys; spray, sprayer.

3. If a word ends in a *y* that is preceded by a consonant, change the *y* to *i* before adding a suffix.

   Examples: try, tries, tried; lady, ladies; dainty, daintiest; steady, steadily; heavy, heavier; study, studious; ally, alliance; defy, defiant; beauty, beautiful; justify, justifiable.

   Exceptions: dry, dryly, dryness; shy, shyly; sly, slyly, slyness; spry, spryly.

   NOTE: This rule does not apply before the suffixes *-ing* and *-ish*. To avoid double *i*, retain the *y* before *-ing* and *-ish*.

   Examples: fly, flying; baby, babyish; relay, relaying.

4. A silent *e* at the end of a word is usually dropped before a suffix that begins with a vowel.

> ***Examples:***
>
> dine + ing = dining
>
> locate + ion = location
>
> use + able = usable
>
> relieve + ed = relieved
>
> admire + ation = admiration

> ***Exceptions:***
>
> Words ending in *ce* and *ge* retain the *e*.
>
> Words ending in *-able* and *-ous* to retain the soft sounds of *c* and *g*.

> ***Examples:***
>
> peace + able = peaceable
>
> courage + ous = courageous

5. The silent *e* is usually kept when followed by a suffix that begins with a consonant.

> ***Examples:***
>
> care + less = careless
>
> late + ly = lately
>
> one + ness = oneness
>
> game + ster = gamester
>
> manage + ment = management

> **NOTE:** This is a case where exceptions must simply be memorized. Some exceptions to rules 4 and 5 are *truly, duly, awful, argument, wholly, ninth, mileage, dyeing, acreage, canoeing,* and *judgment.*

6. In a one-syllable word that ends in a single consonant that is preceded by a single vowel, you must double the final consonant before a suffix beginning with a vowel or with *y*.

> ***Examples:*** *hit, hitting; drop, dropped; big, biggest; mud, muddy; quit, quitter.*

> ***Exceptions:*** *help* becomes *helping,* because *help* ends in *two* consonants; and *need* becomes *needing,* because the final consonant is preceded by *two* vowels.

7. In a multi-syllable word that ends in a single consonant preceded by a single vowel and in which the last syllable is accented, you must double the final consonant when adding a suffix beginning with a vowel.

> ***Examples:*** begin, beginner; admit, admitted; control, controlling; excel, excellence; recur, recurrent; admit, admittance; transmit, transmittal

> ***Exceptions:*** *enter* becomes *entered* because the accent is *not* on the last syllable; *divert* becomes *diverted* because the word ends in *two* conso-

nants; *refrain* becomes *refraining* because *two* vowels precede the final consonant; and *equip* becomes *equipment* because the suffix begins with a consonant.

8. In a word ending in -*er* or -*ur,* you must double the *r* in the past tense if the accent falls on the last syllable.

    Examples: occur, occurred; prefer, preferred; transfer, transferred

9. In a word ending in -*er,* do not double the *r* in the past tense if the accent falls on any syllable other than the last.

    Examples: answer, answered; offer, offered; differ, differed

10. When -*full* is added to the end of a noun to form an adjective, the final *l* is dropped.

    Examples: cheerful, cupful, hopeful

11. All words beginning with *over* should be spelled as one unhyphenated word.

    Examples: overcast, overcharge, overhear

12. All words beginning with the prefix *self-* should be hyphenated.

    Examples: self-control, self-defense, self-evident

13. The letter *q* is always followed by *u.*

    Examples: quiz, bouquet, acquire

14. *Percent* is never hyphenated. It may be spelled as one word (*percent*) or as two words (*per cent*).

15. *Welcome* is one word with one *l.*

16. *All right* is always two words. There is no such word as *alright.*

17. *Already* means "prior to a specified or implied time." *All ready* means "completely ready." The words are not interchangeable.

    Examples: By the time I was *all ready* to go to the play, he had *already* left.

18. *Altogether* means "entirely." *All together* means "in sum" or "collectively." The words are not interchangeable.

    Examples: There are *altogether* too many people to seat in this room when we are *all together.*

19. *Their* is the possessive of *they. They're* is the contraction for *they are. There* is *that place.* They are not interchangeable.

    Examples: They're going to put *their* books over *there.*

20. *Your* is the possessive of *you. You're* is the contraction for *you are.* They are not interchangeable.

    Examples: You're planning to leave *your* muddy boots outside, aren't you?

21. *Whose* is the possessive of *who*. *Who's* is the contraction for *who is*. They are not interchangeable.

> *Examples:* Do you know *who's* ringing the doorbell or *whose* car is in the street?

22. *Its* is the possessive of *it*. *It's* is the contraction for *it is*. They are not interchangeable.

> *Examples:* *It's* not I who doesn't like *its* style.

Of course, these aren't the only spelling rules for the English language, but this is a good start. Studying these rules and practicing them while learning spelling will see you through thousands of perplexing situations. One final hint: If you find that you must look up certain words every time you use them, write them down, correctly spelled, on the inside front cover of your dictionary to save valuable time. Consult this list of your personal spelling "devils" the day before your exam. Chances are, the words that trouble you also perplex others—and that means they may appear on your exam.

If you are following the advice in this book, you've begun compiling a list of words that tend to stump you consistently: your spelling devils. Many of these words may appear on the list, "400 Frequently Misspelled Words," in the Appendix section of this book. These are words that have proven troublesome for most test takers and that frequently appear on civil service exam spelling sections. Reviewing this list before exam day will help you tackle many of the most vexing words.

PRACTICE SPELLING QUESTIONS

Now that you've reviewed some of the most basic spelling rules and exceptions, try your hand at these practice questions.

Exercise 1

> **Directions:** Circle the letter of the correct spelling. If no suggested spelling is correct, circle choice (D). The answers are at the end of the exercise.

1.
- **(A)** occassional
- **(B)** ocassional
- **(C)** occasional
- **(D)** none of these

2.
- **(A)** Wensday
- **(B)** Wednesday
- **(C)** Wendesday
- **(D)** none of these

3.
- **(A)** rythm
- **(B)** ryhthm
- **(C)** rhthym
- **(D)** none of these

4.
- **(A)** matinee
- **(B)** mattinee
- **(C)** matinnee
- **(D)** none of these

5.
(A) availble
(B) available
(C) availible
(D) none of these

6.
(A) conscience
(B) consceince
(C) concience
(D) none of these

7.
(A) wholly
(B) wholey
(C) wholley
(D) none of these

8.
(A) basiclly
(B) basicaly
(C) basically
(D) none of these

9.
(A) bookeeper
(B) bookeepper
(C) bookkeeper
(D) none of these

10.
(A) picknicing
(B) picnicking
(C) picnicing
(D) none of these

11.
(A) sacreligious
(B) sacrelegious
(C) sacrilegious
(D) none of these

12.
(A) February
(B) Ferbuary
(C) Febuary
(D) none of these

13.
(A) obsolescensce
(B) obsolecense
(C) obsolescence
(D) none of these

14.
(A) interferance
(B) interferrence
(C) interference
(D) none of these

15.
(A) outrageous
(B) outragous
(C) outrageouse
(D) none of these

16.
(A) vacuum
(B) vacume
(C) vaccuume
(D) none of these

17.
(A) vegtable
(B) vegertable
(C) vegitable
(D) none of these

18.
(A) caffiene
(B) caffeinn
(C) caffeine
(D) none of these

19.
(A) gauge
(B) guage
(C) gaugue
(D) none of these

20.
(A) exzema
(B) exzcema
(C) ezxema
(D) none of these

ANSWER KEY AND EXPLANATIONS

1. C	5. B	9. C	13. C	17. D
2. B	6. A	10. B	14. C	18. C
3. D	7. A	11. C	15. A	19. A
4. A	8. C	12. A	16. A	20. D

1. **The correct answer is (C).** The correct spelling is *occasional*.

2. **The correct answer is (B).** The correct spelling is *Wednesday*.

3. **The correct answer is (D).** The correct spelling is *rhythm*.

4. **The correct answer is (A).** The correct spelling is *matinee*.

5. **The correct answer is (B).** The correct spelling is *available*.

6. **The correct answer is (A).** The correct spelling is *conscience*.

7. **The correct answer is (A).** The correct spelling is *wholly*.

8. **The correct answer is (C).** The correct spelling is *basically*.

9. **The correct answer is (C).** The correct spelling is *bookkeeper*.

10. **The correct answer is (B).** The correct spelling is *picnicking*.

11. **The correct answer is (C).** The correct spelling is *sacrilegious*.

12. **The correct answer is (A).** The correct spelling is *February*.

13. **The correct answer is (C).** The correct spelling is *obsolescence*.

14. **The correct answer is (C).** The correct spelling is *interference*.

15. **The correct answer is (A).** The correct spelling is *outrageous*.

16. **The correct answer is (A).** The correct spelling is *vacuum*.

17. **The correct answer is (D).** The correct spelling is *vegetable*.

18. **The correct answer is (C).** The correct spelling is *caffeine*.

19. **The correct answer is (A).** The correct spelling is *gauge*.

20. **The correct answer is (D).** The correct spelling is *eczema*.

Exercise 2

Directions: In each of the following groups, there is one misspelled word. Write the letter of that word on the line provided.

1. _____
   - (A) refferee
   - (B) eligible
   - (C) excitement
   - (D) reign

2. _____
   - (A) eighth
   - (B) acheivement
   - (C) aching
   - (D) readiness

3. _____
   - (A) imune
   - (B) orator
   - (C) ascertain
   - (D) pierce

4. _____
   - (A) wield
   - (B) gradually
   - (C) tumbleing
   - (D) philosophical

5. _____
   - (A) superior
   - (B) traffic
   - (C) interminable
   - (D) admittence

6. _____
   - (A) standardize
   - (B) peaceable
   - (C) fatigue
   - (D) involvment

7. _____
   - (A) arbitrary
   - (B) blemish
   - (C) testamony
   - (D) deprivation

8. _____
   - (A) apparently
   - (B) demolition
   - (C) resturant
   - (D) visibility

9. _____
   - (A) vacancy
   - (B) incredible
   - (C) minature
   - (D) interpreter

10. _____
   - (A) allottment
   - (B) baggage
   - (C) equitable
   - (D) colossal

Directions: In the following section, some words are spelled correctly and some are misspelled. If a word is spelled correctly, write the word "correct" on the line to the right. If a word is misspelled, write the correct spelling.

11. enrolement _____

12. grease _____

13. goalkeeper _____

14. qualitey _____

15. disatisfied _____

16. whisle _____

17. abundant _____

18. intellectuel _____

19. antena _____

20. cieling _____

21. controlled _____

22. disgise _____

23. physicain _____

24. noticable _____

25. nineteenth _____

26. consience _____

27. renounce _____

28. enamies _____

29. allergick _____

30. spagetti _____

31. apalogy _____

32. concerning _____

33. pianoes _____

34. celabration _____

35. license _____

36. privilege _____

37. sophmore _____

38. acheiving _____

39. lonliness _____

40. surroundings _____

41. prarie _____

42. legitamate _____

43. secretarial _____

44. dissagreeable _____

45. coincidence _____

46. concientious _____

47. comparision _____

48. salaries _____

49. creditted _____

50. forthcoming _____

ANSWERS AND EXPLANATIONS

1. The correct answer is **(A)**. Refferee should be *referee*.

2. The correct answer is **(B)**. Acheivement should be *achievement*.

3. The correct answer is **(A)**. Imune should be *immune*.

4. The correct answer is **(C)**. Tumbleing should be *tumbling*.

5. The correct answer is **(D)**. Admittence should be *admittance*.

6. The correct answer is **(D)**. Involvment should be *involvement*.

7. The correct answer is **(C)**. Testamony should be *testimony*.

8. The correct answer is **(C)**. Resturant should be *restaurant*.

9. The correct answer is **(C)**. Minature should be *miniature*.

10. The correct answer is **(A)**. Allottment should be *allotment*.

11. The correct spelling is *enrollment*.

12. Correct as written.

13. Correct as written.

14. The correct spelling is *quality*.

15. The correct spelling is *dissatisfied*.

16. The correct spelling is *whistle*.

17. Correct as written.

18. The correct spelling is *intellectual*.

19. The correct spelling is *antenna*.

20. The correct spelling is *ceiling*.

21. Correct as written.

22. The correct spelling is *disguise*.

23. The correct spelling is *physician*.

24. The correct spelling is *noticeable*.

25. Correct as written.

26. The correct spelling is *conscience*.

27. Correct as written.

28. The correct spelling is *enemies*.

29. The correct spelling is *allergic*.

30. The correct spelling is *spaghetti*.

31. The correct spelling is *apology*.

32. Correct as written.

33. The correct spelling is *pianos*.

34. The correct spelling is *celebration*.

35. Correct as written.

36. Correct as written.

37. The correct spelling is *sophomore*.

38. The correct spelling is *achieving*.

39. The correct spelling is *loneliness*.

40. Correct as written.

41. The correct spelling is *prairie*.

42. The correct spelling is *legitimate*.

43. Correct as written.

44. The correct spelling is *disagreeable*.

45. Correct as written.

46. The correct spelling is *conscientious*.

47. The correct spelling is *comparison*.

48. Correct as written.

49. The correct spelling is *credited*.

50. Correct as written.

SUMMING IT UP

- A public safety dispatcher must be clearly and easily understood and must have a strong command of the language. He or she must also readily understand others and be able to draw meaning from excited or garbled messages or speech. This is why vocabulary and spelling are assessed on the public safety dispatcher exam.

- The vocabulary you'll encounter on the exam is more complex than what most people use in everyday speech—but if you know the meaning of more obscure words, you will most certainly be fluent and proficient with simpler words.

- Synonym questions are the most commonly used measure of vocabulary on the public safety dispatcher exam. Test takers use two types of synonym questions. One consists of a key word followed by several answer choices; you must select the word or phrase that is exactly the same as or closest in meaning to the key word. Another question type consists of a sentence containing one uppercased word; you must choose the answer choice that is the best synonym for that word.

- Spelling is not a major component of the public safety dispatcher position, but it's important that your spelling is accurate enough that it's unlikely to be misread or misinterpreted. Dispatchers who prepare written reports must ensure that the reports are correct in content and form; if you are testing for this type of position, you'll probably see spelling questions on your exam.

- Learn and review the spelling rules in this chapter and the 400-word spelling list in the Appendix section of this book. The list consists of words that many test takers find troublesome and that frequently appear on civil service exams.

Clerical Skills

OVERVIEW

- Typing on the Public Safety Dispatcher Exam
- Typing exercises
- Address checking on the Public Safety Dispatcher Exam
- Address-checking exercises
- Name and number comparison questions on the Public Safety Dispatcher Exam
- Comparison exercises
- Summing it up

TYPING ON THE PUBLIC SAFETY DISPATCHER EXAM

Facility in typing is so important to the job of the public safety dispatcher that some municipalities rely solely on a typing test to select candidates for the position. Very few cities waive proof of a candidate's typing skills.

The typing test, like the written test, can take many different forms. It is usually administered on a computer keyboard. Since computers and typing test programs vary, you will receive specific instructions and ample time to practice on the testing equipment before the scored portion of your typing test begins.

An effective public safety dispatcher must be an accurate and swift typist. Some municipalities require a speed as minimal as 25 words per minute (wpm), but these municipalities generally demand 100 percent accuracy: A single error at 25 wpm is enough to disqualify a candidate. If you hope to do well on the typing test, it's imperative that you practice as much as time permits. The more you practice, the more proficient you will become.

To prepare for the typing test, practice both copying and typing from dictation, and be sure to include words and numbers. Limber up by typing whatever pops into your head, or copy the text of the day's junk mail. Aim for total accuracy. The usual rule in scoring typing tests is that a corrected error is still an error; ideally, you should make no mistakes at all. Corrections you make while typing on a computer keyboard are generally not recorded. Watch the screen closely for errors, however. If you make an error, correct it as quickly as possible and keep moving. Any time you lose in making a correction will do you less harm than letting the error pass.

chapter 6

One variety of this test is called a "plain copy" typing test. You're given a few paragraphs to type exactly as you see them on the copy. You must reproduce spacing, paragraph breaks, spelling, punctuation, capitalization, and line breaks precisely as they appear on the original copy. Most plain copy typing tests take 5 minutes. Try practicing this type of test with the exercises that follow. Make sure you correct any errors you spot, and be sure to time yourself (or have someone do it for you).

TYPING EXERCISES

Directions: Space, paragraph, spell, punctuate, capitalize, and begin and end each line precisely as shown in the exercise. Allow exactly 5 minutes to type as many copies of the copy as you can. Each time you complete the paragraph, hit the return key twice and begin again. Continue typing until five minutes have elapsed.

Exercise 1

Your position at the computer is of prime importance. You

should sit easily and naturally, with your hips back in the

chair, your body erect, and both feet flat on the floor. One

foot may be somewhat in front of the other. Your shoulders

should be relaxed, your upper arms close to your body, and

your forearms parallel to the slope of the keyboard. Your

hands should never rest on the keyboard.

Exercise 2

This is an example of the type of material that will be

presented to you at the actual typing examination.

Each competitor will be required to type the practice

material exactly as it appears on the copy. You will be

asked to space, capitalize, punctuate, spell, and begin and

end each line exactly as it is presented in the copy. Each

time you reach the end of the paragraph, you should begin

again and continue to practice typing the paragraph until

the test administrator tells you to stop. You are advised

that it is more important to type accurately than to type

rapidly.

Exercise 3

Because they have often learned to know types of architecture

by decoration, casual observers sometimes fail to

realize that the significant part of a structure is not the

ornamentation but the body itself. Architecture, because of

its close contact with human lives, is peculiarly and intimately

governed by climate. For instance, a home built for

comfort in the cold and snow of the northern areas of this

country would be unbearably warm in a country with weather

such as that of Cuba. A Cuban house, with its open court,

would prove impossible to heat in a northern winter.

Because the purpose of architecture is the construction of

shelters in which human beings may carry on their numerous

activities, the designer must consider not only climatic

conditions, but also the function of a building. Thus,

although the climate of a certain locality requires that an

auditorium and a hospital have several features in common,

the purposes for which they will be used demand some difference

in structure. For centuries, builders have first

complied with these two requirements and later added whatever

ornamentation they wished. Logically, we should see as

mere additions, not as basic parts, the details by which we

identify architecture.

Listening and Typing

Because the work of a public safety dispatcher relies heavily upon information received via telephone, your typing test is just as likely to be based on typing from dictation as it is to be a copying test. To practice typing from dictation, ask a friend or family member to read short passages at varying speeds (but fairly rapidly at times). Find passages that include names, addresses, and telephone numbers. They might also include short sections of reported information, such as "burglary in progress," "my child can't breathe," or "there's a fire in the house across the street." Your friend could read names, addresses, and telephone numbers directly from a phone book and from the clerical speed and accuracy exercises in the next section. The reader should also dictate some longer passages, such as those you practiced keying in the plain copy exercises. Ask your friend to read these passages more slowly and with expression and appropriate pauses so that you can punctuate correctly. If a friend or family member isn't available to dictate, read some material into a recorder and then play it back to yourself.

Typing Numbers

Listening to numbers and relaying them in the same order is very important in the work of a public safety dispatcher, so your exam may contain a section emphasizing number entry. The number line is the keyboard section with which most people are least familiar and least skilled in using. In routine typing, number keys are not used as frequently as letter keys; however, to perform the duties of a public safety dispatcher, it's vital to be comfortable with the number keys.

Type Exercise 4 again and again, making sure you include the spacing and punctuation exactly as they appear here. At first, aim for perfect accuracy; then focus on increasing your typing speed. In the beginning, you may have to look at the number keys on your typewriter. If your computer has an extended keyboard with a numerical keypad, consider using that instead of the row of numbered keys above the lettered section of the keyboard. The numerical keypad is set up like a calculator, and you may find it easier to use than the row of numbers on the basic keyboard. Regardless of which set of keys you choose, be sure that you know how to use both for typing numbers.

Your goal for Exercise 4 should be to type the entire passage correctly, looking only at the paper from which you're copying and the computer screen—not the keyboard or keypad. Proofread it carefully, either onscreen or printed out. Repeat this exercise until you are satisfied with your speed and accuracy. Then try typing the same numbers from dictation.

Exercise 4

8321	9547	6503	8402	0886
9723	7531	7158	4602	0284
1570	2580	8400	4790	4273
682,412	598,211	890,142	797,501	204,673
212 - 1237	914 - 17862	516 - 1418	203 - 9834	4 - 8308
336 - 1451	773 - 4801	926 - 1862	302 - 0964	8 - 2593
$510.66	$923.45	$256.99	$812.59	$908.45@
#67,532	#909,482	#856,304	#168,451	#93,715
21.33%	100%	99.44%	155%	83.8%
@230	@490	@82	@92140	@810

The Alphanumeric Typing Test

On your public safety dispatcher exam, you may also encounter an alphanumeric, computer-administered section. The format explained here is one of several for this test type.

As the test begins, you'll see on the screen an explanation of which keys you will be using and how they function. You need to use the letter, number, shift, return (or enter), delete (or backspace,) and caps lock keys. A test administrator will remain in the room to answer questions.

The computer program will then display an explanation of the typing task itself. A letter-and-number code will appear on the upper right of the screen. You must type the code exactly as you see it, then hit return to bring up the next code. When you see the next code, type that exactly as you see it and hit return, and so on.

The codes generally consist of four letters and three numbers; for example TYHR346 or BZIP801. The more quickly you enter them and hit return, the more quickly the next code will come up and the more codes you'll be able to enter before the test ends. In the explanation phase of the exam, you will have 15 seconds in which to copy five codes. The computer program will tell you how many you copied correctly.

After the explanation phase, you'll be offered a practice session. You're allowed 5 minutes to correctly copy as many codes as you can (again, one at a time). The 5-minute practice session does not count toward your exam score, so this is your chance to experiment.

Follow these four simple steps when taking an alphanumeric typing test:

1. Look at the code and quickly memorize it; four letters and three numbers should pose no problem for such a short-term memory task.

2. Type in the code, keeping your eyes at the center of the screen where the letters and numbers appear.

3. Delete and retype if you spot an error.

4. Hit the return button and repeat the process.

When your 5 minutes have elapsed, your score will flash on the screen. If you scored 14 or higher, you can feel confident about taking the actual exam; you've done well. If your score is lower than 14, don't panic. Remember that this session does not count toward your exam score, and that you used this time to practice. Look at it this way: You now have 5 minutes to use the system with which you have already become comfortable. Your second score—the score that *does* count—will be higher. The actual test session is exactly like the practice session, but with new sets of codes.

Exercise 5 is a sample of the kind of content you'll encounter on a computer-based alphanumeric typing test. Use it as a model to prepare more exercises for additional practice.

Exercise 5

RJKF566	BVEI155	GKZP876
YTMN068	FUQS478	EDBJ582
FULLD727	JMGE610	OLDE751
TTHU950	SQWP010	LEAP274
NORT707	BDEY851	PHYX593
FLIR015	CZDT874	BLDV592
OYJXO55	FTTD123	KHTP805
GYKN094	RHVZ417	IFWK173
WEST301	TGIF629	YCWI142
DRHK967	PDQD157	OLZT809
AVNB893	EAST383	VMHW649
RKBY775	GSAP013	HTCQ858
LGBU919	UQFP180	JFTA862

ADDRESS CHECKING ON THE PUBLIC SAFETY DISPATCHER EXAM

It is impossible to overemphasize the need for speed and accuracy in the work of a dispatcher. Public safety dispatchers must be able to hear, type, and read accurately. Without these skills, the public safety dispatcher could, for example, transpose numbers and potentially send an assisting emergency vehicle to the wrong address. Or misspelling a name might lead the police to detain an innocent person as a suspect in a crime.

When a public safety dispatcher listens to information on the telephone, he or she must be able to immediately enter the information into a computer and promptly relay it to another party. An applicant's ability to perform these tasks accurately and quickly is tested in several ways. Some municipalities give only paper-and-pencil tests of speed and accuracy in checking names, numbers, or both. These types of tests often involve complex instructions.

Other municipalities test for clerical speed and accuracy with a typing test. We've already reviewed what a typing test might entail for a public safety dispatcher position. In this section, we'll look at how you can conquer clerical speed and accuracy exam questions.

5 Steps for Answering Address-Checking Questions

Address-checking questions are not difficult, but they require great speed and often carry heavy penalties for inaccuracy. Some may also have rather complicated directions. To answer address-checking questions swiftly and accurately, you need to learn to spot differences very quickly and make firm, fast decisions. Let's review five steps you can use to improve your speed and accuracy with address-checking questions. Once you have learned this "system," practice will help you build up speed.

1. Read exactly what you see. The best way to read addresses is to read exactly what you see and sound out words by syllable. For example:

- If you see "St.," read "es-tee, period," not "street."

- If you see "NH," read "en aich," not "New Hampshire."

- If you see "1035," read "one zero three five," not "one thousand thirty-five."

Why do this? Let's say you read the abbreviation "Pky" as "Parkway," the word it stands for. Very likely, this means you'll also read "Pkwy" as "Parkway"—and you won't notice the difference between the two abbreviations. Your mind will complete the word without allowing you to focus on the letters. If, however, you read each abbreviation *as* an abbreviation, you will begin to notice that the two abbreviations are not the same. Similarly, if you read "Kansas City, MO" as "Kansas City, Missouri," you are unlikely to catch the difference between it and "Kansas City, MD." But if you read "Kansas City em oh," you will readily pick up the difference between that phrase and "Kansas city em dee."

Read aloud at first so that you'll develop an ear for what you're reading. As you practice, you'll learn to "hear" the correctly sounded addresses in your mind.

2. Use your hands. Because speed is so important in answering address-checking questions, and since it is so easy to lose your place, use both hands during your work on questions with this format. In the hand with which you write, hold your pencil poised at the number on your answer sheet. Run the index finger of your other hand under the addresses being compared. This helps you to focus on one line at a time and will help you avoid jumping from one line to another. By holding your place on both the question and answer sheet, you're less likely to skip a question or fill in the wrong answer space.

One effective way to tackle address-checking questions quickly and accurately is to look for differences in just one area at a time. Every address consists of numbers and words. If you narrow your focus to compare only the numbers or only the words, you are more likely to notice differences and less apt to see what you expect to see rather than what is actually printed on the page.

3. Look for differences in numbers. Look first at the numbers. Read the number in the left column, then skip immediately to the number in the right column. Do the two numbers contain the same number of digits? Are they in the same order? Is any digit out of place?

4. Look for differences in abbreviations. When you are satisfied that the numbers are alike, and if no other difference has "struck you between the eyes," turn your attention to the abbreviations. Keep alert for subtle differences. For example:

Rd	Dr
Wy	Way
NH	NM

5. Look for differences in street or city names. If you've compared the numbers and the abbreviations but have not spotted any differences, look next at the main words of the address. Are the words in the two addresses really the same words? Sound out the words by syllables or spell them out. Is the spelling exactly the same? Are the same letters doubled? Are two letters reversed?

Here are four sets of questions so you can practice looking for differences in numbers, abbreviations, and street or city names (Steps 3, 4, and 5 on page 119).

Practice Set 1

Directions: In the questions that follow, choose **(A)** if the two numbers are exactly alike or **(D)** if the numbers differ in any way.

1. 2003   2003
2. 75864   75864
3. 7300   730
4. 50106   5016
5. 2184   2184
6. 7516   7561
7. 80302   80302
8. 19832   18932
9. 6186   6186
10. 54601   54601
11. 16830   16830
12. 94936   94636
13. 3287   3285
14. 54216   54216
15. 32341   33341

ANSWER KEY AND EXPLANATIONS

1. A	4. D	7. A	10. A	13. D
2. A	5. A	8. D	11. A	14. A
3. D	6. D	9. A	12. D	15. D

1. **The correct answer is (A).** Both are the same.

2. **The correct answer is (A).** Both are the same.

3. **The correct answer is (D).** The first, 7300, is four digits; the second, 730, is three digits.

4. **The correct answer is (D).** The first, 50106, is five digits; the second, 5016, is four digits and does not have a second 0.

5. **The correct answer is (A).** Both are the same.

6. **The correct answer is (D).** The first, 7516, ends in 16; the second ends in 61.

7. **The correct answer is (A).** Both are the same.

8. **The correct answer is (D).** The first, 19832, begins with 198; the second begins with 189.

9. **The correct answer is (A).** Both are the same.

10. **The correct answer is (A).** Both are the same.

11. **The correct answer is (A).** Both are the same.

12. **The correct answer is (D).** The first, 94936, has 9 as its middle (third) digit; the second, 94636, has 6 as its middle digit.

13. **The correct answer is (D).** The first, 3287, ends in 7; the second, 3285, ends in 5.

14. **The correct answer is (A).** Both are the same.

15. **The correct answer is (D).** The first, 32341, has 2 as its second digit; the second, 33341, has 3 as its second digit.

Practice Set 2

Directions: In the following set of practice questions, all differences are in the numbers. Work quickly, focusing only on the numbers. You may find any of the three varieties of differences just described. Place an **(A)** next to the question if the items are alike, and a **(D)** if they are different.

1. 3685 Brite Ave   3865 Brite Ave
2. Ware MA 08215   Ware MA 08215
3. 4001 Webster Rd   401 Webster Rd
4. 9789 Bell Rd   9786 Bell Rd
5. Scarsdale NY 10583   Scarsdale NY 10583
6. 1482 Grand Blvd   1482 Grand Blvd
7. Milwaukee WI 53202   Milwaukee WI 52302
8. 3542 W 48th St   3542 W 84th St
9. 9461 Hansen St   9461 Hansen St
10. 32322 Florence Pkwy   3232 Florence Pkwy
11. Portland OR 97208   Portland OR 99208
12. 3999 Thompson Dr   3999 Thompson Dr
13. 1672 Sutton Pl   1972 Sutton Pl
14. Omaha NE 68127   Omaha NE 68127
15. 1473 S 96th St   1743 S 96th St
16. 3425 Geary St   3425 Geary St
17. Dallas TX 75234   Dallas TX 75234
18. 4094 Horchow Rd   4904 Horchow Rd
19. San Francisco CA 94108   San Francisco CA 94108
20. 1410 Broadway   141 Broadway
21. 424 Fifth Ave   4240 Fifth Ave
22. Westport CT 06880   Westport CT 06880
23. 1932 Wilton Rd   1923 Wilton Rd
24. 2052 Victoria Sta   2502 Victoria Sta
25. 1982 Carlton Pl   1982 Carlton Pl

ANSWER KEY AND EXPLANATIONS

1. D	6. A	11. D	16. A	21. D
2. A	7. D	12. A	17. A	22. A
3. D	8. D	13. D	18. D	23. D
4. D	9. A	14. A	19. A	24. D
5. A	10. D	15. D	20. D	25. A

1. **The correct answer is (D).** The first address includes the number 3685; in the second address, the middle two digits of this number are transposed (3865).

2. **The correct answer is (A).** Both are the same.

3. **The correct answer is (D).** The first address includes a four-digit number, 4001; the second includes a three-digit number, 401.

4. **The correct answer is (D).** The number in the first address, 9789, ends in 9; the number in the second address ends in 6.

5. **The correct answer is (A).** Both are the same.

6. **The correct answer is (A).** Both are the same.

7. **The correct answer is (D).** In the number in the first address, the second digit is 3 and third is 2; in the number in the second address, the second digit is 2 and the third is 3.

8. **The correct answer is (D).** The number in the first address is 48; the number in the second is 84.

9. **The correct answer is (A).** Both are the same.

10. **The correct answer is (D).** The first address includes a five-digit number, 32322; the second address includes a four-digit number, 3232.

11. **The correct answer is (D).** In the number of the first address, the second digit is 7; in the number in the second address, the second digit is 9.

12. **The correct answer is (A).** Both are the same.

13. **The correct answer is (D).** In the number of the first address, the second digit is 6; in the number in the second address, the second digit is 9.

14. **The correct answer is (A).** Both are the same.

15. **The correct answer is (D).** The second and third digits of the two address numbers have been transposed: 47 and 74.

16. **The correct answer is (A).** Both are the same.

17. **The correct answer is (A).** Both are the same.

18. **The correct answer is (D).** The second and third digits of the two address numbers have been transposed: 09 and 90.

19. **The correct answer is (A).** Both are the same.

20. **The correct answer is (D).** The first address has a four-digit number, 1410; the second has a three-digit number, 141.

21. **The correct answer is (D).** The first address has a three-digit number, 424;

the second has a four-digit number, 4240.

22. The correct answer is (A). Both are the same.

23. The correct answer is (D). The third and fourth digits of the two address numbers have been transposed: 32 and 23.

24. The correct answer is (D). The second and third digits of the two address numbers have been transposed: 05 and 50.

25. The correct answer is (A). Both are the same.

Practice Set 3

Directions: For each question, look for any discrepancies between abbreviations. Remember to sound out the abbreviations exactly as you see them.

1.	3238 NW 3rd St	3238 NE 3rd St
2.	7865 Harkness Blvd	7865 Harkness Blvd
3.	Seattle WA 98102	Seattle WY 98102
4.	342 Madison Ave	342 Madison St
5.	723 Broadway E	723 Broadway E
6.	4731 W 88th Dr	4731 W 88th Rd
7.	Boiceville NY 12412	Boiceville NY 12412
8.	9021 Rodeo Dr	9021 Rodeo Dr
9.	2093 Post St	2093 Post Rd
10.	New Orleans LA 70153	New Orleans LA 70153
11.	5332 SW Bombay St	5332 SW Bombay St
12.	416 Wellington Pkwy	416 Wellington Hwy
13.	2096 Garden Ln	2096 Garden Wy
14.	3220 W Grant Ave	3220 W Grant Ave
15.	Charlotte VT 05445	Charlotte VA 05445
16.	4415 Oriental Blvd	4415 Oriental Blvd
17.	6876 Raffles Rd	6876 Raffles Rd
18.	891 S Hotel Hwy	891 E Hotel Hwy
19.	9500 London Br	9500 London Br
20.	24A Motcomb St	24A Motcomb St
21.	801 S Erleigh Ln	801 S Erleigh La
22.	839 Casco St	839 Casco St
23.	Freeport ME 04033	Freeport NE 04033
24.	3535 Island Ave	3535 Island Av
25.	2186 Missourie Ave NE	2186 Missourie Ave NW

ANSWER KEY AND EXPLANATIONS

1. D	6. D	11. A	16. A	21. D
2. A	7. A	12. D	17. A	22. A
3. D	8. A	13. D	18. D	23. D
4. D	9. D	14. A	19. A	24. D
5. A	10. A	15. D	20. A	25. D

1. **The correct answer is (D).** The first address includes NW (for Northwest); the second includes NE (for Northeast).

2. **The correct answer is (A).** Both are the same.

3. **The correct answer is (D).** The first address is in WA (Washington); the second address is in WY (Wyoming).

4. **The correct answer is (D).** The first address includes Ave (for Avenue); the second includes St (for Street).

5. **The correct answer is (A).** Both are the same.

6. **The correct answer is (D).** The first address includes Dr (for Drive); the second includes Rd (for Road).

7. **The correct answer is (A).** Both are the same.

8. **The correct answer is (A).** Both are the same.

9. **The correct answer is (D).** The first address includes St (for Street); the second includes Rd (for Road).

10. **The correct answer is (A).** Both are the same.

11. **The correct answer is (A).** Both are the same.

12. **The correct answer is (D).** The first address includes Pkwy (for Parkway); the second includes Hwy (for Highway).

13. **The correct answer is (D).** The first address includes Ln (Lane); the second includes Wy (Way).

14. **The correct answer is (A).** Both are the same.

15. **The correct answer is (D).** The first address is located in VT (Vermont); the second is located in VA (Virginia).

16. **The correct answer is (A).** Both are the same.

17. **The correct answer is (A).** Both are the same.

18. **The correct answer is (D).** The first address is on S (South) Hotel; the second is on E (East) Hotel.

19. **The correct answer is (A).** Both are the same.

20. **The correct answer is (A).** Both are the same.

21. **The correct answer is (D).** The two addresses contain different abbreviations for Lane (Ln vs. La).

22. **The correct answer is (A).** Both are the same.

23. **The correct answer is (D).** The first address is located in ME (Maine); the second is located in NE (Nebraska).

24. **The correct answer is (D).** The addresses contain different abbreviations for Avenue (Ave vs. Av).

25. **The correct answer is (D).** The first address is on Missourie Ave NE (Northeast); the second is on Missourie Ave NW (Northwest).

Practice Set 4

Directions: Look for discrepancies in the following list. Place an **(A)** next to the question if the items are alike, and a **(D)** if they are different.

1. Brookfield   Brookville
2. Wayland   Wayland
3. Ferncliff   Farmcliff
4. Spring   Springs
5. New City   New City
6. Beech   Beach
7. Torrington   Torington
8. Brayton   Brayton
9. Collegaite   Collegiate
10. Weston   Wetson

ANSWER KEY AND EXPLANATIONS

1. D	3. D	5. A	7. D	9. D
2. A	4. D	6. D	8. A	10. D

1. **The correct answer is (D).** The first is Brook*field*; the second is Brook*ville*.

2. **The correct answer is (A).** Both are the same.

3. **The correct answer is (D).** The first is *Fern*cliff; the second is *Farm*cliff.

4. **The correct answer is (D).** The first is Spring; the second ends in an *s*.

5. **The correct answer is (A).** Both are the same.

6. **The correct answer is (D).** The first, Beech, is spelled with *ee*; the second is spelled with *ea*.

7. **The correct answer is (D).** The first contains a double *r*; the second does not.

8. **The correct answer is (A).** Both are the same.

9. **The correct answer is (D).** In the first word, Collegaite, *a* comes before *i* (fourth- and third-to-last letters); in the second word, Collegiate, the order of these two letters is reversed.

10. **The correct answer is (D).** In the first word, Weston, the *s* comes before the *t*; in the second, the *t* comes before the *s*.

ADDRESS-CHECKING EXERCISES

In these questions, you may find differences in the two addresses in numbers, abbreviations, or main words, or you may find no difference at all. Work quickly, but do not time yourself on these practice questions.

Exercise 1

Directions: Look for discrepancies in the following list. Place an **(A)** next to the question if the items are alike, and a **(D)** if they are different.

1.	8690 W 134th St	8960 W 134th St
2.	1912 Berkshire Wy	1912 Berkshire Wy
3.	5331 W Professor St	5331 W Proffesor St
4.	Philadelphia PA 19124	Philadelphia PN 19124
5.	7450 Saguenay St	7450 Saguenay St
6.	8650 Christy St	8650 Christey St
7.	Lumberville PA 18933	Lumberville PA 19833
8.	114 Alabama Ave NW	114 Alabama Av NW
9.	1756 Waterford St	1756 Waterville St
10.	2214 Wister Wy	2214 Wister Wy
11.	2974 Repplier Rd	2974 Repplier Dr
12.	Essex CT 06426	Essex CT 06426
13.	7676 N Bourbon St	7616 N Bourbon St
14.	2762 Rosengarten Wy	2762 Rosengarden Wy
15.	239 Windell Ave	239 Windell Ave
16.	4667 Edgeworth Rd	4677 Edgeworth Rd
17.	2661 Kennel St SE	2661 Kennel St SW
18.	Alamo TX 78516	Alamo TX 78516
19.	3709 Columbine St	3709 Columbine St
20.	9699 W 14th St	9699 W 14th Rd
21.	2207 Markland Ave	2207 Markham Ave
22.	Los Angeles CA 90013	Los Angeles CA 90018
23.	4608 N Warnock St	4806 N Warnock St
24.	7118 S Summer St	7118 S Summer St
25.	New York, NY 10016	New York, NY 10016

26.	4514 Ft Hamilton Pk	4514 Ft Hamilton Pk
27.	5701 Koszciusko St	5701 Koscusko St
28.	5422 Evergreen St	4522 Evergreen St
29.	Gainesville FL 32611	Gainesville FL 32611
30.	5018 Church St	5018 Church Ave
31.	1079 N Blake St	1097 N Blake St
32.	8072 W 20th Rd	8072 W 20th Dr
33.	Onoro ME 04473	Orono ME 04473
34.	2175 Kimbell Rd	2175 Kimball Rd
35.	1243 Mermaid Rd	1243 Mermaid St
36.	4904 SW 134th St	4904 SW 134th St
37.	1094 Hancock St	1049 Hancock St
38.	Des Moines IA 50311	Des Moines IA 50311
39.	4832 S Rinaldi Rd	4832 S Rinaldo Rd
40.	2015 Dorchester Rd	2015 Dorchester Rd
41.	5216 Woodbine St	5216 Woodburn St
42.	Boulder CO 80302	Boulder CA 80302
43.	4739 N Marion St	479 N Marion St
44.	3720 Nautilus Wy	3720 Nautilus Way
45.	3636 Gramercy Pk	3636 Gramercy Pk
46.	757 Johnson Ave	757 Johnston Ave
47.	3045 Brighton 12th St	3054 Brighton 12th St
48.	237 Ovington Ave	237 Ovington Ave
49.	Kalamazoo MI 49007	Kalamazoo MI 49007
50.	Missoula MT 59812	Missoula MS 59812
51.	Stillwater OK 74704	Stillwater OK 47404
52.	4746 Empire Blvd	4746 Empire Bldg
53.	6321 St Johns Pl	6321 St Johns Pl
54.	2242 Vanderbilt Ave	2242 Vanderbilt Ave
55.	542 Ditmas Blvd	542 Ditmars Blvd
56.	4603 W Argyle Rd	4603 W Argyle Rd
57.	653 Knickerbocker Ave NE	653 Knickerbocker Ave NE
58.	3651 Midwood Terr	3651 Midwood Terr

59. Chapel Hill NC 27514	Chaple Hill NC 27514
60. 3217 Vernon Pl NW	3217 Vernon Dr NW
61. 1094 Rednor Pkwy	1049 Rednor Pkwy
62. 986 S Doughty Blvd	986 S Douty Blvd
63. Lincoln NE 68508	Lincoln NE 65808
64. 1517 LaSalle Ave	1517 LaSalle Ave
65. 3857 S Morris St	3857 S Morriss St
66. 6104 Saunders Expy	614 Saunders Expy
67. 2541 Appleton St	2541 Appleton Rd
68. Washington DC 20052	Washington DC 20052
69. 6439 Kessler Blvd S	6439 Kessler Blvd S
70. 4786 Catalina Dr	4786 Catalana Dr
71. 132 E Hampton Pkwy	1322 E Hampton Pkwy
72. 1066 Goethe Sq S	1066 Geothe Sq S
73. 1118 Jerriman Wy	1218 Jerriman Wy
74. 5798 Gd Central Pkwy	5798 Gd Central Pkwy
75. Delaware OH 43015	Delaware OK 43015
76. Corvallis OR 97331	Corvallis OR 97331
77. 4231 Keating Ave N	4231 Keating Av N
78. 5689 Central Pk Pl	5869 Central Pk Pl
79. 1108 Lyndhurst Dr	1108 Lyndhurst Dr
80. 842 Chambers Ct	842 Chamber Ct
81. Athens OH 45701	Athens GA 45701
82. Tulsa OK 74171	Tulsa OK 71471
83. 6892 Beech Grove Ave	6892 Beech Grove Ave
84. 2939 E Division St	2939 W Division St
85. 1554 Pitkin Ave	1554 Pitkin Ave
86. 905 St Edwards Plz	950 St Edwards Plz
87. 1906 W 152nd St	1906 W 152nd St
88. 3466 Glenmore Ave	3466 Glenville Ave
89. Middlebury VT 05753	Middlebery VT 05753
90. Evanston IL 60201	Evanston IN 60201
91. 9401 W McDonald Ave	9401 W MacDonald Ave

92. 5527 Albermarle Rd		5527 Albermarle Rd
93. 9055 Carter Dr		9055 Carter Rd
94. Greenvale NY 11548		Greenvale NY 11458
95. 1149 Cherry Gr S		1149 Cherry Gr S

ANSWER KEY AND EXPLANATIONS

1. D	20. D	39. D	58. A	77. D
2. A	21. D	40. A	59. D	78. D
3. D	22. D	41. D	60. D	79. A
4. D	23. D	42. D	61. D	80. D
5. A	24. A	43. D	62. D	81. D
6. D	25. A	44. D	63. D	82. D
7. D	26. A	45. A	64. A	83. A
8. D	27. D	46. D	65. D	84. D
9. D	28. D	47. D	66. D	85. A
10. A	29. A	48. A	67. D	86. D
11. D	30. D	49. A	68. A	87. A
12. A	31. D	50. D	69. A	88. D
13. D	32. D	51. D	70. D	89. D
14. D	33. D	52. D	71. D	90. D
15. A	34. D	53. A	72. D	91. D
16. D	35. D	54. A	73. D	92. A
17. D	36. A	55. D	74. A	93. D
18. A	37. D	56. A	75. D	94. D
19. A	38. A	57. A	76. A	95. A

1. **The correct answer is (D).** The first address number is 8690; in the second address, the number is 8960.

2. **The correct answer is (A).** Both are the same.

3. **The correct answer is (D).** The first address contains Professor with a double *s;* the second contains Proffesor with a double *f.*

4. **The correct answer is (D).** The first address contains PA; the second contains PN.

5. **The correct answer is (A).** Both are the same.

6. **The correct answer is (D).** The first address contains Christy with no *e;* the second spells Christey with an *e.*

7. **The correct answer is (D).** The number in the first address is 18933; in the second, the number is 19833 (second and third digits transposed).

8. **The correct answer is (D).** The first has Ave as an abbreviation for Avenue; the second uses Av.

9. **The correct answer is (D).** The first address is in Waterford; the second is in Waterville.

10. **The correct answer is (A).** Both are the same.

11. **The correct answer is (D).** The first address is a Road (Rd); the second is a Drive (Dr).

12. **The correct answer is (A).** Both are the same.

13. **The correct answer is (D).** The number of the first address is 7676; the number of the second is 7616.

14. **The correct answer is (D).** The first address includes Rosengarten spelled with a *t*; the second includes Rosengarden spelled with a *d*.

15. **The correct answer is (A).** Both are the same.

16. **The correct answer is (D).** The number of the first address is 4667; the number of the second is 4677.

17. **The correct answer is (D).** The first address is Kennel St *SE*; the second is Kennel St *SW*.

18. **The correct answer is (A).** Both are the same.

19. **The correct answer is (A).** Both are the same.

20. **The correct answer is (D).** The first address is a Street (St); the second is a Road (Rd).

21. **The correct answer is (D).** The street name in the first address is Markland; in the second, it is Markham.

22. **The correct answer is (D).** The ZIP Code in the first address is 90013; in the second, it is 90018.

23. **The correct answer is (D).** The street number in the first address is 4608; in the second, it is 4806.

24. **The correct answer is (A).** Both are the same.

25. **The correct answer is (A).** Both are the same.

26. **The correct answer is (A).** Both are the same.

27. **The correct answer is (D).** The street name in the first address is Koszciusko; in the second, it is Koscusko.

28. **The correct answer is (D).** The number in the first address is 5422; in the second, it is 4522.

29. **The correct answer is (A).** Both are the same.

30. **The correct answer is (D).** The first address is a Street (St); the second is an Avenue (Ave).

31. **The correct answer is (D).** The number in the first address is 1079; in the second, it is 1097.

32. **The correct answer is (D).** The first address is a Road (Rd); the second is a Drive (Dr).

33. **The correct answer is (D).** The town name in the first address is Onoro; in the second, it is Orono.

34. **The correct answer is (D).** The first address is on Kimbell; the second is on Kimball.

35. **The correct answer is (D).** The first address is a Road (Rd); the second is a Street (St).

36. **The correct answer is (A).** Both are the same.

37. **The correct answer is (D).** The number of the first address is 1094; the number of the second is 1049.

38. **The correct answer is (A).** Both are the same.

39. **The correct answer is (D).** The first address is Rinaldi; the second is Rinaldo.

40. **The correct answer is (A).** Both are the same.

41. The correct answer is (D). The first address contains Woodbine; the second contains Woodburn.

42. The correct answer is (D). The first address is in Colorado (CO); the second is in California (CA).

43. The correct answer is (D). The number in the first address is four digits long (4739); in the second, it is three digits (479).

44. The correct answer is (D). In the first address, Way is abbreviated (Wy); in the second, it is spelled out.

45. The correct answer is (A). Both are the same.

46. The correct answer is (D). The first address is on Johnson; the second is on Johnston (with a *t*).

47. The correct answer is (D). The number in the first address is 3045; in the second, it is 3054.

48. The correct answer is (A). Both are the same.

49. The correct answer is (A). Both are the same.

50. The correct answer is (D). The first address is in Montana (MT); the second is in Mississippi (MS).

51. The correct answer is (D). The number of the first address is 74704; the number of the second is 47404.

52. The correct answer is (D). The first address refers to a Boulevard (Blvd); the second refers to a Building (Bldg).

53. The correct answer is (A). Both are the same.

54. The correct answer is (A). Both are the same.

55. The correct answer is (D). The first address is on Ditmas; the second is on Ditmars.

56. The correct answer is (A). Both are the same.

57. The correct answer is (A). Both are the same.

58. The correct answer is (A). Both are the same.

59. The correct answer is (D). The first address is in Chapel Hill; the second is in Chaple Hill.

60. The correct answer is (D). The first address is a Place (Pl); the second is a Drive (Dr).

61. The correct answer is (D). The number of the first address is 1094; the number of the second is 1049.

62. The correct answer is (D). The first address is on Doughty; the second is on Douty.

63. The correct answer is (D). The ZIP Code of the first address is 68508; the ZIP Code of the second is 65808.

64. The correct answer is (A). Both are the same.

65. The correct answer is (D). The first address is on Morris; the second is on Morriss.

66. The correct answer is (D). The number of the first address is 6104 (four digits); the number of the second is 614 (three digits).

67. The correct answer is (D). The first address is a Street (St); the second is a Road (Rd).

68. The correct answer is (A). Both are the same.

69. The correct answer is (A). Both are the same.

70. The correct answer is (D). The first address is on Catalina; the second is on Catalana.

71. **The correct answer is (D).** The number of the first address is 132 (three digits); the number of the second is 1322 (four digits).

72. **The correct answer is (D).** The first address is on Goethe; the second is on Geothe.

73. **The correct answer is (D).** The number of the first address is 1118; the number of the second is 1218.

74. **The correct answer is (A).** Both are the same.

75. **The correct answer is (D).** The first address is in Ohio (OH); the second is in Oklahoma (OK).

76. **The correct answer is (A).** Both are the same.

77. **The correct answer is (D).** In the first address, Avenue is abbreviated Ave; in the second, it is abbreviated Av.

78. **The correct answer is (D).** The number of the first address is 5689; the number of the second is 5869.

79. **The correct answer is (A).** Both are the same.

80. **The correct answer is (D).** The first address is on Chambers; the second is on Chamber (no *s*).

81. **The correct answer is (D).** The first address is in Ohio (OH); the second is in Georgia (GA).

82. **The correct answer is (D).** The ZIP Code of the first address is 74171; the ZIP Code of the second is 71471.

83. **The correct answer is (A).** Both are the same.

84. **The correct answer is (D).** The first address is on *E* Division; the second is on *W* Division.

85. **The correct answer is (A).** Both are the same.

86. **The correct answer is (D).** The number of the first address is 905; the number of the second is 950.

87. **The correct answer is (A).** Both are the same.

88. **The correct answer is (D).** The first address is on Glenmore; the second is on Glenville.

89. **The correct answer is (D).** The first address is in Middlebury; the second is in Middlebery.

90. **The correct answer is (D).** The first address is in Illinois (IL); the second is in Indiana (IN).

91. **The correct answer is (D).** The first address is on McDonald; the second is on MacDonald.

92. **The correct answer is (A).** Both are the same.

93. **The correct answer is (D).** The first address is a Drive (Dr); the second is a Road (Rd).

94. **The correct answer is (D).** The ZIP Code of the first address is 11548; the ZIP Code of the second is 11458.

95. **The correct answer is (A).** Both are the same.

Exercise 2

Directions: Each question consists of a set of names and addresses. In each question, the name and address in Column II should be exactly like the name and address in Column I. However, some addresses in Column II contain mistakes.

- Write **(A)** next to the question number if there is a mistake *only* in the NAME.

- Write **(B)** next to the question number if there is a mistake *only* in the ADDRESS.

- Write **(C)** next to the question number if there are mistakes in *both* NAME *and* ADDRESS.

- Write **(D)** next to the question number if there are NO MISTAKES.

Column I	Column II
1. Mrs. Myrna McCardle 332 East 128th St. Chicago, IL 60637	Mrs. Myra McCardle 332 East 128th St. Chicago, IL 60637
2. Jorge T. Garcia, M.D. 843 Alameda Street Austin, TX 78712	Jorge T. Garcia, M.D. 843 Alameda Street Austin, TX 78712
3. Ms. Lillian Loomis 862 S.E. Byram Blvd Durham, NC 27706	Ms. Lillian Loomia 862 S.E. Bryan Blvd. Durham, NC 27706
4. Prof. Jeanette Jesperson 761 Palo Alto Drive Stanford, CA 94305	Prof. Jeanette Jesperson 716 Palo Alto Drive Stamford, CA 94305
5. Mr. Brett H. Meyers 72 Nannyhagen Road Haverford, PA 19042	Mr. Brett H. Meyers 72 Nannyhagen Road Haverford, PA 19402
6. George and Sylvia Shields 362 West 96th Street New York, NY 10028	George and Sylvia Sheilds 362 West 96th Street New York, NY 10028

7. Dr. and Mrs. P.J. Clarke   Dr. and Mrs. P.J. Clarke
   2146 Old Lyme Highway   2146 Old Lyme Highway
   New London, CT 06320   New London, CA 06320

8. Mr. Milton F. Gladstone   Mr. Milton P. Gladstone
   72 Conshohocken Rd.   72 Conshahocken Rd.
   Athens, OH 45701   Athena, OH 45701

9. Francis X. O'Rourke   Francis X. O'Rourke
   1918 Meridian Way   1918 Meridian Way
   Norman, OK 73069   Norman, OK 73069

10. Mrs. Anne C. Warren   Mrs. Anna C. Warren
    38-42 Marvela Drive   38-42 Marvella Drive
    Santa Cruz, CA 95064   Santa Cruz, CA 95064

11. Miss Maude Silverstone   Miss Maude Silverstone
    48601 Maryland Ave. NW   48610 Maryland Ave. NW
    Washington, DC 20052   Washington, DC 20052

12. Hoh Sun-Wah, Ph.D.   Moh Sun-Wah, Ph.D.
    4862 Southern Artery   4862 Southern Arterial
    Omaha, NE 68178   Omaha, NE 68178

13. Sr. Mary Donohue   Sr. Mary Donoghue
    378 Brigham Drive   378 Brigham Drive
    Provo, UT 84601   Provo, UT 86401

14. Mr. Thomas Trimmingham   Mr. Thomas Trimingham
    603 East Taunton Street   603 East Taunton Street
    Atlanta, GA 30322   Atlanta, GA 30322

15. Miss Sussana Oliviero   Miss Sussana Oliviero
    215 Sorority Way   215 Sorority Way
    Tallahassee, FL 32306   Tallahassee, FL 32306

ANSWER KEY AND EXPLANATIONS

1. A	4. B	7. B	10. C	13. C
2. D	5. B	8. C	11. B	14. A
3. C	6. A	9. D	12. C	15. D

1. **The correct answer is (A).** The first name of the addressee in Column I is Myrna; in the second, it is Myra.

2. **The correct answer is (D).** No errors.

3. **The correct answer is (C).** The last name of the addressee in Column I is Loomis; in the second, it is Loomia. Also, the first address is on Byram; the second is on Bryan.

4. **The correct answer is (B).** The number of the first address is 761; the number of the second is 716. Also, the first address is in Stanford; the second is in Stamford.

5. **The correct answer is (B).** The ZIP Code of the first address is 19042; the ZIP Code of the second is 19402.

6. **The correct answer is (A).** The last name of the addressees in Column I is Shields; in the second, it is Sheilds.

7. **The correct answer is (B).** The first address is in CT; the second is in CA.

8. **The correct answer is (C).** The middle initial of the addressee in Column I is F; the middle initial of the addressee in Column II is P. Also, the first address is in Conshohocken; the second is in Conshahocken.

9. **The correct answer is (D).** No errors.

10. **The correct answer is (C).** The first name of the addressee in Column I is Anne; the first name of the addressee in Column II is Anna. Also, the address in Column I is on Marvela; in Column II, it is on Marvella.

11. **The correct answer is (B).** The ZIP Code of the address in Column I is 48601; in Column II, it is 48610.

12. **The correct answer is (C).** The addressee's first name in Column I is Hoh; in Column II, it is Moh. Also, the address in Column I is on Artery; in Column II, it is on Arterial.

13. **The correct answer is (C).** The last name of the addressee in Column I is Donohue; the last name in Column II is Donoghue. Also, the ZIP Code of the address in Column I is 84601; in Column II, it is 86401.

14. **The correct answer is (A).** The addressee's last name in Column I is Trimmingham; in Column II, it is Trimingham.

15. **The correct answer is (D).** No errors.

NAME AND NUMBER COMPARISON QUESTIONS ON THE PUBLIC SAFETY DISPATCHER EXAM

You may see name-and-number and number-and-letter comparison questions in one of many different formats and question styles. In general, though, the basic comparison task is always the same. The biggest difference lies in the directions. It is unlikely that you will find more than one form of comparison question on your exam, but there is no way of predicting which kind of question you will encounter. Therefore, if you find any comparison questions on your exam, it's extremely important that you *read the directions* very carefully.

COMPARISON EXERCISES

Try the five comparison exercises that follow. Each has a different style of question. Each has different directions that you must master before you attempt to answer the questions. For the most part, the strategies that you learned for address checking will work well here, too. Of course, if you are not comparing columns, you must adjust to the requirements of the exercise. The final exercise is considerably more complicated than the others in terms of directions.

Exercise 1

Directions: Each question consists of letters or numbers in Columns I and II. For each question, compare each line of Column I with its corresponding line in Column II. Decide how many lines in Column II are exactly the same as their counterparts in Column I.

- Choose **(A)** if only ONE line in Column II is exactly the same as its corresponding line in Column I.
- Choose **(B)** if TWO lines in Column II are exactly the same as their corresponding lines in Column I.
- Choose **(C)** if THREE lines in Column II are exactly the same as their corresponding lines in Column I.
- Choose **(D)** if ALL FOUR lines in Column II are exactly the same as their corresponding lines in Column I.

Column I	Column II
1. 3816	3816
5283	5832
4686	4868
1252	1252
2. acdt	acdt
xuer	xuer
Itbf	Ibtf
oypn	oypn

3. 9063   9063

    itop   itop

    nzne   nzne

    7549   7549

4. TYBF   TYIF

    5631   5361

    BcOp   BcOP

    ag7B   ag7B

5. Ibct   lbct

    1803   1803

    Xtux   Xtux

    45NM   45NM

6. AbuR   AbuR

    52VC   52VC

    rehg   rehg

    3416   3416

7. awg3   awg3

    tyE3   ty3E

    abhn   abnh

    24po   24op

8. 6tru   6tru

    sw4k   sw4K

    lgh8   lgh8

    u2up   u2up

9. agxp   agXp

    ruy5   ruy5

    aglb   agLb

    8a9c   8z9c

10 agbt   agbt

  1LiI   lliI

  ty4f   ty4f

  arwd   erwd

11. 4tT4   4tt4

  mp8s   mp8s

  bh43   bh43

  9ewz   9ewz

12. r2D2   R2D2

  zboc   zboc

  LQ6t   Lq6T

  0851   0851

13. tzng   yzng

  5F09   5F09

  bAlIr   bAlr

  6406   6406

14. 151Y   151Y

  Pti7   Pti7

  4uy3   4uyE

  htmn   hynm

15. rvC8   rvC8

  pg53   pg53

  1080   1080

  ednp   edhp

16. rTux   rTux

  lgad   lgab

  84fp   84fb

  uEms   uEms

17. rpIt   rlpt

    8eoz   8oez

    agew   agew

    T59v   T59v

18. 38mo   38m0

    Sebc   Sbce

    UPRF   URPF

    a5y3   a5y3

19. 25dq   25bq

    uz4R   uz4R

    ylng   yLng

    stRe   sire

20. 4fKD   4fKd

    swhC   swhC

    nbQt   bNQt

    L073   L073

ANSWER KEY AND EXPLANATIONS

1. B	5. C	9. A	13. B	17. B
2. C	6. D	10. B	14. B	18. A
3. D	7. A	11. C	15. C	19. A
4. A	8. C	12. B	16. B	20. B

1. **The correct answer is (B).** Alike: 3816, 3816; 1252, 1252. Different: 5<u>2</u>83, 5<u>8</u>32; 4<u>6</u>86, 4<u>8</u>68.

2. **The correct answer is (C).** Alike: acdt, acdt, xuer, xuer; oypn, oypn. Different: <u>I</u>tbf, <u>l</u>btf.

3. **The correct answer is (D).** All alike.

4. **The correct answer is (A).** Alike: ag7B, ag7B. Different: TY<u>B</u>F, TY<u>I</u>F; 5<u>631</u>, 5<u>361</u>; BcO<u>p</u>, BcO<u>P</u>.

5. **The correct answer is (C).** Alike: 1803, 1803; Xtux, Xtux; 45NM, 45NM. Different: <u>I</u>bct, <u>l</u>bct.

6. **The correct answer is (D).** All alike.

7. **The correct answer is (A).** Alike: awg3, awg3. Different: ty<u>E3</u>, ty<u>3E</u>; ab<u>hn</u>, ab<u>nh</u>; 24<u>po</u>, 24<u>op</u>.

8. **The correct answer is (C).** Alike: 6tru, 6tru; lgh8, lgh8; u2up, u2up. Different: sw4<u>k</u>, sw4<u>K</u>.

9. **The correct answer is (A).** Alike: ruy5, ruy5. Different: ag<u>x</u>p, ag<u>X</u>p; Ag<u>l</u>b, ag<u>L</u>b; 8<u>a</u>9c, 8<u>z</u>9c.

10. **The correct answer is (B).** Alike: agbt, agbt; ty4f, ty4f. Different: 1<u>L</u>iI, 1<u>1</u>iI; <u>a</u>rwd, <u>e</u>rwd.

11. **The correct answer is (C).** Alike: mp8s, mp8s; bh43, bh43; 9ewz, 9ewz. Different: 4t<u>T</u>4, 4tt<u>4</u>.

12. **The correct answer is (B).** Alike: zboc, zboc; 0851, 0851. Different: <u>r</u>2D2, <u>R</u>2D2; LQ6<u>t</u>, Lq6<u>T</u>.

13. **The correct answer is (B).** Alike: 5F09, 5F09; 6406, 6406. Different: bA<u>lI</u>r, bA<u>lr</u>; <u>t</u>zng, <u>y</u>zng.

14. **The correct answer is (B).** Alike: 151Y, 151Y; Pti7, Pti7. Different: 4uy<u>3</u>, 4uy<u>E</u>; ht<u>mn</u>, hy<u>nm</u>.

15. **The correct answer is (C).** Alike: rvC8, rvC8, pg53, pg53; 1080, 1080. Different: ed<u>n</u>p, ed<u>h</u>p.

16. **The correct answer is (B).** Alike: rTux, rTux; uEms, uEms. Different: lga<u>d</u>, lga<u>b</u>; 84f<u>p</u>, 84f<u>b</u>.

17. **The correct answer is (B).** Alike: agew, agew; T59v, T59v. Different: rp<u>I</u>t, rl<u>p</u>t; 8<u>eo</u>z, 8<u>oe</u>z.

18. **The correct answer is (A).** Alike: a5y3, a5y3. Different: 38m<u>o</u>, 38m<u>0</u>; S<u>eb</u>c, S<u>bce</u>; U<u>P</u>RF, U<u>RP</u>F.

19. **The correct answer is (A).** Alike: uz4R, uz4R. Different: 25<u>d</u>q, 25<u>b</u>q; y<u>l</u>ng, y<u>L</u>ng; st<u>R</u>e, s<u>i</u>re.

20. **The correct answer is (B).** Alike: swhC, swhC; L073, L073. Different: 4fK<u>D</u>, 4fK<u>d</u>; <u>n</u>bQt, <u>b</u>NQt.

Exercise 2

Directions: Each of the following questions consists of three sets of names and name codes. For each question, the two names and name codes on the same line should be exactly the same. Look carefully at each set of names and codes and mark your answer next to the question number.

- Write **(A)** if ALL THREE sets contain mistakes.
- Write **(B)** if TWO of the sets contain mistakes.
- Write **(C)** if only ONE set contains mistakes.
- Write **(D)** if NO MISTAKES are in any of the sets.

Column I		Column II	
1. Macabe, John N.	V 53162	Macade, John N.	V 53162
Howard, Joan S.	J 24791	Howard, Joan S.	124791
Ware, Susan B.	A 45068	Ware, Susan B.	A 45968
2. Powell, Michael C.	78537 F	Powell, Michael C.	78537 F
Martinez, Pablo J.	24435 P	Martinez, Pablo J.	24435 P
MacBane, Eliot M.	98674 E	MacBane, Eliot M.	98674 E
3. Fitz-Kramer Machines	259090	Fitz-Kramer Machines	259090
Marvel Cleaning Service	482657	Marvel Cleaning Service	482657
Donato, Carl G.	637418	Danato, Carl G.	687418
4. Davison Trading Corp.	43108 T	Davidson Trading Corp.	43108 T
Cotwald Lighting Fixtures	76065 L	Cotwald Lighting Fixtures	70056 L
R. Crawford Plumbers	23157 C	R. Crawford Plumbers	23157 G
5. Fraiman Eng. Corp.	M4773	Friaman Eng. Corp.	M4773
Neuman, Walter B.	N7745	Neumen, Walter B.	N7745
Pierce, Eric M.	W6304	Pierce, Eric M.	W6304
6. Constable, Eugene	B 64837	Comstable, Eugene	B 64837
Derrick, Paul	H 27119	Derrik, Paul	H 27119
Heller, Karen	S 49606	Heller, Karen	S 46906
7. Hernando Delivery Co.	D 7456	Hernando Delivery Co.	D 7456
Barettz Electrical Supplies	N 5392	Barettz Electrical Supplies	N 5392
Tanner, Abraham	M 4798	Tanner, Abraham	M 4798

8. | Kalin Associates | R 38641 | Kaline Associates | R 38641 |
| Sealey, Robert E. | P 63533 | Sealey, Robert E. | P 63553 |
| Scalsi Office Furniture | R 36742 | Scalsi Office Furniture | R 36742 |

9. | Janowsky, Philip M | 742213 | Janowsky, Philip M. | 742213 |
| Hansen, Thomas H. | 934816 | Hanson, Thomas H. | 934816 |
| L. Lester and Son Inc. | 294568 | L. Lester and Son Inc. | 294568 |

10. | Majthenyi, Alexander | P 4802 | Majthenyi, Alexander | B 4802 |
| Prisco Pools, Inc. | W 3641 | Frisco Pools, Inc. | W 3641 |
| DePaso, Nancy G. | X 4464 | DePasoa, Nancy G. | X 4464 |

11. | Hardy, Thomas G. | 374093 | Hardy, Thomas G. | 374093 |
| Carlin, Oren F. | 581158 | Carling, Oren F. | 581158 |
| van Rijn, Marike | 248652 | von Rijn, Marike | 248652 |

12. | Kozy Kitchens, Inc. | Z 48621 | Kozy Kitchens, Inc. | Z 46821 |
| Mullins, Iris | L 51790 | Mollins, Iris | L 51790 |
| The Cheese Shop | M 48164 | The Cheese Shop | M 48614 |

13. | Bryant College | 431798 | Bryant College | 431798 |
| Harbison, James T. | 468319 | Harbinson, James T. | 486319 |
| Riverfront Stadium | 791645 | Riverside Stadium | 791645 |

14. | Brunswick Lanes | T 44198 | Runswick Lanes | T 44198 |
| T. Greisis & Son | Q 53817 | T. Greisis & Son | Q 53817 |
| DiPasquale, Gino | B 43921 | DiPasquale, Gino | B 43921 |

15. | Hisogi, Mitsuki | 563141 | Hisogi, Mitsuki | 536141 |
| Janover, Richard L. | 453120 | Janover, Richard L. | 453210 |
| Britten, Barbara B. | 673498 | Brittan, Barbara B. | 673498 |

ANSWER KEY AND EXPLANATIONS

1. A	4. A	7. D	10. A	13. B
2. D	5. B	8. B	11. B	14. C
3. C	6. A	9. C	12. A	15. A

1. **The correct answer is (A).** Macabe, Macade; J24791, 124791; A 45068, A 45968.

2. **The correct answer is (D).** No errors.

3. **The correct answer is (C).** Donato, Danato; 637418; 687418.

4. **The correct answer is (A).** Davison, Davidson; 76065 L, 70056 L; 23157 C, 23157 G.

5. **The correct answer is (B).** Fraiman, Friaman; Neuman, Neumen.

6. **The correct answer is (A).** Constable, Comstable; Derrick, Derrik; S 49606, S 46906.

7. **The correct answer is (D).** No errors.

8. **The correct answer is (B).** Kalin, Kaline; P 63533, P 63553.

9. **The correct answer is (C).** Hansen, Hanson.

10. **The correct answer is (A).** P 4802, B 4802; Prisco, Frisco; DePaso, DePasoa.

11. **The correct answer is (B).** Carlin, Carling; van Rijn, von Rijn.

12. **The correct answer is (A).** Z 48621, Z 46821; Mullins, Mollins; M 48164, M 48614.

13. **The correct answer is (B).** Harbison, Harbinson; Riverfront, Riverside.

14. **The correct answer is (C).** Brunswick, Runswick.

15. **The correct answer is (A).** 563141, 536141; 453120, 453210; Britten, Brittan.

Exercise 3

Directions: Each question lists four names or numbers. The names or numbers may or may not be exactly the same. Compare the four names or numbers in each question, and next to the question number:

- Write **(A)** if ALL FOUR names or numbers are DIFFERENT.
- Write **(B)** if TWO of the names or numbers are exactly the same.
- Write **(C)** if THREE of the names or numbers are exactly the same.
- Write **(D)** if all FOUR names or numbers are exactly the same.

1. W.E. Johnston
   W.E. Johnson
   W.E. Johnson
   W.B. Johnson

2. Vergil L. Muller
   Vergil L. Muller
   Vergil L. Muller
   Vergil L. Muller

3. 5261383
   5263183
   5623183
   5263183

4. Atherton R. Warde
   Asheton R. Warde
   Atherton P. Warde
   Athertin P. Warde

5. 8125690
   8126690
   8125609
   8125609

6. E. Owens McVey
   E. Owen McVey
   E. Owen McVay
   E. Owen McVey

7. Emily Neal Rouse
   Emily Neal Rowse
   Emily Neal Roose
   Emily Neal Rowse

8. Francis Ramsdell
   Francis Ransdell
   Francis Ramsdell
   Francis Ramsdell

9. 2395890
   2395890
   2395890
   2395890

10. 1926341
    1962341
    1963241
    1926341

11. H. Merritt Audubon
    H. Merriott Audobon
    H. Merritt Audobon
    H. Merritt Audubon

12. 6219354
    6219354
    6219345
    6219354

13. Cornelius Detwiler
    Cornelius Detwiler
    Cornelius Detwiler
    Cornelius Detwiler

14. 2312793
    2312973
    2312973
    2312973

15. Drusilla S. Ridgeley
    Drusilla S. Ridgeley
    Drucilla S. Ridgeley
    Drucilla S. Ridgely

16. Andrei I. Tourantzev
    Andrei I. Toumantzev
    Andrei I. Toumantzov
    Andrei I. Tourantzov

17. 0065407
    1065407
    0065407
    0064507

18. 6452054
    6452054
    6452654
    6452054

19. 8501268
    8501286
    8501268
    8501268

20. Ella Burk Newham
    Ella Burk Newnam
    Ella Burk Newham
    Ella Burk Newham

ANSWER KEY AND EXPLANATIONS

1. B	5. B	9. D	13. D	17. B
2. D	6. B	10. B	14. C	18. C
3. B	7. B	11. B	15. B	19. C
4. A	8. C	12. C	16. A	20. C

1. **The correct answer is (B).** Same: E. Johnson, E. Johnson. Different: E. Johnston; B. Johnson.

2. **The correct answer is (D).** All alike.

3. **The correct answer is (B).** Same: 2631, 2631. Different: 2613, 6231.

4. **The correct answer is (A).** Different: Atherton R., Asheton R., Atherton P., Athertin P.

5. **The correct answer is (B).** Same: 5609, 5609. Different: 5690, 6690.

6. **The correct answer is (B).** Same: Owen McVey, Owen McVey. Different: Owens McVey, Owen McVay.

7. **The correct answer is (B).** Same: Rowse, Rowse. Different: Rouse, Roose.

8. **The correct answer is (C).** Same: Ramsdell, Ramsdell, Ramsdell. Different: Ransdell.

9. **The correct answer is (D).** All alike.

10. **The correct answer is (B).** Same: 263, 263. Different: 623, 632.

11. **The correct answer is (B).** Same: Merritt Audubon, Merritt Audubon. Different: Merriott Audobon, Merritt Audobon.

12. **The correct answer is (C).** Same: 54, 54, 54. Different: 45.

13. **The correct answer is (D).** All alike.

14. **The correct answer is (C).** Same: 973, 973, 973. Different: 793.

15. **The correct answer is (B).** Same: Drusilla Ridgeley, Drusilla Ridgeley. Different: Drucilla Ridgeley, Drucilla Ridgely.

16. **The correct answer is (A).** Different: Tourantzev, Toumantzev, Toumantzov, Tourantzov

17. **The correct answer is (B).** Same: 00654, 00654. Different: 10654, 00645.

18. **The correct answer is (C).** Same: 054, 054, 054. Different: 654.

19. **The correct answer is (C).** Same: 68, 68, 68. Different: 86.

20. **The correct answer is (C).** Same: Newham, Newham, Newham. Different: Newnam.

Exercise 4

Directions: Each question gives the name and identification number of an employee. Choose the ONE answer that has exactly the same identification number and name as those given in the question, and circle the letter of your answer.

1. 176823 Katherine Blau
   - (A) 176823 Catherine Blau
   - (B) 176283 Katherine Blau
   - (C) 176823 Katherine Blau
   - (D) 176823 Katherine Blaw

2. 673403 Boris T. Frame
   - (A) 673403 Boris P. Frame
   - (B) 673403 Boris T. Frame
   - (C) 673403 Boris T. Fraim
   - (D) 673430 Boris T. Frame

3. 498832 Hyman Ziebart
   - (A) 498832 Hyman Zeibart
   - (B) 498832 Hiram Ziebart
   - (C) 498832 Hyman Ziebardt
   - (D) 498832 Hyman Ziebart

4. 506745 Barbara O'Dey
   - (A) 507645 Barbara O'Day
   - (B) 506745 Barbara O'Day
   - (C) 506475 Barbara O'Day
   - (D) 506745 Barbara O'Dey

5. 344223 Morton Sklar
   - (A) 344223 Morton Sklar
   - (B) 344332 Norton Sklar
   - (C) 344332 Morton Sklaar
   - (D) 343322 Morton Sklar

6. 816040 Betsy B. Voight
   - (A) 816404 Betsy B. Voight
   - (B) 814060 Betsy B. Voight
   - (C) 816040 Betsy B. Voight
   - (D) 816040 Betsey B. Voight

7. 913576 Harold Howritz
   - (A) 913576 Harold Horwitz
   - (B) 913576 Harold Howritz
   - (C) 913756 Harold Howritz
   - (D) 913576 Harald Howritz

8. 621190 Jayne T. Downs
   - (A) 621990 Janie T. Downs
   - (B) 621190 Janie T. Downs
   - (C) 622190 Janie T. Downs
   - (D) 621190 Jayne T. Downs

9. 004620 George McBoyd
   - (A) 006420 George McBoyd
   - (B) 006420 George MacBoyd
   - (C) 006420 George McBoid
   - (D) 004620 George McBoyd

10. 723495 Alice Appleton
    - (A) 723495 Alice Appleton
    - (B) 723594 Alica Appleton
    - (C) 723459 Alice Appleton
    - (D) 732495 Alice Appleton

11. 856772 Aaron B. Haynes
    - (A) 856722 Aaron B. Haynes
    - (B) 856722 Arron B. Haynes
    - (C) 856722 Aaron B. Haynes
    - (D) 856772 Aaron B. Haynes

12. 121434 Veronica Pope
    - (A) 121343 Veronica Pope
    - (B) 121434 Veronica Pope
    - (C) 121434 Veronica Popa
    - (D) 121343 Veronica Popa

13. 376900 Barry R. Jantzen
    (A) 376900 Barry R. Jantsen
    (B) 379600 Barry R. Jantzen
    (C) 376900 Barry R. Jantzen
    (D) 376900 Barry R. Jantzon

14. 804866 Margery Melton
    (A) 804866 Marjery Melton
    (B) 808466 Margery Melton
    (C) 804866 Margery Mellon
    (D) 804866 Margery Melton

15. 762409 Philip L. Phillipi
    (A) 762409 Philip L. Philippi
    (B) 762409 Phillip L. Philipi
    (C) 762490 Philip L. Phillipi
    (D) 762409 Philip L. Phillipi

ANSWER KEY AND EXPLANATIONS

1. C	4. D	7. B	10. A	13. C
2. B	5. A	8. D	11. D	14. D
3. D	6. C	9. D	12. B	15. D

1. **The correct answer is (C).** 176823 Katherine Blau. (A) Catherine; (B) 176283; (D) Blaw.

2. **The correct answer is (B).** 673403 Boris T. Frame. (A) P.; (C) Fraim; (D) 673430.

3. **The correct answer is (D).** 498832 Hyman Ziebart. (A) Zeibart; (B) Hiram; (C) Ziebardt.

4. **The correct answer is (D).** 506745 Barbara O'Dey. (A) 507645 O'Day; (B) O'Day; (C) 506475 O'Day.

5. **The correct answer is (A).** 344223 Morton Sklar. (B) 344332 Norton; (C) 344332 Sklaar; (D) 343322.

6. **The correct answer is (C).** 816040 Betsy B. Voight. (A) 816404; (B) 814060; (D) Betsey.

7. **The correct answer is (B).** 913576 Harold Howritz. (A) Horwitz; (C) 913756 Horwitz; (D) Harald.

8. **The correct answer is (D).** 621190 Jayne T. Downs. (A) 621990 Janie; (B) Janie; (C) 622190 Janie.

9. **The correct answer is (D).** 004620 George McBoyd. (A) 006420; (B) 006420 MacBoyd; (C) 006420 McBoid.

10. **The correct answer is (A).** 723495 Alice Appleton. (B) 723594 Alica; (C) 723459; (D) 732495.

11. **The correct answer is (D).** 856772 Aaron B. Haynes. (A) 856722; (B) 856722 Arron; (C) 856722.

12. **The correct answer is (B).** 121434 Veronica Pope. (A) 121343; (C) Popa; (D) 121343 Popa.

13. **The correct answer is (C).** 376900 Barry R. Jantzen. (A) Jantsen; (B) 379600; (D) Jantzon.

14. **The correct answer is (D).** 804866 Margery Melton. (A) Marjery; (B) 808466; (C) Mellon.

15. **The correct answer is (D).** 762409 Philip L. Phillipi. (A) Philippi; (B) Phillip Philipi; (C) 762490 Philippi.

Exercise 5

This final exercise is considerably more complicated than the previous comparison questions because of the complexity of the directions. The procedure you must follow is somewhat related to the one you followed in the address-checking questions at the beginning of this chapter. Note also that this exercise offers you five answer choices rather than the four in the previous exercises.

> **Directions:** In the following questions, compare the three names or numbers and mark your answer next to the question number.
>
> - Write **(A)** if ALL THREE names or numbers are exactly ALIKE.
>
> - Write **(B)** if only the FIRST and SECOND names or numbers are exactly ALIKE.
>
> - Write **(C)** if only the FIRST and THIRD names or numbers are exactly ALIKE.
>
> - Write **(D)** if only the SECOND and THIRD names or numbers are exactly ALIKE.
>
> - Write **(E)** if ALL THREE names or numbers are DIFFERENT.

Tips To Get You Started

- When comparing names, look first for the shortest, easiest comparisons. If the name has first or middle initials, check them first. Then look for Jr., Sr., II, M.D., and the like.

- The next area for easy comparison is names that include Mc, Mac, Van, von, de, De, and so on. If you find a difference between first and second names in any of these regards, mark a minus sign (–) in the space between the names to keep track. Then do the same for any differences between the second and third names.

- If after the "easy" comparisons, you already have minus signs between first and second and between second and third, you can concentrate on comparing first and third; first along "easy" lines, then the main names.

- If the first and third differ as well, you can choose (E) with confidence and move on to the next question.

- If after making the "easy" comparisons you have no minus signs or only one, then look at the names themselves. Start with the first names or last names, but do so consistently. Be on the lookout for added or dropped "e" or "s" in particular. Check for spelling, double letters, and letters dropped into the middle of names. Again, mark a minus sign between first and second and between second and third names if you find any differences. The minus signs help you eliminate comparisons and narrow your field.

- Two minus signs in a question signal you to compare the first and third names, and choose (C) or (E) as indicated. The absence of minus signs tells you immediately that you must choose (A). If the first and second names are exactly alike and the second and third names are exactly alike, then the first and third must be exactly alike. Take a look at the following examples.

A. Henry H. Liede   Henry M. Liede   Henry H. Leide

Begin with the "easy" comparisons. You see a middle initial, which is a good starting place. The middle initial of the first name is H, whereas that of the second name is M, so put a minus sign between the first and second names. The middle initial of the second name is M, but that of the third name is H, so put a minus also between the second and third names. Your only possible comparison is between the first and third names. You already know that they have the same middle initial. A very quick look tells you that the first name, Henry, is alike in both. Look carefully, though, at the spellings of the last names. In the first name it is spelled Liede; in the third name it is spelled Leide. All three names are different, so the answer is (E). NOTE: Do not bother to look at the spelling of the last name in the second name. It is already out of the comparison because of the middle initial.

B. Gerald M. Rosmarin   Gerald M. Rosmarin   Gerald M. Rosemarin

Start with the middle initials. All three are M. Next, look at first names: Differences tend to be more obvious among first names. All three are alike. Now look carefully at the last names. The first and second are identical; however, the third name has an *e* that does not appear in name two. Mark a minus sign between two and three, and mark (B) as the correct answer. Do not waste time comparing names three and one, because you've already determined that the first name is the same as the second.

C. Frima V. Spiner, M.D.   Frima V. Spiner, M.D.   Frima V. Spiner, M.D.

With a single glance, you can make two "easy" comparisons in this set. All three names have the middle initial V, and all three end with M.D. The first name is short although uncommon. You can easily see that all three are alike. So far, you have marked no minus signs. Next, check the third name. There are no differences between the third and the other two. The first is the same as the second, and the second is the same as the third. Therefore, the first and third must also be alike. The answer is (A).

D. Emilio Scaramuzza   Emilio Scaramuzzo   Emilio Scaramuzza

None of the names in this set has a middle initial, so begin by comparing first names. All three are alike. Compare last names, paying special attention to doubled letters. You might expect that in one name, the letter "z" might not be doubled or that the letter "r" might be doubled in addition to or instead of the *z*. In this example, though, this is not the case. Look carefully and you'll see that the first name ends with the letter *a* and the second ends with the letter *o*. Put a minus sign between one and two. Now, the second name ends with the letter *o*, and the third ends with an *a*. Mark a minus sign between the second and third names. You cannot answer (E) just because you have placed minus signs in two places, however. You must still compare the last names of the first and third names. One and three are exactly alike, so the answer is (C).

E. Craig R. Curcio   Graig R. Curcio   Graig R. Curcio

The middle initials are alike, so check first names. The first name starts with Craig (beginning with a C); in the second name you have Graig (beginning with a G). Place a minus sign between name one and two. The third name begins with G, just like the second. Now compare the second and third last names. Both are alike and you've completed your comparison of the second and third names, so the answer is (D). Do not bother to compare any part of the third name with the first. If the third name is exactly like the second, and the second name differs from the first, the first and third cannot be alike.

Comparing numbers is essentially the same as comparing names, except that the task is not as neatly divided into steps. There is no easy comparison with which to begin; at the outset, you must be alert for number reversals and actual number differences. You may find it worthwhile to divide each number into segments when comparing; this helps you develop a rhythm for reading them and may make differences easier to spot.

F.   5282864   5282864   5282684

Compare one and two. They are identical. Compare two and three. Three reverses the numbers 8 and 6. Place a minus sign between two and three, and do not bother to compare one and three. The correct answer is (B).

G.   6983429   6985429   6983429

Compare the first and second numbers. The middle digit of the first number is 3; the middle digit of the second is 5. Mark a minus sign between the first and second numbers, and compare the second to the third. The middle digit of the second is 5; the middle digit of the third is 3. Mark another minus sign. Now compare one and three. They are exactly alike, so the answer is (C).

Now try some practice questions on your own.

1. Cyriac Aleyamma   Cyriac Aleyamma   Cyriac Aleyamma
2. Eric O. Hartman   Eric O. Hartman   Eric O. Harpman
3. Stephen Mescall   Steven Mescall   Stephan Mescall
4. Frank E. Roemer   Frank F. Roemer   Frank F. Reomer
5. Rose T. Waldhofer   Rose T. Waldhofer   Rose T. Walderhofer
6. 4726840   4728640   4726840
7. 9616592   9616952   9616592
8. 8349135   8319435   8349135
9. 4243275   4243275   4243275
10. 3245270   3245270   3245270
11. Susan B. Vizoski   Susan B. Vizoski   Suzan B. Vizoski
12. M.R. vonWeisenseel M.R. vonWeisenseel   M.R. vonWeisensteel
13. Barbara T. Scarry   Barbara T. Scarey   Barbara T. Scarrey
14. Roy L. Gildesgame   Roy L. Gildegame   Roy L. Gildesgame
15. Jaime Chiquimia   Jaime Chiquimia   Jaime Chiquimia
16. 7621489   7624189   7621849
17. 9625874   9625974   9625874
18. 5767140   5761740   5761740
19. 2454308   2454308   2454380
20. 7622378   7622378   7622378

ANSWER KEY AND EXPLANATIONS

1. A	5. B	9. A	13. E	17. C
2. B	6. C	10. A	14. C	18. D
3. E	7. C	11. B	15. A	19. B
4. E	8. C	12. B	16. E	20. A

1. **The correct answer is (A).** All alike.

2. **The correct answer is (B).** Alike: Eric O. Hartman, Eric O. Hartman. Different: Eric O. Harpman.

3. **The correct answer is (E).** Different: Stephen, Steven, Stephan.

4. **The correct answer is (E).** Different: E. Roemer, F. Roemer, F. Reomer.

5. **The correct answer is (B).** Alike: Waldhofer, Waldhofer. Different: Walderhofer

6. **The correct answer is (C).** Alike: 4726840, 4726840. Different: 4728640

7. **The correct answer is (C).** Alike: 9616592, 9616592. Different: 9616952.

8. **The correct answer is (C).** Alike: 8349135, 8349135. Different: 8319435.

9. **The correct answer is (A).** All alike.

10. **The correct answer is (A).** All alike.

11. **The correct answer is (B).** Alike: Susan B. Vizoski, Susan B. Vizoski. Different: Suzan.

12. **The correct answer is (B).** Alike: M.R. vonWeisenseel, M.R. vonWeisenseel. Different: vonWeisensteel.

13. **The correct answer is (E).** Different: Scarry, Scarey, Scarrey.

14. **The correct answer is (C).** Alike: Gildesgame, Gildesgame. Different: Gildegame.

15. **The correct answer is (A).** All alike.

16. **The correct answer is (E).** Different: 1489, 4189, 1849.

17. **The correct answer is (C).** Alike: 9625874, 9625874. Different: 9625974.

18. **The correct answer is (D).** Alike: 5761740, 5761740. Different: 5767140.

19. **The correct answer is (B).** Alike: 2454308, 2454308. Different: 2454380.

20. **The correct answer is (A).** All alike.

SUMMING IT UP

- An effective public safety dispatcher must be an accurate and swift typist. If you hope to do well on the typing section of the public safety dispatcher exam, be sure to practice as much as you can, and practice both copying and typing from dictation. Include words and numbers in your drills and aim for total accuracy. The typing section of the public safety dispatcher exam may take one of several forms: plain copy typing, typing from dictation, numbers typing, or alphanumeric typing.

- The usual rule in scoring typing tests is that a corrected error is still an error; ideally, you should make no mistakes. Corrections you make on a computer keyboard are generally not recorded. Watch the screen closely for errors, however. If you make an error, correct it as quickly as possible and keep moving.

- Address-checking questions require great speed and may carry heavy penalties for inaccuracy. You may need to follow complicated directions. Follow these five steps to increase your accuracy: (1) read exactly what you see; (2) use your hands; (3) look for differences in numbers; (4) look for differences in abbreviations; (5) look for differences in street or city names. Practice with the exercises in this chapter so that you're able to spot differences quickly and make firm, fast decisions.

- Your exam may include name-and-number and number-and-letter comparison questions; these can appear in one of a number of different formats, but the basic comparison task is always the same. The biggest difference lies in the directions. With name-and-number and number-and-letter comparison questions, it is extremely important that you read the directions thoroughly and carefully. For the most part, the strategies you learn for address checking will work well here, too. Follow "Tips to Get You Started" in this chapter for help in answering this type of question quickly and accurately.

Following Oral Directions

chapter 7

OVERVIEW

- Oral directions exercises on the Public Safety Dispatcher Exam
- Tips for answering oral directions exercises
- Summing it up

ORAL DIRECTIONS EXERCISES ON THE PUBLIC SAFETY DISPATCHER EXAM

Every written exam tests your ability to follow written directions. Some directions are quite simple; others are complex. In any event, it's important that you read each set of directions carefully and be absolutely certain that you know what is expected of you before you begin answering the questions. If the directions are complex, you may need to refer to them as you answer questions. Rereading directions takes time, but it is time well spent if it prevents you from answering incorrectly because you misunderstood what was expected of you.

Similarly, because the responsibilities of the public safety dispatcher are so heavily telephone-based, many public safety dispatcher qualification exams include a section that measures a test taker's ability to follow oral directions. The example we provide in this book is one of the many forms in which you might encounter this type of exam section. The questions and type of directions on your actual exam may differ from the exercise that follows, but it will nonetheless give you a fair idea of what you can expect.

The key to success with questions testing your ability to follow oral directions is to maintain total concentration on the task at hand. Many of the instructions consist of asking you to take one step on the worksheet followed by another step on the answer sheet. For example, you may hear oral directions similar to this:

> Find the smallest number on line 3 and draw one line under that number. Now, on your answer sheet, find the number under which you just drew one line and blacken space (C).

This is a relatively simple set of instructions. The moment you hear the words "line 3," you should direct your attention there and begin searching for the lowest number. But you must not stop paying attention to the rest of the instructions, or you will not know what to do with that number on line 3.

"Draw one line" is uncomplicated. The two-second pause that a reader takes after announcing this instruction should be adequate time for you to find the smallest number and draw a single line under it. The second part of the instruction is also uncomplicated—but remember, you cannot let your attention be drawn away from listening to what you must do next. You need to concentrate on what the reader is saying to find out which lettered space you must blacken. You then have 5 seconds to find the number and blacken the space.

If you hear more complicated directions, you are generally given slightly more time to follow them. For example, if the reader instructs you to circle each even number between 12 and 25, you will be given at least 10 seconds to find the numbers and actually circle them. In the example above, after the instructions that tell you what letters to darken, you are allowed 5 seconds for each combination.

The most difficult directions to follow are multi-step ones such as this:

> If January comes before June, and Monday comes after Wednesday, write the letter E in the box on the left; if not, write the letter A in the circle on the right.

Take questions like these one step at a time. Yes, January comes before June, so the first part of the opening phrase is true. Monday does *not* come after Wednesday, so the second part of this phrase is false. The instructions, however, use *and* to connect these two parts, so what immediately follows should only be performed if both parts of the statement are true. In this statement, one part is false, so you must perform the second action: Write the letter *A* in the circle on the right.

TIPS FOR ANSWERING ORAL DIRECTIONS EXERCISES

Try your best to stay calm during this section of your public safety dispatcher exam. If you miss part of an instruction, try to follow through as best you can, or just let that instruction pass and be ready for the next one. Your reader is not permitted to repeat an instruction, so you will hear it only once. Still, a missed question here or there in this section is not likely to rule out your candidacy. Take it in stride and resolve to focus carefully on the next set of instructions.

To practice taking this part of the public safety dispatcher exam, you'll need someone to read aloud the oral instructions in this chapter and in the Practice Tests at the end of the book. On the actual exam, you will not see or hear the oral instructions before exam day—so to get the most out of your practice, you should treat the "oral instructions" questions in this book as if they were actual exam questions. Do not look at them before answering the practice questions, and do not record yourself reading the instructions to play back for practice.

Answer Sheet for Following Oral Directions Exercise

1. Ⓐ Ⓑ Ⓒ Ⓓ Ⓔ
2. Ⓐ Ⓑ Ⓒ Ⓓ Ⓔ
3. Ⓐ Ⓑ Ⓒ Ⓓ Ⓔ
4. Ⓐ Ⓑ Ⓒ Ⓓ Ⓔ
5. Ⓐ Ⓑ Ⓒ Ⓓ Ⓔ
6. Ⓐ Ⓑ Ⓒ Ⓓ Ⓔ
7. Ⓐ Ⓑ Ⓒ Ⓓ Ⓔ
8. Ⓐ Ⓑ Ⓒ Ⓓ Ⓔ
9. Ⓐ Ⓑ Ⓒ Ⓓ Ⓔ
10. Ⓐ Ⓑ Ⓒ Ⓓ Ⓔ
11. Ⓐ Ⓑ Ⓒ Ⓓ Ⓔ
12. Ⓐ Ⓑ Ⓒ Ⓓ Ⓔ
13. Ⓐ Ⓑ Ⓒ Ⓓ Ⓔ
14. Ⓐ Ⓑ Ⓒ Ⓓ Ⓔ
15. Ⓐ Ⓑ Ⓒ Ⓓ Ⓔ
16. Ⓐ Ⓑ Ⓒ Ⓓ Ⓔ
17. Ⓐ Ⓑ Ⓒ Ⓓ Ⓔ
18. Ⓐ Ⓑ Ⓒ Ⓓ Ⓔ
19. Ⓐ Ⓑ Ⓒ Ⓓ Ⓔ
20. Ⓐ Ⓑ Ⓒ Ⓓ Ⓔ
21. Ⓐ Ⓑ Ⓒ Ⓓ Ⓔ
22. Ⓐ Ⓑ Ⓒ Ⓓ Ⓔ
23. Ⓐ Ⓑ Ⓒ Ⓓ Ⓔ

24. Ⓐ Ⓑ Ⓒ Ⓓ Ⓔ
25. Ⓐ Ⓑ Ⓒ Ⓓ Ⓔ
26. Ⓐ Ⓑ Ⓒ Ⓓ Ⓔ
27. Ⓐ Ⓑ Ⓒ Ⓓ Ⓔ
28. Ⓐ Ⓑ Ⓒ Ⓓ Ⓔ
29. Ⓐ Ⓑ Ⓒ Ⓓ Ⓔ
30. Ⓐ Ⓑ Ⓒ Ⓓ Ⓔ
31. Ⓐ Ⓑ Ⓒ Ⓓ Ⓔ
32. Ⓐ Ⓑ Ⓒ Ⓓ Ⓔ
33. Ⓐ Ⓑ Ⓒ Ⓓ Ⓔ
34. Ⓐ Ⓑ Ⓒ Ⓓ Ⓔ
35. Ⓐ Ⓑ Ⓒ Ⓓ Ⓔ
36. Ⓐ Ⓑ Ⓒ Ⓓ Ⓔ
37. Ⓐ Ⓑ Ⓒ Ⓓ Ⓔ
38. Ⓐ Ⓑ Ⓒ Ⓓ Ⓔ
39. Ⓐ Ⓑ Ⓒ Ⓓ Ⓔ
40. Ⓐ Ⓑ Ⓒ Ⓓ Ⓔ
41. Ⓐ Ⓑ Ⓒ Ⓓ Ⓔ
42. Ⓐ Ⓑ Ⓒ Ⓓ Ⓔ
43. Ⓐ Ⓑ Ⓒ Ⓓ Ⓔ
44. Ⓐ Ⓑ Ⓒ Ⓓ Ⓔ
45. Ⓐ Ⓑ Ⓒ Ⓓ Ⓔ
46. Ⓐ Ⓑ Ⓒ Ⓓ Ⓔ

47. Ⓐ Ⓑ Ⓒ Ⓓ Ⓔ
48. Ⓐ Ⓑ Ⓒ Ⓓ Ⓔ
49. Ⓐ Ⓑ Ⓒ Ⓓ Ⓔ
50. Ⓐ Ⓑ Ⓒ Ⓓ Ⓔ
51. Ⓐ Ⓑ Ⓒ Ⓓ Ⓔ
52. Ⓐ Ⓑ Ⓒ Ⓓ Ⓔ
53. Ⓐ Ⓑ Ⓒ Ⓓ Ⓔ
54. Ⓐ Ⓑ Ⓒ Ⓓ Ⓔ
55. Ⓐ Ⓑ Ⓒ Ⓓ Ⓔ
56. Ⓐ Ⓑ Ⓒ Ⓓ Ⓔ
57. Ⓐ Ⓑ Ⓒ Ⓓ Ⓔ
58. Ⓐ Ⓑ Ⓒ Ⓓ Ⓔ
59. Ⓐ Ⓑ Ⓒ Ⓓ Ⓔ
60. Ⓐ Ⓑ Ⓒ Ⓓ Ⓔ
61. Ⓐ Ⓑ Ⓒ Ⓓ Ⓔ
62. Ⓐ Ⓑ Ⓒ Ⓓ Ⓔ
63. Ⓐ Ⓑ Ⓒ Ⓓ Ⓔ
64. Ⓐ Ⓑ Ⓒ Ⓓ Ⓔ
65. Ⓐ Ⓑ Ⓒ Ⓓ Ⓔ
66. Ⓐ Ⓑ Ⓒ Ⓓ Ⓔ
67. Ⓐ Ⓑ Ⓒ Ⓓ Ⓔ
68. Ⓐ Ⓑ Ⓒ Ⓓ Ⓔ
69. Ⓐ Ⓑ Ⓒ Ⓓ Ⓔ

70. Ⓐ Ⓑ Ⓒ Ⓓ Ⓔ
71. Ⓐ Ⓑ Ⓒ Ⓓ Ⓔ
72. Ⓐ Ⓑ Ⓒ Ⓓ Ⓔ
73. Ⓐ Ⓑ Ⓒ Ⓓ Ⓔ
74. Ⓐ Ⓑ Ⓒ Ⓓ Ⓔ
75. Ⓐ Ⓑ Ⓒ Ⓓ Ⓔ
76. Ⓐ Ⓑ Ⓒ Ⓓ Ⓔ
77. Ⓐ Ⓑ Ⓒ Ⓓ Ⓔ
78. Ⓐ Ⓑ Ⓒ Ⓓ Ⓔ
79. Ⓐ Ⓑ Ⓒ Ⓓ Ⓔ
80. Ⓐ Ⓑ Ⓒ Ⓓ Ⓔ
81. Ⓐ Ⓑ Ⓒ Ⓓ Ⓔ
82. Ⓐ Ⓑ Ⓒ Ⓓ Ⓔ
83. Ⓐ Ⓑ Ⓒ Ⓓ Ⓔ
84. Ⓐ Ⓑ Ⓒ Ⓓ Ⓔ
85. Ⓐ Ⓑ Ⓒ Ⓓ Ⓔ
86. Ⓐ Ⓑ Ⓒ Ⓓ Ⓔ
87. Ⓐ Ⓑ Ⓒ Ⓓ Ⓔ
88. Ⓐ Ⓑ Ⓒ Ⓓ Ⓔ
89. Ⓐ Ⓑ Ⓒ Ⓓ Ⓔ
90. Ⓐ Ⓑ Ⓒ Ⓓ Ⓔ

answer sheet

Following Oral Directions Worksheet

Directions: Listening carefully to each set of instructions, mark each item on this worksheet as directed. Then complete each question by marking the answer sheet as directed. For each answer, you will darken the answer for a number-letter combination. Should you fall behind and miss an instruction, don't panic. Let it go and listen for the next one. If, when you start to darken a space, you find that you have already darkened another space for that number, either erase the first mark and darken the space for the new combination or let the first mark stay and do not darken a space for the new combination. Write with a pencil that has a clean eraser. When you finish, you should have no more than one space darkened for each number.

1. 45 _____   43 _____   83 _____

2.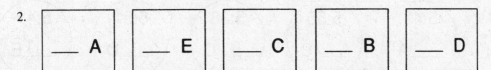

3. 69   87   50   54   25   47   20   80   27

4.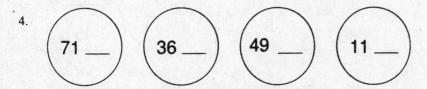

5.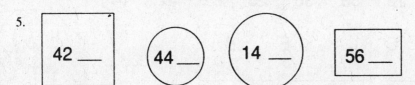

6.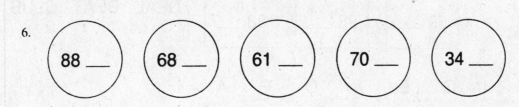

7. 28   67   29   77   26

8.
| A CHESTNUT STREET _____ | B HYDE PARK _____ | C PRUDENTIAL PLAZA _____ |

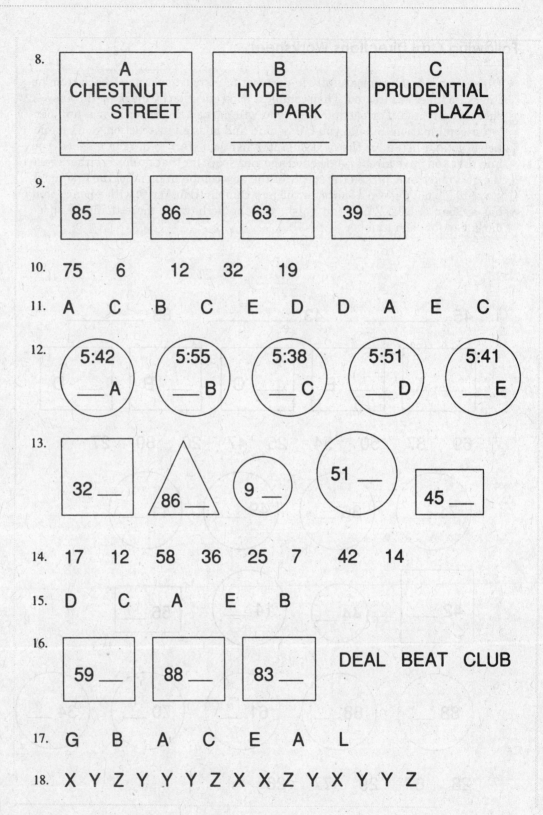

9.   85 ___   86 ___   63 ___   39 ___

10.   75   6   12   32   19

11.   A   C   B   C   E   D   D   A   E   C

12.   5:42 ___A   5:55 ___B   5:38 ___C   5:51 ___D   5:41 ___E

13.   32 ___   86 ___   9 ___   51 ___   45 ___

14.   17   12   58   36   25   7   42   14

15.   D   C   A   E   B

16.   59 ___   88 ___   83 ___   DEAL   BEAT   CLUB

17.   G   B   A   C   E   A   L

18.   X   Y   Z   Y   Y   Y   Z   X   X   Z   Y   X   Y   Y   Z

Following Oral Directions Exercise

Total Time: *25 minutes*

> **Directions:** Give the following instructions to a friend and have him or her read them aloud to you at 80 words per minute. Do NOT read them to yourself. Your friend will need a timepiece that measures seconds. Listen carefully and do exactly what your friend tells you to do with the worksheet *and* with the answer sheet. Your friend will tell what to do with each item on the worksheet. After each set of instructions, your friend will give you time to mark your answer by darkening a circle on the answer sheet. **Before proceeding further, tear out the worksheet on pages 163–164 of this test. Then hand this book to your friend.**

To the Reader: The directions are to be read at a rate of 80 words per minute. Do not read aloud the material that is in parentheses. Once you have begun the test itself, do not repeat any directions. The next three paragraphs consist of approximately 120 words. Read these three paragraphs aloud to the candidate in about one and one-half minutes.

On the job, you will have to listen to directions and then do what you have been told to do. In this test, I will read instructions to you. Try to understand them as I read them; I cannot repeat them. Once we begin, you may not ask any questions until the end of the test.

On the job, you won't have to deal with pictures, numbers, and letters like those in the test, but you will have to listen to instructions and follow them. We are using this test to see how well you can follow instructions.

You are to mark your test booklet according to the instructions that I'll read to you. After each set of instructions, I'll give you time to record your answers on the separate answer sheet.

The actual test begins now.

Look at line 1 on your worksheet. (*Pause slightly.*) Next to the left-hand number write the letter "E." (*Pause 2 seconds.*) Now, on your answer sheet, find the space for the number beside which you wrote, and darken space "E." (*Pause 5 seconds.*)

Now look at line 2 on your worksheet. (*Pause slightly.*) There are five boxes. Each box has a letter. (*Pause slightly.*) In the fifth box, write the answer to this question: Which of the following numbers is largest: 18, 9, 15, 19, or 13? (*Pause 5 seconds.*) Now, on your answer sheet, darken the space for the number-letter combination that is in the box in which you just wrote. (*Pause 5 seconds.*) In the fourth box on the same line, do nothing. In the third box, write "5." (*Pause 2 seconds.*) Now, on your answer sheet, darken the space for the number-letter combination that is in the box in which you just wrote. (*Pause 5 seconds.*) In the second box, write the answer to this question: How many hours are there in a day? (*Pause 2 seconds.*) Now, on your answer sheet, darken the space for the number-letter combination that is in the box in which you just wrote. (*Pause 5 seconds.*)

Look at line 3 on your worksheet. (*Pause slightly.*) Draw a line under every number that is greater than 50 but less than 85. (*Pause 12 seconds.*) Now, on your answer sheet, for each number under which you drew a line, darken space "D" as in dog. (*Pause 25 seconds.*)

Look at line 4 on your worksheet. (*Pause slightly.*) Write a "B" as in baker in the third circle. (*Pause 2 seconds.*) Now, on your answer sheet, find the number in that circle, and darken space "B" as in baker for that number. (*Pause 5 seconds.*)

Look at line 4 again. (*Pause slightly.*) Write "C" in the first circle. (*Pause 2 seconds.*) Now, on your answer sheet, find the number in that circle and darken space "C" for that number. (*Pause 5 seconds.*)

Look at line 5 on your worksheet. (*Pause slightly.*) There are two circles and two boxes of different sizes with numbers in them. (*Pause slightly.*) If 4 is more than 6 and if 9 is less than 7, write "D" as in dog in the smaller box. (*Pause slightly.*) Otherwise write "A" in the larger circle. (*Pause 2 seconds.*) Now, on your answer sheet, darken the space for the number-letter combination for the box or circle in which you just wrote. (*Pause 5 seconds.*)

Now look at line 6 on your worksheet. (*Pause slightly.*) Write an "E" in the second circle. (*Pause 2 seconds.*) Now, on your answer sheet, find the number in that circle and darken space "E" for that number. (*Pause 5 seconds.*)

Now look at line 6 again. (*Pause slightly.*) Write a "B" as in baker in the middle circle. (*Pause 2 seconds.*) Now, on your answer sheet, find the number in that circle and darken space "B" as in baker for that number. (*Pause 5 seconds.*)

Look at line 7 on your worksheet. (*Pause slightly.*) Draw a line under the largest number in the line. (*Pause 2 seconds.*) Now, on your answer sheet, find the number and darken space "C" for that number. (*Pause 5 seconds.*)

Now look at line 7 again. (*Pause slightly.*) Draw a circle around the smaller number in the line. (*Pause 2 seconds.*) Now, on your answer sheet, find the number around which you just drew a circle and darken space "A" for that number. (*Pause 5 seconds.*)

Now look at line 8 on your worksheet. (*Pause slightly.*) There are three boxes with words and letters in them. (*Pause slightly.*) Each box represents a station in a large city. Station A delivers mail in the Chestnut Street area, Station B delivers mail in Hyde Park, and Station C delivers mail in the Prudential Plaza. Mr. Adams lives in Hyde Park. Write the number 30 on the line inside the box that represents the station that delivers Mr. Adams' mail. (*Pause 2 seconds.*) Now, on your answer sheet, find number 30 and darken the space for the letter that is in the box in which you just wrote. (*Pause 5 seconds.*)

Now look at line 9 on your worksheet. (*Pause slightly.*) Write a "D" as in dog in the third box. (*Pause 2 seconds.*) Now, on your answer sheet, find the number that is in the box you just wrote in, and darken space "D" as in dog for that number. (*Pause 5 seconds.*)

Look at line 10 on your worksheet. (*Pause slightly.*) Draw a line under all the even numbers in line 10. (*Pause 5 seconds.*) Find the second number with a line drawn under it. (*Pause 2 seconds.*) On your answer sheet, blacken space "C" for that number. (*Pause 5 seconds.*)

Look at line 11 on your worksheet. (*Pause slightly.*) Count the number of "Cs" in line 11 and write the number at the end of the line. (*Pause 3 seconds.*) On your answer sheet, blacken the letter "E" for that number. (*Pause 5 seconds.*)

Now look at line 12 on your worksheet. (*Pause slightly.*) The time written in each circle represents the last pickup of the day from a particular street box. Write the last two numbers of the earliest pickup time on the line next to the letter in that circle. (*Pause 2 seconds.*) Now on your answer sheet blacken the space for the number-letter combination in the circle in which you just wrote. (*Pause 5 seconds.*)

Look at line 12 on your worksheet again. (*Pause slightly.*) Find the second earliest pickup time and write the last two numbers of the second earliest pickup time on the line next to the letter in that circle. (*Pause 2 seconds.*) Now, on your answer sheet, blacken the space for the number-letter combination in the circle in which you just wrote. (*Pause 5 seconds.*)

Look at line 13 on your worksheet. (*Pause slightly.*) If there are 365 days in a leap year, write the letter "B" as in baker in the small circle. (*Pause 2 seconds.*) If not, write the letter "A" in the triangle. (*Pause 2 seconds.*) Now, on your answer sheet, blacken the space for the letter-number combination in the figure in which you just wrote. (*Pause 5 seconds.*)

Look at line 13 again. (*Pause slightly.*) Write the letter "D" as in dog in the box with the lower number. (*Pause 2 seconds.*) Now, on your answer sheet, blacken the space for the letter-number combination in the figure in which you just wrote. (*Pause 5 seconds.*)

Look at line 14 on your worksheet. (*Pause slightly.*) Draw two lines under all the numbers that are greater than 12, but less than 41. (*Pause 8 seconds.*) Count the number of numbers under which you drew two lines and blacken the letter "B" as in baker for that number on your answer sheet. (*Pause 10 seconds.*)

Still on line 14 of the worksheet, (*pause slightly*) circle all the even numbers. (*Pause 2 seconds.*) Count all the numbers that you marked in any way, and blacken the letter "E" for that number on your answer sheet. (*Pause 10 seconds.*)

Look at line 15 on your worksheet. (*Pause slightly.*) Circle the fourth letter in the line. (*Pause 2 seconds.*) Add together the number of hours in a day, the number of months in a year, and the number of days in a week. (*Pause 10 seconds.*) Now on your answer sheet, blacken the circled letter for that number. (*Pause 5 seconds.*)

Look at line 16 on your worksheet. (*Pause slightly.*) Write the first letter of the third word in the second box. (*Pause 5 seconds.*) On your answer sheet, mark the number-letter combination in the box in which you just wrote. (*Pause 5 seconds.*)

Look again at line 16. (*Pause slightly.*) Write the third letter of the second word in the first box. (*Pause 5 seconds.*) On your answer sheet, mark the number-letter combination in the box in which you just wrote. (*Pause 5 seconds.*)

Look once more at line 16. (*Pause slightly.*) Write the second letter of the second word in the third box. (*Pause 5 seconds.*) Now, on your answer sheet, mark the number-letter combination in the box in which you just wrote. (*Pause 5 seconds.*)

Look at line 17 on your worksheet. (*Pause slightly.*) Draw a wavy line under the middle letter in the line. (*Pause 2 seconds.*) On your answer sheet, blacken that letter for answer space 36. (*Pause 5 seconds.*)

Look at line 18 on your worksheet. (*Pause slightly.*) Count the number of "Ys" in the line and write the number at the end of the line. (*Pause 2 seconds.*) Add 27 to that number (*pause 2 seconds*) and blacken "B" as in baker for the space that represents the total of 27 plus the number of "Ys." (*Pause 5 seconds.*)

END OF EXAMINATION

Correctly Filled Worksheet

1. 45 ___*E*___   43 _____   83 _____

2.
| ___ A | *24* E | *5* C | ___ B | *19* D |

3. <u>69</u>   87   50   <u>54</u>   25   47   20   <u>80</u>   27

4. 71 *C*   36 ___   49 *B*   11 ___

5. 42 ___   44 ___   14 *A*   56 ___

6. 88 ___   68 *E*   61 *B*   70 ___   34 ___

7. 28   67   29   <u>77</u>   (26)

8.
| A CHESTNUT STREET | B HYDE PARK *30* | C PRUDENTIAL PLAZA |
| _____ | _____ | _____ |

9.
| 85 ___ | 86 ___ | 63 *D* | 39 ___ |

10. 75   <u>6</u>   <u>12</u>   <u>32</u>   19

11. A   C   B   C   E   D   D   A   E   C   *3*

12.

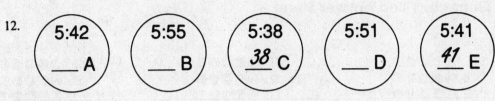

13.

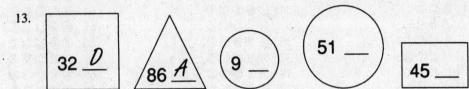

14. <u>17</u> (12) (58) (36) <u>25</u> 7 (42) (14)

15. D C A (E) B

16.

| 59 _A_ | 88 _C_ | 83 _E_ | DEAL   BEAT   CLUB |

17. G B A <u>C</u> E A L

18. X Y Z Y Y Y Z X X Z Y X Y Y Z   _7_

Correctly Filled Answer Sheet

1. Ⓐ Ⓑ Ⓒ Ⓓ Ⓔ	31. Ⓐ Ⓑ Ⓒ Ⓓ Ⓔ	61. Ⓐ ● Ⓒ Ⓓ Ⓔ
2. Ⓐ Ⓑ Ⓒ Ⓓ Ⓔ	32. Ⓐ Ⓑ Ⓒ ● Ⓔ	62. Ⓐ Ⓑ Ⓒ Ⓓ Ⓔ
3. Ⓐ Ⓑ Ⓒ Ⓓ ●	33. Ⓐ Ⓑ Ⓒ Ⓓ Ⓔ	63. Ⓐ Ⓑ Ⓒ ● Ⓔ
4. Ⓐ ● Ⓒ Ⓓ Ⓔ	34. Ⓐ ● Ⓒ Ⓓ Ⓔ	64. Ⓐ Ⓑ Ⓒ Ⓓ Ⓔ
5. Ⓐ Ⓑ ● Ⓓ Ⓔ	35. Ⓐ Ⓑ Ⓒ Ⓓ Ⓔ	65. Ⓐ Ⓑ Ⓒ Ⓓ Ⓔ
6. Ⓐ Ⓑ Ⓒ Ⓓ Ⓔ	36. Ⓐ Ⓑ ● Ⓓ Ⓔ	66. Ⓐ Ⓑ Ⓒ Ⓓ Ⓔ
7. Ⓐ Ⓑ Ⓒ Ⓓ ●	37. Ⓐ Ⓑ Ⓒ Ⓓ Ⓔ	67. Ⓐ Ⓑ Ⓒ Ⓓ Ⓔ
8. Ⓐ Ⓑ Ⓒ Ⓓ Ⓔ	38. Ⓐ Ⓑ ● Ⓓ Ⓔ	68. Ⓐ Ⓑ Ⓒ Ⓓ ●
9. Ⓐ Ⓑ Ⓒ Ⓓ Ⓔ	39. Ⓐ Ⓑ Ⓒ Ⓓ Ⓔ	69. Ⓐ Ⓑ Ⓒ ● Ⓔ
10. Ⓐ Ⓑ Ⓒ Ⓓ Ⓔ	40. Ⓐ Ⓑ Ⓒ Ⓓ Ⓔ	70. Ⓐ Ⓑ Ⓒ Ⓓ Ⓔ
11. Ⓐ Ⓑ Ⓒ Ⓓ Ⓔ	41. Ⓐ Ⓑ Ⓒ Ⓓ ●	71. Ⓐ Ⓑ ● Ⓓ Ⓔ
12. Ⓐ Ⓑ ● Ⓓ Ⓔ	42. Ⓐ Ⓑ Ⓒ Ⓓ Ⓔ	72. Ⓐ Ⓑ Ⓒ Ⓓ Ⓔ
13. Ⓐ Ⓑ Ⓒ Ⓓ Ⓔ	43. Ⓐ Ⓑ Ⓒ Ⓓ ●	73. Ⓐ Ⓑ Ⓒ Ⓓ Ⓔ
14. ● Ⓑ Ⓒ Ⓓ Ⓔ	44. Ⓐ Ⓑ Ⓒ Ⓓ Ⓔ	74. Ⓐ Ⓑ Ⓒ Ⓓ Ⓔ
15. Ⓐ Ⓑ Ⓒ Ⓓ Ⓔ	45. Ⓐ Ⓑ Ⓒ Ⓓ ●	75. Ⓐ Ⓑ Ⓒ Ⓓ Ⓔ
16. Ⓐ Ⓑ Ⓒ Ⓓ Ⓔ	46. Ⓐ Ⓑ Ⓒ Ⓓ Ⓔ	76. Ⓐ Ⓑ Ⓒ Ⓓ Ⓔ
17. Ⓐ Ⓑ Ⓒ Ⓓ Ⓔ	47. Ⓐ Ⓑ Ⓒ Ⓓ Ⓔ	77. Ⓐ Ⓑ ● Ⓓ Ⓔ
18. Ⓐ Ⓑ Ⓒ Ⓓ Ⓔ	48. Ⓐ Ⓑ Ⓒ Ⓓ Ⓔ	78. Ⓐ Ⓑ Ⓒ Ⓓ Ⓔ
19. Ⓐ Ⓑ Ⓒ ● Ⓔ	49. Ⓐ ● Ⓒ Ⓓ Ⓔ	79. Ⓐ Ⓑ Ⓒ Ⓓ Ⓔ
20. Ⓐ Ⓑ Ⓒ Ⓓ Ⓔ	50. Ⓐ Ⓑ Ⓒ Ⓓ Ⓔ	80. Ⓐ Ⓑ Ⓒ ● Ⓔ
21. Ⓐ Ⓑ Ⓒ Ⓓ Ⓔ	51. Ⓐ Ⓑ Ⓒ Ⓓ Ⓔ	81. Ⓐ Ⓑ Ⓒ Ⓓ Ⓔ
22. Ⓐ Ⓑ Ⓒ Ⓓ Ⓔ	52. Ⓐ Ⓑ Ⓒ Ⓓ Ⓔ	82. Ⓐ Ⓑ Ⓒ Ⓓ Ⓔ
23. Ⓐ Ⓑ Ⓒ Ⓓ Ⓔ	53. Ⓐ Ⓑ Ⓒ Ⓓ Ⓔ	83. Ⓐ Ⓑ Ⓒ Ⓓ ●
24. Ⓐ Ⓑ Ⓒ Ⓓ ●	54. Ⓐ Ⓑ Ⓒ ● Ⓔ	84. Ⓐ Ⓑ Ⓒ Ⓓ Ⓔ
25. Ⓐ Ⓑ Ⓒ Ⓓ Ⓔ	55. Ⓐ Ⓑ Ⓒ Ⓓ Ⓔ	85. Ⓐ Ⓑ Ⓒ Ⓓ Ⓔ
26. ● Ⓑ Ⓒ Ⓓ Ⓔ	56. Ⓐ Ⓑ Ⓒ Ⓓ Ⓔ	86. ● Ⓑ Ⓒ Ⓓ Ⓔ
27. Ⓐ Ⓑ Ⓒ Ⓓ Ⓔ	57. Ⓐ Ⓑ Ⓒ Ⓓ Ⓔ	87. Ⓐ Ⓑ Ⓒ Ⓓ Ⓔ
28. Ⓐ Ⓑ Ⓒ Ⓓ Ⓔ	58. Ⓐ Ⓑ Ⓒ Ⓓ Ⓔ	88. Ⓐ Ⓑ ● Ⓓ Ⓔ
29. Ⓐ Ⓑ Ⓒ Ⓓ Ⓔ	59. ● Ⓑ Ⓒ Ⓓ Ⓔ	89. Ⓐ Ⓑ Ⓒ Ⓓ Ⓔ
30. Ⓐ ● Ⓒ Ⓓ Ⓔ	60. Ⓐ Ⓑ Ⓒ Ⓓ Ⓔ	90. Ⓐ Ⓑ Ⓒ Ⓓ Ⓔ

SUMMING IT UP

- Because a large part of a public safety dispatcher's job consists of recording and relaying information by telephone, it's likely that you will see a section on your public safety dispatcher exam that measures your ability to follow oral directions.

- The questions and type of directions you encounter on your actual exam may differ from those in the exercise in this chapter, but this exercise will nonetheless help train you to listen carefully and follow directions as they are spoken.

- On your actual exam, don't panic if you miss part of an instruction. Try to follow through as best you can, or just let that instruction pass and prepare for the next one.

- Keep in mind that your reader is not permitted to repeat an instruction, so you will hear it only once.

- To practice taking this part of the public safety dispatcher exam, enlist the help of a friend or colleague to read aloud the oral instructions. Treat the "oral instructions" questions in this book as if they were actual exam questions: Do not look at them before answering the practice questions, and do not record yourself reading the instructions to play back for practice.

Personality Assessments

OVERVIEW

- **Personality assessments on the Public Safety Dispatcher Exam**
- **Personality assessment variations**
- **How personality assessments differ from interviews**
- **Sample personality assessment**
- **Reviewing your responses**
- **Summing it up**

PERSONALITY ASSESSMENTS ON THE PUBLIC SAFETY DISPATCHER EXAM

You may have read in the sample job announcement for a police service representative (Chapter 2) that applicants for the position must undergo a personality assessment. Many municipalities rely on an oral interview to assess whether a candidate has the emotional and psychological stability and the personality type to deal with the rigors and stresses of a public safety dispatcher job. However, some agencies administer assessments—in paper-and-pencil, audiocassette or CD recording, or computer-based format—in conjunction with or as a replacement for oral interviews. These assessments aim to evaluate the behaviors and personalities of candidates to help determine whether they will be successful as public safety dispatchers.

PERSONALITY ASSESSMENT VARIATIONS

Personality assessments for the type of person generally sought for a public safety dispatcher position saves government agencies time and money. Entry-level dispatchers receive extensive training, so it is to an agency's benefit to determine before this training period which candidates are best for the job—those who will not only learn quickly but will also adapt easily to the many mental and emotional challenges involved in dispatching. Because the occupation is often stressful and fast-paced, agencies want to ensure that they are hiring individuals who have the personality traits needed to remain calm under pressure. Let's look at some of the types of questions you might encounter on a personality assessment.

chapter 8

True-or-False Questions

You probably already know that you should not try to second-guess questions on a personality assessment. There are no "correct" responses, even if certain answers *seem* to be correct. Moreover, inconsistency in answering questions that purport to probe specific attitudes and behaviors may indicate that you're being untruthful. It's best simply to strive to be as honest as possible when answering the questions.

The MMPI

The most commonly used standardized personality assessment is the Minnesota Multiphasic Personality Inventory (MMPI). The most recent version of the MMPI, the MMPI-2-RF, consists of 338 questions (older versions, such as the MMPI-2, may include up to 567 questions) to which test takers must answer "True" or "False." The statements are free-ranging: No single answer is of special significance; what's important is the totality of the pattern that emerges from all answers.

Here are some sample MMPI-type questions for which you would answer True (T) or False (F).

_____ I like school.

_____ I like to cook.

_____ Someone is trying to poison me.

_____ I like to tease animals.

_____ I would rather win than lose in a game.

_____ I do not like everyone I know.

_____ I am not afraid of mice.

_____ I like repairing a door latch.

_____ I dread the thought of an earthquake.

_____ My parents often objected to the kind of people I went around with.

A variation of the MMPI might be a locally constructed assessment, on which you would answer "Yes" or "No" rather than "True" or "False" for each statement:

_____ I often have difficulty making decisions.

_____ I often think that someone is out to get me.

_____ I enjoy going to plays more than to parties.

_____ I sometimes feel self-conscious.

_____ Most people are dishonest.

_____ We had a lot of family trouble when I was young.

_____ I often have headaches.

The HPI

The Hogan Personality Inventory (HPI) is another widely used personality assessment. The HPI consists of 206 true-or-false items that aim to predict occupational success. It assesses the following seven personality characteristics:

1. adjustment

2. ambition

3. sociability

4. interpersonal sensitivity

5. prudence

6. inquisitiveness

7. learning approach

It also assesses six personality factors that may help predict a candidate's potential for job success:

1. service orientation

2. stress tolerance

3. reliability

4. clerical potential

5. sales potential

6. managerial potential

HPI assessment questions are similar to the true-and-false statements you would see on the MMPI:

____ I enjoy making friends.

____ I consider myself a lively person.

____ I do not have a great deal of self-confidence.

____ I think crowded public events (rock concerts, sports events) are very exciting.

____ I try to get details correct in my work.

Self-Evaluation

Some personality assessments require candidates to evaluate a variety of behaviors and character traits in themselves. This requires not only self-assessment but also an understanding of how your elders and peers might rate you regarding certain traits. The traits evaluated in such assessments often relate to a candidate's energy, adventuresomeness, fearfulness, friendliness, gentleness, and compassion.

HOW PERSONALITY ASSESSMENTS DIFFER FROM INTERVIEWS

Standardized personality assessments require only true-false or multiple-choice responses. You do not need to calculate or use logic to determine your answers. As a result, scores can be derived quickly—almost immediately if the test is computer-based. These tests usually don't rely on the answers to individual questions for interpretation but rather on the sum of responses to a group of questions, such as those related to personal integrity—although key questions may be scattered throughout the personality assessment (we'll discuss this later in the chapter).

Length of Assessment

Standardized tests don't probe as deeply as subjective tests that require you to write your answers or explain them verbally to an interviewer. You are responding to very narrowly phrased questions. The examiner cannot explore the meaning of your true-or-false (or yes-or-no) responses, and you don't have the opportunity to explain them. To help counteract the fact that such responses can be misunderstood, personality assessments generally include a great number of questions (usually hundreds).

On the other hand, a standardized personality assessment can cover a much larger field than a more subjective assessment. It doesn't take long to answer several hundred true-or-false questions. (The HPI, for example, is administered over 15 to 20 minutes.) From an employer's point of view, the more information one can gather about an applicant, the better.

Time Limits

For the sample questions in this chapter, you are given no time limit. However, an actual personality assessment is timed. The idea is to answer quickly without dwelling too much on any one question; a time limit is intended to keep you moving through the questions without thinking too much. A timed personality assessment doesn't allow you the luxury of analyzing each question in depth or agonizing over your answer, but you usually have enough time to read each question and briefly consider which is the most truthful response.

That said, don't answer questions without considering what your response means. For example, let's say you receive a warning from the test administrator that your time is nearly up. Avoid feeling pressured into speeding through the rest of the questions and answering without reading thoroughly. With a personality assessment, you're far better off having not answered some questions than having accidentally labeled yourself a dishonest or unscrupulous person.

SAMPLE PERSONALITY ASSESSMENT

The following are sample questions drawn from a variety of standardized personality assessments. Find a quiet place where you're unlikely to be disturbed, and answer these questions without pausing, as if you were taking an official personality assessment. Although there is no time limit, work through them as efficiently as possible, and try not to spend too much time on any one question.

Directions: Please answer all questions in the space provided or on a separate sheet of paper. If you are using a separate sheet, number it from 1–30 before you start. Answer these questions by circling "Y" for "Yes" or "N" for "No."

1. Y N   Would you jump (or go under) a subway turnstile if you were sure you wouldn't be caught?

2. Y N   Have you ever found a crook so clever or entertaining that you rooted for him or her to get away with a crime?

3. Y N   Is taking damaged goods from your employer all right?

4. Y N   Do you always tell the truth?

5. Y N   Have you ever been tempted to take company property but didn't?

6. Y N   Do you think that police officers are usually honest?

7. Y N   While shopping, have you ever been tempted to take something without paying?

8. Y N   Is it okay to cheat on your taxes?

9. Y N   Did anyone ever show you how you could cheat your company out of money?

10. Y N   Have you ever thought about committing a burglary?

Directions: For the following items, please circle "Y" for "Yes" or "N" for "No" concerning any of the following activities you may have been involved in within the last six years. IN THE LAST SIX YEARS, DID YOU:

11. Y N   Sell illegal drugs?

12. Y N   Steal?

13. Y N   Get drunk?

14. Y N   File a false insurance claim deliberately?

15. Y N   Smoke pot?

16. Y N   Knowingly buy stolen or "hot" merchandise?

17. Y N   Give a friend company merchandise without charging for it?

18. Y N   Snort cocaine?

19. Y N   Do something only to cause trouble in your workplace?

20. Y N   Threaten somebody or use force to take something of value?

Directions: For the following items, please indicate your choice by circling the letter in front of the option you have selected. Be sure to answer all questions honestly.

21. What color is marijuana?
    (A) black
    (B) white
    (C) green
    (D) red

22. What color is cocaine?
    (A) black
    (B) white
    (C) green
    (D) red

23. Cocaine makes the user
    (A) hyperactive.
    (B) lazy.
    (C) hungry.
    (D) none of the above.

24. What was the worth of the most valuable thing you have stolen?
    (A) $2000 or more
    (B) $1000 to $2000
    (C) $100 to $1000
    (D) $25 to $100
    (E) $0 to $25

25. Have you ever taken a towel from a hotel or motel?
    (A) Yes
    (B) No

26. "If given a chance, everybody would cheat on their taxes." This statement is
    (A) definitely true.
    (B) mostly true.
    (C) uncertain.
    (D) mostly false.
    (E) definitely false.

27. "Everybody would steal if given the chance to do it without being caught." This statement is
    (A) definitely true.
    (B) mostly true.
    (C) uncertain.
    (D) mostly false.
    (E) definitely false.

28. "The reason people steal lies with the environment and the society in which we live." This statement is
    (A) definitely true.
    (B) mostly true.
    (C) uncertain.
    (D) mostly false.
    (E) definitely false.

29. "A person who will lie will steal." This statement is
    (A) definitely true.
    (B) mostly true.
    (C) uncertain.
    (D) mostly false.
    (E) definitely false.

30. A fellow employee is caught taking something from your employer that is worth about three dollars. This is the first time it has happened. What should be done?
    (A) The person's employment should be terminated.
    (B) The person should be severely reprimanded.
    (C) The person should be warned that more serious action will be taken if he or she does it again.
    (D) The person should give back what he or she has taken with no further consequences.

REVIEWING YOUR RESPONSES

Take a look at your answers to the sample questions. As we've discussed, there are no correct answers to any of these questions—but some answers may be better than others. Below, we'll discuss why this is true.

Key Questions

Earlier in this chapter, we mentioned the concept of key questions. You'll very likely encounter several of them in any personality assessment you take. In the sample inventory you just took, Question 4 was a key question: *Do you always tell the truth?* Look at your response. If you answered "Yes," read the question again until you completely understand what your answer means.

The key word here is *always*. Of course, the average person *usually* tells the truth—but this question asks whether you *always* tell the truth. On personality assessments, you'll find that statements containing the words *always* or *never* are almost never true for you. Words like *sometimes, usually, often, infrequently,* or *rarely* provide a "hedge" and are thus a lot "safer" to answer with a definite "True" or "False" (or "Yes" or "No").

The main point to remember about key questions is that, although they are expressed in absolute terms *(always* or *never)*, they describe behavior that may be *often* but *not always* correct or incorrect. To the question "Have you ever killed someone?" you can easily give a clear "No" response—but to the key question "Have you ever told a lie?" it's likely that you cannot truthfully and absolutely respond with "No." Key questions are used to test the value of the rest of your responses. Claiming that you always and without question tell the truth may cast serious doubt on the truthfulness of the rest of your responses.

Questions of Integrity and Honesty

The first twenty questions in the sample assessment above relate to honesty, integrity, and possible criminal behavior. Questions 1–10 are intended to assess a person's attitudes toward different types of behavior; they aren't meant to question whether you've done anything wrong. By contrast, the second group (Questions 11–20) ask directly whether you have committed certain acts, some of which are crimes.

You may have noticed that some questions may appear to be variations on the same theme and are simply worded differently. Questions 3, 5, 7, and 10 of the sample assessment all seek to determine your attitude—to varying degrees—toward stealing. For instance, Question 3 asks about taking from an employer something that doesn't belong to you; Question 10 asks about burglary, which is a serious crime. In a personality assessment containing about 100 questions of this type, you can expect to see several questions at the level of Question 3. You might be asked whether it is okay to use your employer's postage stamps, or whether it is okay to take your employer's pencils for your own use.

You need not worry about being consistent in your responses to these questions. Perhaps you believe that taking your employer's pencils is okay but that using your employer's postage stamps is not. Most people have mixed views on what constitutes stealing, and those who write and administer personality assessments recognize this fact. Scoring is not based on consistency of response, but on a continuum from "angel" to "thief." The angel is unbelievable—but nobody wants to hire a thief.

Question 5 illuminates a curious aspect of integrity and honesty questions. Suppose you were tempted to take something and gave in to the temptation. In that case, the appropriate answer is "No." However, if you were never tempted in the first place, the appropriate answer is also "No." In fact, technically, if we were to substitute the word *merchandise* for *property,* you would also answer "No" if you had never worked in a wholesale or retail firm—and therefore never even had the opportunity to be tempted to take your employer's merchandise. The point here is that you must always respond to the question or statement exactly as it is written. Don't read anything into the question that isn't there.

The Importance of Following Directions

As we discussed above, Questions 3, 5, 7, and 10 explore your attitudes about theft. By contrast, Questions 12 and 17 ask directly whether you have stolen anything. This is a good example of the importance of carefully reading the directions that precede groups of questions. The instructions before Questions 11–20 read as follows:

> For the following items, please circle "Y" for "Yes" or "N" for "No" concerning any of the following activities you may have been involved in within the last six years. IN THE LAST SIX YEARS, DID YOU:

These instructions are particularly clear; the same point is made twice. The first sentence refers to *activities you may have been involved in within the last six years*. The second sentence asks outright, "DID YOU?" It's clear here that the questions that follow will ask whether you personally have done any of the things listed. If you don't read the directions carefully, you can easily misinterpret what these questions are asking.

Two examples are Question 14, which includes the word *deliberately,* and Question 16, which includes the word *knowingly*. Both of them exclude actions you may have committed accidentally. Be sure to answer them accordingly. For example, if you filed twice for the same insurance claim because you forgot about the first filing or because the company took a long time to pay, it's true that you may have filed a false claim—but you didn't do it *deliberately,* so your honest answer is "No."

Another example is Question 17, which concerns a situation that's likely to occur only if you have experience in a retail position (the phrase "company merchandise" suggests this). Answer the question *exactly* as it is written. In this question, you weren't asked to admit whether you might have given away company merchandise if you had the opportunity; you were asked whether you actually *did* do it. A personality assessment may contain many such questions. Be sure that you avoid putting yourself into the situation outlined in the question if you've never been in that situation.

Pay Attention to Shades of Meaning

Questions 21–30 of the sample assessment demonstrate the reasoning behind the careful phrasing of personality assessment questions.

In Questions 21–23, you are asked about your knowledge of illegal drugs. The theory is that an applicant whose responses suggest that he or she knows a great deal about this subject is probably using drugs, and one who claims to know absolutely nothing may be trying to hide his or her knowledge of it. Although that is the theory, most administrators seek confirming evidence before tagging an applicant as a drug user based on questions of this sort. That's because none of these questions ask directly whether you have ever used an illegal drug. Knowing about a drug doesn't necessarily mean that you have used it. It's quite possible that you picked up what you know from books, movies, or a school course on drug use.

Questions of this type can have very fine shades of meaning. Changing a word or two can produce a totally different question. For instance, Question 23 might have read:

Cocaine makes <u>you</u>

(A) hyperactive.

(B) lazy.

(C) hungry.

(D) none of the above.

Note the underlined word here. The original question stem reads: "Cocaine makes *the user,*" not "you"; it is asking about your knowledge of the subject, not about your personal experience with cocaine. The lesson here is to read each question very carefully before choosing your response.

Questions 24 and 25 ask directly whether you have ever stolen anything and whether you believe that taking an item of low value is okay. But note how Question 24 is phrased: *What was the worth of the most valuable thing you have stolen?* The question already assumes that you will have stolen something. The only way to answer in the negative—that is, that you have never stolen anything—is to choose response (E). The *$0* in "$0 to $25" is an indirect way to say that, but it's the only response that allows you to do so.

Questions 26–30 offer the opportunity to "shade" your responses. In general, test administrators assume that an applicant who believes that everybody (or almost everybody) is dishonest is by definition including himself or herself in that category. On the other hand, everyone knows that some people *are* dishonest. Unlike the first twenty questions, these multiple-choice questions allow you to choose a non-absolute response. Note, too, that Question 30 differs in format from Questions 26–29, which present generalized statements and ask you to assess your belief in them. Question 30 presents a real-life (albeit hypothetical) situation, and asks you to judge what should be done.

You may find some questions on personality assessments intrusive—or worse. For instance, Questions 11–20 in this chapter may strike you as being of questionable legality, because some of the response choices appear to require that test takers incriminate themselves. Thus far, no one who has taken such personality assessments has legally challenged this sort of question, however, and these particular questions haven't been proven illegal. In any case, the administrators of a personality assessment are not looking to entrap test takers; they are seeking the best candidate for the job. You may choose not to answer certain questions, but bear in mind that this will likely result in your not getting the job for which you're applying.

SUMMING IT UP

- Many municipalities and agencies administer standardized personality assessments instead or in conjunction with interviews. Entry-level dispatchers receive extensive training, so it benefits an agency to determine before the training period which candidates are best for the job.

- The most commonly used standardized personality assessment is the Minnesota Multiphasic Personality Inventory. Another widely used standardized personality assessment, the Hogan Personality Inventory, aims to predict occupational success. On these assessments, the question format requires a true or false (or yes or no) response. Another type of personality assessment requires candidates to evaluate their own behaviors and character traits, both from their own perspective and from the perspectives of their elders and peers.

- The scores for standardized personality assessments are based less on answers to individual questions than on the sum of responses to a group of questions, such as those related to personal integrity. You are responding to narrowly phrased questions and given a time limit on such assessments because you are meant to answer quickly without dwelling too much on any one question.

- Although you should not spend too much time on any one question in a personality assessment, avoid answering any question unless you have the time to read the directions completely and thoroughly. It's better to have run out of time to complete all the questions than to have accidentally labeled yourself unfit or unsuitable for a public safety dispatcher position.

- Key questions, though expressed in absolute terms (using words such as *always* or *never*) nonetheless describe behavior that may be *often* but *not always* correct or incorrect. For this reason, be absolutely sure that you answer them as honestly as you can. For example, claiming that you *always* tell the truth may cast serious doubt on whether the rest of your responses are truthful.

- Questions meant to evaluate honesty and integrity may be phrased to determine your attitudes toward different types of behavior, or they may directly ask whether you have committed certain acts. Don't worry about being consistent in your responses. However, it's vital that you respond to the question or statement exactly as it is written, and that you carefully and thoroughly read every set of directions. Misreading directions can easily cause you to misinterpret what the questions are asking.

PART IV
TWO PRACTICE TESTS

ANSWER SHEET PRACTICE TEST 1

1. Ⓐ Ⓑ Ⓒ Ⓓ	21. Ⓐ Ⓑ Ⓒ Ⓓ	41. Ⓐ Ⓑ Ⓒ Ⓓ	61. Ⓐ Ⓑ Ⓒ Ⓓ
2. Ⓐ Ⓑ Ⓒ Ⓓ	22. Ⓐ Ⓑ Ⓒ Ⓓ	42. Ⓐ Ⓑ Ⓒ Ⓓ	62. Ⓐ Ⓑ Ⓒ Ⓓ
3. Ⓐ Ⓑ Ⓒ Ⓓ	23. Ⓐ Ⓑ Ⓒ Ⓓ	43. Ⓐ Ⓑ Ⓒ Ⓓ	63. Ⓐ Ⓑ Ⓒ Ⓓ
4. Ⓐ Ⓑ Ⓒ Ⓓ	24. Ⓐ Ⓑ Ⓒ Ⓓ	44. Ⓐ Ⓑ Ⓒ Ⓓ	64. Ⓐ Ⓑ Ⓒ Ⓓ
5. Ⓐ Ⓑ Ⓒ Ⓓ	25. Ⓐ Ⓑ Ⓒ Ⓓ	45. Ⓐ Ⓑ Ⓒ Ⓓ	65. Ⓐ Ⓑ Ⓒ Ⓓ
6. Ⓐ Ⓑ Ⓒ Ⓓ	26. Ⓐ Ⓑ Ⓒ Ⓓ	46. Ⓐ Ⓑ Ⓒ Ⓓ	66. Ⓐ Ⓑ Ⓒ Ⓓ
7. Ⓐ Ⓑ Ⓒ Ⓓ	27. Ⓐ Ⓑ Ⓒ Ⓓ	47. Ⓐ Ⓑ Ⓒ Ⓓ	67. Ⓐ Ⓑ Ⓒ Ⓓ
8. Ⓐ Ⓑ Ⓒ Ⓓ	28. Ⓐ Ⓑ Ⓒ Ⓓ	48. Ⓐ Ⓑ Ⓒ Ⓓ	68. Ⓐ Ⓑ Ⓒ Ⓓ
9. Ⓐ Ⓑ Ⓒ Ⓓ	29. Ⓐ Ⓑ Ⓒ Ⓓ	49. Ⓐ Ⓑ Ⓒ Ⓓ	69. Ⓐ Ⓑ Ⓒ Ⓓ
10. Ⓐ Ⓑ Ⓒ Ⓓ	30. Ⓐ Ⓑ Ⓒ Ⓓ	50. Ⓐ Ⓑ Ⓒ Ⓓ	70. Ⓐ Ⓑ Ⓒ Ⓓ
11. Ⓐ Ⓑ Ⓒ Ⓓ	31. Ⓐ Ⓑ Ⓒ Ⓓ	51. Ⓐ Ⓑ Ⓒ Ⓓ	71. Ⓐ Ⓑ Ⓒ Ⓓ
12. Ⓐ Ⓑ Ⓒ Ⓓ	32. Ⓐ Ⓑ Ⓒ Ⓓ	52. Ⓐ Ⓑ Ⓒ Ⓓ	72. Ⓐ Ⓑ Ⓒ Ⓓ
13. Ⓐ Ⓑ Ⓒ Ⓓ	33. Ⓐ Ⓑ Ⓒ Ⓓ	53. Ⓐ Ⓑ Ⓒ Ⓓ	73. Ⓐ Ⓑ Ⓒ Ⓓ
14. Ⓐ Ⓑ Ⓒ Ⓓ	34. Ⓐ Ⓑ Ⓒ Ⓓ	54. Ⓐ Ⓑ Ⓒ Ⓓ	74. Ⓐ Ⓑ Ⓒ Ⓓ
15. Ⓐ Ⓑ Ⓒ Ⓓ	35. Ⓐ Ⓑ Ⓒ Ⓓ	55. Ⓐ Ⓑ Ⓒ Ⓓ	75. Ⓐ Ⓑ Ⓒ Ⓓ
16. Ⓐ Ⓑ Ⓒ Ⓓ	36. Ⓐ Ⓑ Ⓒ Ⓓ	56. Ⓐ Ⓑ Ⓒ Ⓓ	76. Ⓐ Ⓑ Ⓒ Ⓓ
17. Ⓐ Ⓑ Ⓒ Ⓓ	37. Ⓐ Ⓑ Ⓒ Ⓓ	57. Ⓐ Ⓑ Ⓒ Ⓓ	77. Ⓐ Ⓑ Ⓒ Ⓓ
18. Ⓐ Ⓑ Ⓒ Ⓓ	38. Ⓐ Ⓑ Ⓒ Ⓓ	58. Ⓐ Ⓑ Ⓒ Ⓓ	78. Ⓐ Ⓑ Ⓒ Ⓓ
19. Ⓐ Ⓑ Ⓒ Ⓓ	39. Ⓐ Ⓑ Ⓒ Ⓓ	59. Ⓐ Ⓑ Ⓒ Ⓓ	79. Ⓐ Ⓑ Ⓒ Ⓓ
20. Ⓐ Ⓑ Ⓒ Ⓓ	40. Ⓐ Ⓑ Ⓒ Ⓓ	60. Ⓐ Ⓑ Ⓒ Ⓓ	80. Ⓐ Ⓑ Ⓒ Ⓓ

Practice Test 1

80 Questions • 180 Minutes

Directions: Choose the best answer to each question based upon the accompanying information and your own judgment. Regulations, codes, and procedures are not necessarily accurate for the municipality in which you are taking this exam. You must accept the rules as stated; do *not* base answers upon any actual knowledge that you may have.

1. Under certain circumstances, a dispatcher should make specific recommendations for special action to be taken. A dispatcher should recommend that an extra contingent of rescue workers be sent to the scene of a flaming one-story building that houses

   (A) 80 high school students.

   (B) 80 kindergarten children.

   (C) 80 residents of a nursing home.

   (D) 80 office workers.

2. A hysterical woman advises you that her son's dog is sick. You should refer her to

   (A) the animal hospital.

   (B) the local children's hospital.

   (C) the ambulance service.

   (D) none of the above.

3. 911 operator Maria Ruiz receives the following information on her computer screen:

   Place of Occurrence: 1520 Clarendon Road, Brooklyn

   Time of Occurrence: 6:32 a.m.

   Type of Building: Two-family frame dwelling

   Event: Fire, suspected arson

   Suspect: Male, white, approx. 6-feet tall, wearing blue jeans

   Witness: Mary Smith of 1523 Clarendon Road, Brooklyn

   Operator Ruiz is about to notify the fire department and to radio an alert for the suspect. Which of the following expresses the information *most clearly* and *accurately*?

   (A) At 6:32 a.m. Mary Smith of 1523 Clarendon Road, Brooklyn, saw a white male wearing approximately 6-foot blue jeans running from the building across the street.

   (B) A white male wearing blue jeans ran from the house at 1520 Clarendon Road at 6:32 a.m. Mary Smith saw him.

   (C) At 6:32 a.m. a 6-foot white male wearing blue jeans ran from a burning two-family frame structure at 1520 Clarendon Road, Brooklyn. He was observed by a neighbor, Mary Smith.

   (D) A two-family frame house is on fire at 1520 Clarendon Road in Brooklyn. A white male in blue jeans probably did it. Mary Smith saw him run.

4. Operator Warren Wu receives an emergency call from a token clerk. From the information the clerk gives, Wu types the following into his computer:

Time of Occurrence: 1:22 a.m.

Place of Occurrence: Uptown-bound platform, 59th Street Station, 7th Avenue line

Victim: Juana Martinez

Crime: Purse-snatching

Description of Suspect: Unknown, male, fled down steps to lower platform

Operator Wu will now radio the transit police. Which of the following expresses the information *most clearly* and *accurately?*

(A) Juana Martinez had her purse snatched on the subway platform at 59th Street Station. She didn't see him.

(B) A purse was just snatched by a man who ran down the steps from the 7th Avenue token booth at 59th Street Station. Her name is Juana Martinez.

(C) It is 1:22 a.m. The person who snatched Juana Martinez's purse is downstairs at 59th Street Station.

(D) Call from the 59th Street Station, uptown-bound 7th Avenue token booth. A Juana Martinez reports that her purse was just snatched by a man who fled down the steps to a lower platform.

ANSWER QUESTIONS 5–10 ON THE BASIS OF THE FOLLOWING PASSAGE.

Police officers Brown and Redi are on patrol in a radio car on a Saturday afternoon in the fall. They receive a radio message that a burglary is in progress on the fifth floor of a seven-floor building on the corner of 7th Street and Main. They immediately proceed to that location to investigate and take appropriate action.

The officers start for the fifth floor, using the main elevator. As they reach that floor and open the door, they hear noises, followed by the sound of the freight elevator door in the rear of the building closing and the **elevator** descending. They quickly run through the open door of the Fine Jewelry Company and observe that the office safe is open and empty. The officers then proceed to the rear of the building and use the rear staircase to reach the ground floor. They open the rear door and go out onto the street where they observe four individuals running up the street, crossing at the corner. At that point, the police officers get a clear view of the suspects. There are three males and one female. One of the males appears to be white, one is Hispanic, and the other male is black. The female is white.

The white male is bearded. He is dressed in blue jeans, white sneakers, and a red and blue jacket. He is carrying a white duffel bag on his shoulder. The Hispanic male limps slightly and has a large dark moustache. He is wearing brown pants, a green shirt, and brown shoes. He is carrying a blue duffel bag on his shoulder. The black male is clean-shaven, wearing black pants, a white shirt, a green cap, and black shoes. He is carrying what appears to be a toolbox. The white female is carrying a sawed-off shotgun, has long brown hair, and is wearing white jeans, a blue blouse, and blue sneakers. She has a red kerchief around her neck.

The officers chase the suspects for two blocks without being able to catch them. They then quickly return to their radio car to report what has happened. Dispatcher Marian Koslowksi takes their report and sends out a bulletin to all cars in the area. Her bulletin alerts officers to watch for a/an:

5. armed suspect. This suspect is a
   (A) white female.
   (B) black male.
   (C) Hispanic male.
   (D) white male.

6. female suspect whose hair is
   (A) short and light in color.
   (B) long and light in color.
   (C) short and dark in color.
   (D) long and dark in color.

7. suspect who limps while running. This suspect is a
   (A) white female.
   (B) black male.
   (C) Hispanic male.
   (D) white male.

8. bearded white male carrying a
   (A) blue duffel bag.
   (B) yellow duffel bag.
   (C) red duffel bag.
   (D) white duffel bag.

9. female wearing
   (A) a green cap.
   (B) a red jacket.
   (C) blue sneakers.
   (D) a white shirt.

10. black male carrying a
    (A) crowbar.
    (B) sawed-off shotgun.
    (C) red kerchief.
    (D) toolbox.

11. Waynesboro Hospital calls 911 to say that they have a person in the emergency room with a gunshot wound to the head. This is a case of
    (A) robbery.
    (B) harassment.
    (C) larceny.
    (D) assault.

12. The superintendent of Smith View Apartments was seen changing the locks on a woman's apartment because she refused to pay her rent. This is considered
    (A) aggravated harassment.
    (B) illegal eviction.
    (C) theft of service.
    (D) larceny.

13. A group of teenagers were pickpocketing people who were waiting on line at the roller rink. This is a case of
    (A) criminal mischief.
    (B) robbery.
    (C) larceny.
    (D) burglary.

14. Mr. Gleason and his family went to dinner at the Shore Rock Restaurant. When dinner was finished, they left without paying. They stated that they did not like the service. This is considered
    (A) larceny.
    (B) robbery.
    (C) theft of service.
    (D) assault.

15. Sometimes the calls that are made to the emergency number are not really emergencies at all. The emergency operator should refer these callers to the proper agencies. Which one of the following callers should be referred to another agency?

(A) A caller reporting a leak in the bedroom ceiling.

(B) A caller reporting that an occupied elevator is stuck between floors.

(C) A caller reporting a man snapping a large whip on the sidewalk.

(D) A caller reporting a strong odor of gas.

16. Operator Juana Diaz receives a telephoned complaint about poor emergency service. The facts as she records them are as follows:

> **Date of Event:** June 26
>
> **Time of Event:** 8:30 a.m.
>
> **Complainant:** Martha Brown
>
> **Address:** 1030 Whitcomb Street, Apt. 7A
>
> **Complaint:** Requested ambulance took 35 minutes to arrive

Operator Diaz must prepare a report on this call for her supervisor to investigate or to turn over to the dispatcher of Emergency Services. Which one of the following expresses the above information *most clearly* and *accurately*?

(A) Martha Brown said on June 26 an ambulance took 35 minutes to come at 8:30 a.m.

(B) On June 26, an ambulance came at 8:30 a.m. after 35 minutes to 1030 Whitcomb Street, said Martha Brown.

(C) To 1030 Whitcomb Street came an ambulance at 8:30 a.m. after 35 minutes on June 26. Martha Brown said it.

(D) According to Martha Brown of 1030 Whitcomb Street, an ambulance requested on June 26 took 35 minutes, arriving at 8:30 a.m.

ANSWER QUESTIONS 17–21 ON THE BASIS OF THE FOLLOWING PASSAGE.

PROCEDURES CONCERNING TARDINESS, VACATION, PERSONAL DAYS, AND ATTENDANCE

As a new employee, you are allowed 13 sick days, 5 personal days, and 25 vacation days. After 1 year of service, you are allowed 27 days vacation. When you are reporting sick for work, you must notify your command within 10 hours prior to the start of your tour. If you fail to report to your command, you will be reported as AWOL (absent without leave). When returning to work, you must notify your command within 5 hours before reporting back. If you fail to follow this procedure, you will receive a report of violation.

Lateness is not tolerated. When reporting late for work, you must notify your command 2 hours before the start of your tour. If you are in a training class, you must also make a courtesy call to the training center to advise them of your lateness. If you fail to follow this procedure, you will be docked 1 hour of pay for every hour that you are late.

17. Operator John King was to report to work at 11:30 p.m. At 10:30 p.m. he reported to the command that he would be late. Operator King was
    (A) right by notifying the command at 10:30 p.m.
    (B) right because he notified the training class of his lateness.
    (C) wrong because he failed to give 2 hours' notice.
    (D) None of the above.

18. Operator John King will now be
    (A) docked for every hour he is late.
    (B) marked AWOL.
    (C) fired from the job.
    (D) None of the above.

19. Operator Randolph Hill is a new employee in training. He is to report to work at 12:00 a.m. He notified the command at 2:00 p.m. that he was reporting sick. Did he correctly follow the sick procedure?
    (A) No, because he failed to notify the command according to procedure.
    (B) No, because he failed to also notify the training center.

    (C) Yes, because he notified the command within the required time.
    (D) None of the above.

20. Operator Joyce Collins is a new employee. According to procedure, how many times can she call in late?
    (A) 13 times per year.
    (B) 1 time per year.
    (C) 5 times per year.
    (D) None.

21. Operator Gwen McClain has been on the job for two years. How many vacation days can she take?
    (A) 25 days.
    (B) 30 days.
    (C) 15 days.
    (D) None of the above.

ANSWER QUESTION 22 ON THE BASIS OF THE FOLLOWING INFORMATION.

The procedure to be followed upon receipt of the information that a suicide is being attempted is the following:

1. Ask the precise location where the attempt is occurring.

2. Ask for the sex and race of the attempter, plus approximate age and name if known.

3. Ask for the name of the person reporting the attempt.

4. Request the address from which the report is coming.

5. Ask if the caller knows the victim. If so, (a) ask about motive; and (b) request names of others who might be of influence in dissuading the victim.

6. Notify the nearest appropriate rescue squad.

22. 911 operator Henry Hansen receives the message: "Someone is about to jump off the bridge." Hansen first asks, "Which bridge?" He then asks, "Is the jumper a man or a woman? Of what race? About how old is the person? What is his name?" Operator Hansen then asks the caller for his name and from what address he/she is calling. Hansen's next question is, "Do you know this person?" The caller responds, "No, I just happened to be looking out the window." Henry Hansen should now

(A) notify the newspapers about the attempted suicide.

(B) ask the caller why the jumper is attempting suicide.

(C) alert the rescue squad.

(D) ask for the race and age of the caller.

23. It is December 14 and a 911 operator has transmitted the following set of facts to Fire Dispatcher Mary Carey:

Location of fire: 122 Barley Road

Time of report: 4:18 a.m.

Type of structure: Chemicals factory

Origin of fire: Unknown

Extent of involvement: Active and total; heavy, foul-smelling smoke

Fire Dispatcher Carey has committed three full detachments to the scene. She is now preparing a written report of the night's activity. Which of the following conveys all the information *most clearly* and *accurately*?

(A) A chemical factory caught fire all by itself at 4:18 a.m. on Barley Road. Three fire engines put it out.

(B) At 4:18 a.m. on December 14, a fire of unknown origin was reported at a chemicals factory at 122 Barley Road. I dispatched three detachments to the scene and cautioned about the possibility of toxic fumes.

(C) There was a big fire in the chemicals factory at 122 Barley Road early this morning. It was not dangerous because no one is at work at that time, but I sent three detachments to put it out.

(D) Three detachments went to put out the fire at the chemicals factory on Barley Road this morning. The 911 operator told me that the cause was unknown.

24. Emergency communications technician Rita Mulligan receives four very excited calls in rapid succession. Each caller reports that a man has been running back and forth on the block of West 47th Street between 7th and 8th Avenues, shouting obscenities and waving a small handgun. The four descriptions vary in some details. Which of the

following four descriptions should Ms. Mulligan choose to transmit to the police radio dispatcher?

(A) White, 40 years old, wearing a black hat and red sneakers.

(B) Black, 25 years old, wearing a black hat and red sneakers.

(C) White, 25 years old, wearing a black hat and red sneakers.

(D) White, 30 years old, wearing a red hat and black sneakers.

ANSWER QUESTION 25 ON THE BASIS OF THE FOLLOWING INFORMATION.

When an emergency radio dispatcher receives word from the 911 operator that a suspicious package has been noticed at a specific location, the dispatcher must do the following:

1. Notify the police bomb-disarming unit.

2. Check the police jurisdiction grid to identify the precinct in which the suspicious package is located.

3. Pinpoint the nearest squad car and direct it to the location.

4. Check the fire jurisdiction grid to identify the fire company that protects the location.

5. Notify the firehouse for standby alert.

25. In a clear and accurate message, a 911 operator has informed Dispatcher Pedro Melendez of the address, precise location, and description of a suspicious package. Melendez has directed the bomb unit to the scene and has ascertained that the package is in the 35th precinct. Pedro Melendez should now

(A) call the 35th precinct and request that a squad car be sent to the scene to direct evacuation if necessary.

(B) call the 35th precinct and ask for the location of the nearest fire house.

(C) notify the nearest fire company as to the action in progress.

(D) search for the nearest patrol car and send it to the "bomb" site.

ANSWER QUESTION 26 ON THE BASIS OF THE FOLLOWING INFORMATION.

When a police dispatcher receives a call for reinforcements, the dispatcher must do the following:

1. Ask for the calling officer's badge number to be sure that the request is not a diversionary tactic.

2. Ask if an ambulance is needed.

3. Press 222, the emergency signal.

4. Press 456, the signal for all available cars to call in immediately.

5. Tell the location of the action to all responding cars.

6. Notify the hostage negotiation team to be ready.

26. Car 66 has arrived at the scene of a bank robbery in progress, and officers Klein and Carilli realize that there are a number of well-armed robbers inside. Officer Klein radios the police dispatcher and requests that reinforcements be sent at once. Dispatcher Barbara Blake asks Officer Klein for her badge number. Ms. Blake then asks if an ambulance is needed and learns that one is not necessary at this time. The next step dispatcher Blake should take is to

(A) send an ambulance on a nonemergency alert.

(B) press 222, then 456.

(C) broadcast the location of the action to all cars in the area.

(D) tell the location of the action individually to each responding car.

27. At 11 a.m. on Saturday, June 11, Dispatcher Frances Szulk receives a bulletin with the following information:

Location: Bicycle path alongside Shady Parkway, approximately 3,000 yards south of Highland train station

Occurrence: Discovery of body of fully clothed Hispanic female in early 20s

Reporter: Bill Sawyer, age 12

Identity of Victim: Unknown

Dispatcher Szulk must now send a patrol car to the scene. Which of the following conveys all the information *most clearly* and *accurately*?

(A) A woman was found by Bill Sawyer on the Shady Parkway. He doesn't know her.

(B) There is a body on the bicycle path on Shady Parkway near the train station. She is a Hispanic woman and Bill Sawyer, a 12-year-old, found her.

(C) The body of an unknown Hispanic woman was found at 11 a.m. by 12-year-old Bill Sawyer, on the bicycle path of Shady Parkway south of the Highland train station.

(D) On Saturday, June 11, Bill Sawyer found a dead body of a woman on the bicycle path. He called to say he didn't know her or why she died, but she had her clothes on.

28. An emergency operator receives many calls. Many of these calls do require action by the operator, but some are greater emergencies than others. Of the following calls, to which should an operator assign *lowest* priority?

(A) A dog is running loose in a residential neighborhood.

(B) An open fire hydrant is gushing into the roadway.

(C) There is a panhandler at the bus stop.

(D) A wire of unknown purpose is dangling over the sidewalk.

ANSWER QUESTION 29 ON THE BASIS OF THE FOLLOWING INFORMATION.

When a 911 operator receives notice of an accident that has just occurred in the street, the operator must do the following:

1. Ask for the exact location of the accident.

2. Ask about the number of people involved.

3. Inquire about the extent of the injuries.

4. If there are serious injuries, send ambulance(s).

5. Dispatch two patrol cars.

6. Ask if there is fire.

7. If there is fire, sound the alarm at the firehouse.

8. Ask if there are seriously disabled vehicles.

9. If necessary, send tow trucks.

29. 911 operator Tim Weitz receives a call informing him that a taxi has just hit a boy on a bicycle. Weitz learns the precise location of the accident and finds out that the boy seems badly hurt, but that the cabby is standing over him and no one else was involved. Operator Weitz sends an ambulance to the scene and dispatches the nearest two patrol cars. Then he asks if the cab is on fire and is assured that it is not. The next thing Tim Weitz must do is

(A) send a fire engine.

(B) send a tow truck.

(C) ask about the condition of the cab.

(D) ask if the bicycle has been damaged.

ANSWER QUESTION 30 ON THE BASIS OF THE FOLLOWING INFORMATION.

If the caller on the line is threatening to kill someone, the operator must

1. ask the caller for street address and apartment number.

2. write these alongside code 202 and pass the slip of paper to the nearest operator so that he or she can dispatch the police at once.

3. ask for the name of the caller.

4. ask questions about the intended victim and the situation leading to the threat.

5. keep the caller on the telephone until police arrive.

30. The caller screams at operator Jenny Wong that her son has just come home high again and he is rummaging through her pocketbook, and this time she will kill him. Operator Wong asks the woman where she lives. Next, Jenny Wong should

(A) press code 202.

(B) write down the exact address.

(C) tell the operator next to her to send the police.

(D) ask the woman what kind of drugs her son takes.

ANSWER QUESTIONS 31–36 ON THE BASIS OF THE FOLLOWING PASSAGE.

The following memorandum is on the police dispatcher's desk. The dispatcher must become thoroughly familiar with its content in order to alert both police officers assigned to the court house and patrol officers to the situation, and to rapidly process any reports of sightings that may come in from the field.

MEMORANDUM

This memorandum concerns the murder trial of George Jackson that is now in progress. Information has been received from reliable sources that the accused may attempt to escape from the courtroom, aided by members of the "Blue Circle" gang with which the accused was connected prior to his arrest.

Known members of this gang include Patsy "Boots" Brescia, a short, swarthy individual who invariably dresses conservatively. Although this member of the gang has no arrest record, he is known to carry firearms at all times and is now wanted by authorities in this state.

Fred Fick, alias Frederick Fidens: This individual is 6 feet, 4 inches tall; weighs 230 pounds; and may be identified by a knife scar on the right cheek. He has been convicted of felonious assault, manslaughter, and burglary.

Patrick Ahern: This individual is 6 feet, 2 inches tall and weighs 145 pounds. He is known to be extremely dangerous when under the influence of drugs. Ahern's convictions include those for robbery, breaking and entering, and Sullivan Law violation. He is wanted for kidnapping by the California authorities.

All officers, including those not assigned to the murder trial, are expected to be on the lookout for anyone acting peculiarly. If you observe anyone who answers any of the descriptions given above, or anyone else whose actions arouse your suspicion, send another officer to call the chief court officer. Avoid any indication that you are suspicious. Above all, avoid any action that may even remotely jeopardize the safety of spectators. While every precaution will be taken to prevent the admission to the courtroom of anyone carrying arms, do not gamble on the success of these precautions. These men are dangerous and, if convinced that their own safety is in peril, will not hesitate to use their weapons.

31. The memorandum indicates that, of the members of the "Blue Circle" gang mentioned,
    - (A) all have been arrested at least once.
    - (B) only one has never been arrested.
    - (C) two have never been arrested.
    - (D) three have never been arrested.

32. Of the members of the gang mentioned in the memorandum,
    - (A) at least one, if apprehended, may be extradited (returned to another state).
    - (B) at least two are said to be wanted by authorities in other states.
    - (C) at least three have been guilty of felonies.
    - (D) any one is likely to act peculiarly.

33. The memorandum does not state that Fred Fick has ever been convicted of
    (A) burglary.
    (B) manslaughter.
    (C) robbery.
    (D) felonious assault.

34. From information given in the memorandum, Patrick Ahern may best be described as
    (A) short and stocky.
    (B) tall and heavy.
    (C) tall and thin.
    (D) short and thin.

35. According to the memorandum, the member of the "Blue Circle" gang who is known to use drugs is
    (A) "Boots" Brescia.
    (B) Patrick Ahern.
    (C) Fred Fick.
    (D) George Jackson.

36. "Boots" Brescia may most readily be identified by
    (A) his swarthy complexion.
    (B) the scar on his right cheek.
    (C) his flashy clothes.
    (D) his footwear.

ANSWER QUESTIONS 37–39 BASED ON THE INFORMATION PROVIDED BELOW.

When receiving information from a caller in regard to a ringing alarm, the information should be taken in the following order:

1. What is the address or location of the ringing alarm?

2. How long has the alarm been ringing?

3. Is the alarm coming from a building or car?

4. If the alarm is coming from a building, find out if there are any open doors.

5. If the alarm is coming from a car, obtain the color, plate number, and type of auto.

6. Get name and address of the caller.

37. An anonymous caller states that an alarm is coming from the house across the street. He is unable to sleep and would like the police to respond to the location as soon as possible. What will your next course of action be?
    (A) Ask the caller for his name.
    (B) Ask how long has the alarm been ringing.
    (C) Obtain the address of the house.
    (D) None of the above.

38. What would be your next course of action?
    (A) Find out how long the alarm has been ringing.
    (B) Find out if anyone is in the house.
    (C) Obtain the color, plate number, and type of auto.
    (D) None of the above.

39. Your final course of action should be to
    (A) tell the caller the police are responding.
    (B) get the name and address of the caller.
    (C) get the caller's name.
    (D) None of the above.

ANSWER QUESTION 40 ON THE BASIS OF THE FOLLOWING INFORMATION.

When a 911 operator receives a call in a familiar foreign language, the operator should do the following:

1. If not certified in that language, transfer the call to an operator who is certified in that language.

2. If certified:

   a. Ask the caller for telephone number, name, and address.

   b. Ask about the nature of the emergency.

3. Determine which emergency service is appropriate to the problem.

4. Transmit the information to the appropriate dispatcher.

40. Operator Marisol Gonzalez receives a call from a distraught woman who tells her, in Spanish, that drug sales are being carried on in the hallway outside her apartment door. Operator Gonzalez is fluent in Spanish, though not certified, and easily obtains from the woman her telephone number, name, and address. Then Ms. Gonzalez transmits this information to a police dispatcher so that the drug sales can be observed in progress and the suspects arrested. Marisol Gonzalez's actions are

   (A) correct; she is perfectly competent to deal with the Spanish-speaking woman, and action must be taken quickly when dealing with drug sales.

   (B) incorrect; if she is not certified, her Spanish is not adequate for dealing with the excited woman.

   (C) correct; it would be too upsetting to the distraught woman to have her call transferred to another operator.

   (D) incorrect; the rules require that only foreign language–certified operators handle foreign language calls.

41. An emergency operator transmits the following information to the police dispatcher, who must radio it to patrol cars and ambulance:

   Location: Intersection of Grand Street and Torrance Avenue

   Occurrence: Hit and run accident

   Victim: Very old Asian man

   Witness: Joan Johnson of 332 Grand Street, Apt. 3B

   Vehicle: Red sports car with out-of-state license plates

   Which of the following expresses the information *most clearly* and *accurately*?

   (A) A very old Asian man was hit by Joan Johnson in a red sports car at 332 Grand Street, Apt. 3B.

   (B) Joan Johnson was hit by a very old Asian man at the intersection of Grand Street and Torrance Avenue. The red sports car was from out of state.

   (C) Joan Johnson of 332 Grand Street, Apt. 3B, reports that a very old Asian man was hit by a red sports car at Grand and Torrance.

   (D) A red sports car from out of state hit an old Asian man in front of Joan Johnson of 332 Grand Street, Apt. 3B.

ANSWER QUESTION 42 ON THE BASIS OF THE FOLLOWING INFORMATION.

When an emergency operator receives a call reporting a fire, the operator must ask for the following information in this order:

1. The exact address of the building or the nearest intersection.

2. The kind of building—apartment, private house, factory, store, theater, school, etc.

3. The number of floors—2-story, low-rise, mid-rise, or high-rise.

4. If the building is customarily occupied, vacant, or abandoned.

5. Whether or not the building is actually occupied.

6. Identity of the owner of the building.

7. Identity of the caller.

42. Operator Hans Kohl has received a report of a fire and has asked the caller where the fire is. He has learned that the building is a boarded-up small apartment house. Operator Kohl's next question should be

(A) Is the fire out yet?

(B) Do you know if anyone was living there?

(C) How did the fire start?

(D) Do you know who owns the building?

43. Police officer George Mullins arrives at the scene of a jewelry store robbery. Witnesses surround him, all eager to give descriptions of the getaway car. Officer Mullins must call the dispatcher to broadcast the description of the car throughout the city. Which of the following descriptions should he assume to be correct?

(A) White Ford, 2-door, California plate 482-ACE

(B) Cream Buick, 2-door, New York plate 483-GE

(C) Yellow Mercury, 4-door, New Jersey plate 495-BGF

(D) Cream Ford, 2-door, New Jersey plate 482-BCE

ANSWER QUESTION 44 ON THE BASIS OF THE FOLLOWING INFORMATION.

If an operator receives a call from a woman about to give birth, the operator must do the following in the following order:

1. Ask the caller for her telephone number, address, and name. If an apartment building, ask apartment number.

2. Ask how emergency personnel can gain entrance to building and unit.

3. Ask about any problems that may require immediate special services—prematurity or heavy bleeding, for instance.

4. Transmit information to police and ambulance services.

5. Ask caller if anyone else—doctor, family member—should be alerted.

44. Operator Raoul Castellano receives a call from a woman who tells him that she is in heavy labor and the baby is coming very fast. Operator Castellano asks the woman for her telephone number, name, and address. Then he learns that the apartment house front door is always open and the woman has unlocked her own apartment door. In answer to Castellano's inquiry, the woman says that she is just entering her seventh month of pregnancy. Operator Castellano's next act should be to

(A) call the hospital to alert them of the imminent arrival of a premature newborn.

(B) ask the woman for the name and number of her doctor.

(C) transmit all the information to the police and emergency medical services.

(D) ask who is caring for the other children.

45. The following information appears on the screen in front of Police Dispatcher Mike Thorkelson:

Occurrence: Dog bite, left calf

Victim: Calliope Petropolis, age 9

Address of Victim: 730 Ninth Avenue, Apt. 5G

Location of occurrence: In front of 680 Tenth Avenue

Caller: Artemis Canellos, 688 Tenth Avenue

Description of dog: Terrier-sized brown-and-white mongrel

Location of dog: Unknown

Thorkelson must transmit this information to the police canine control unit. Which of the following expresses this information *most completely* and *accurately*?

(A) A brown-and-white mongrel bit Artemis Canellos at 730 Ninth Avenue. She is nine. It bit her left leg.

(B) Calliope Petropolis, a nine-year-old of 730 Ninth Avenue, Apt. 5G, was bitten on the leg by a brown-and-white mongrel. The occurrence took place near 680 Tenth Avenue and was reported by one Artemis Canellos of #688. The dog is at large.

(C) Nine-year-old Calliope Petropolis was bitten by a brown-and-white mutt at 730 Ninth Avenue. Artemis Canellos reported that it was her left calf. She doesn't know where the dog is.

(D) A dog bit Calliope Petropolis in front of 680 Tenth Avenue. Calliope is 9, reported Artemis Canellos of Apt. 5G. No one knows where the dog is.

46. 911 operator Jim Goldman receives a call from a citizen who complains of a foul odor coming from the trunk of a car parked in his neighborhood. This is not an emergency situation, but operator Goldman takes down information to pass on to the police department. The caller is Frank Connolly of 923 188th Road. The car is a nearly new blue Lincoln Town Car. It has been parked at the same spot, in front of 947 188th Street, for at least two weeks. The car bears New York license plate SBT-383. With which of the following will operator Goldman express the information *most clearly* and *accurately*?

(A) Frank Connolly of 923 188th Road reports an odor coming from a blue Lincoln Town Car, NY SBT-383, parked in front of 947 188th Street for two weeks.

(B) A blue Lincoln at 923 188th Road has a bad smell for two weeks. Its number is SBT-383. Mr. Connolly told about it.

(C) License plate SBT-383 from New York is on a blue Lincoln Town Car. It smells, says Frank Connolly of 923 188th Road.

(D) Frank Connolly complains that a blue Lincoln with New York license plate SBT-383 has been smelling bad for two weeks. He lives at 923; it is at 947.

ANSWER QUESTION 47 ON THE BASIS OF THE FOLLOWING INFORMATION.

When a caller to 911 makes a bizarre or highly improbable report, the operator must follow a special line of questioning to determine if the caller is a danger to the public, requiring massive, immediate response, or to himself or herself, requiring a nonintimidating reaction. The order of questioning is as follows:

1. Telephone number of phone being used and location from which call is being made.

2. Name, address, and home phone number of caller.

3. Detailed description of event being reported.

   a. If alien landing, description, how many, how armed.

   b. Demands being made of caller.

4. What the caller is planning to do about it.

47. 911 operator Akeel Hakim receives a call from an agitated citizen who reports that a space ship has just touched down in the vacant lot across the street and that aliens are pouring out of it. Hakim gets from the caller the phone number and address from which he is calling and determines that these are the home number and address of the caller. Next he should ask:

(A) What are you going to do about it?

(B) Do they speak English?

(C) Tell me what they look like and how many there are.

(D) What do they want?

48. Mrs. Wood calls 911 and states that the unoccupied elevator in her building is not working. You should

(A) send a patrol car to check the elevator.

(B) tell her to call back in 1 hour if the elevator is still not working.

(C) tell her to call building repair or superintendent/landlord of the building

(D) hang up on her.

49. On July 21 at 10:30 p.m., emergency operator Lorraine Wilson receives a call from a furious citizen who complains about nighttime activity in the church parking lot next door. He says that his name is Peter Lynch and he lives at 168 Cayman Road. He says that the parking lot of St. Mary's church at 170 Cayman Road is "sin center" at night. He demands that the parking lot gate be locked at night to discourage the drag racing, drinking, and sexual activity that have been going on there. Operator Wilson knows that this is not an emergency and that she needn't pass the call to a dispatcher, but as long as she has the information, she prepares a written report. Which of the following expresses the information *most clearly* and *accurately*?

(A) Peter Lynch of St. Mary's on 170 Cayman Road says the parking lot should be locked at 10:30 p.m. People drink there at night.

(B) Peter Lynch of 168 Cayman Road complains of nighttime rowdiness in the parking lot of St. Mary's at 170 Cayman. He requests that the lot be padlocked at night.

(C) There is drinking and sex in the St. Mary's parking lot at night at 170 Cayman Road. Peter Lynch says it should be padlocked on July 21st.

(D) Padlocking the parking lot of St. Mary's is the solution to nightly disturbances at 170 Cayman Road, according to Peter Lynch of 168 Cayman Road at 10:30 p.m. on July 21st.

50. Mrs. Swanson calls 911 to find out if alternate street parking is suspended today. You should

(A) ask the operator next to you, because she drives.

(B) tell her that you think so, because of all the snow outside.

(C) tell her to watch the news.

(D) refer her to the alternate street parking hotline.

ANSWER QUESTIONS 51–55 ON THE BASIS OF THE FOLLOWING PASSAGE.

EMPLOYEE LEAVE REGULATIONS

As a full-time permanent City employee under the Career and Salary Plan, operator Peter Smith earns an annual leave allowance. This consists of a certain number of days off per year with pay and may be used for vacation, personal business, or for observing religious holidays. As a newly appointed employee, during his first 8 years of City service he will earn an annual leave allowance of 20 days off per year (an average of 1-2/3 days off per month). After he has finished 8 full years of working for the City, he will begin earning an additional 5 days off per year. His annual leave allowance will then be 25 days per year and will remain at this amount for 7 full years. He will begin earning an additional 2 days off per year after he has completed a total of 15 years of City employment. Therefore, in his sixteenth year of working for the City, Smith will be earning 27 days off a year as his 'annual leave allowance' (an average of 2-1/4 days off per month).

A sick leave allowance of 1 day per month is also given to Operator Smith, but it can be used only in case of actual illness. When Smith returns to work after using sick leave allowance, he must have a doctor's note if the absence is for a total of more than 3 days, but he may also be required to show a doctor's note for absences of 1, 2, or 3 days.

51. According to the preceding passage, Mr. Smith's annual leave allowance consists of a certain number of days off per year that he
   (A) does not get paid for.
   (B) gets paid for at time and a half.
   (C) may use for personal business.
   (D) may not use for observing religious holidays.

52. According to the preceding passage, after Mr. Smith has been working for the City for 9 years, his annual leave allowance will be
   (A) 20 days per year.
   (B) 25 days per year.
   (C) 27 days per year.
   (D) 37 days per year.

53. According to the preceding passage, Mr. Smith will begin earning an average of 2-1/4 days off per month as his annual leave allowance after he has worked for the City for
   (A) 7 full years.
   (B) 8 full years.
   (C) 15 full years.
   (D) 17 full years.

54. According to the preceding passage, Mr. Smith is given a "sick leave allowance" of
   (A) 1 day every 2 months.
   (B) 1 day per month.
   (C) 1-2/3 days per month.
   (D) 2-1/4 days per month.

55. According to the preceding passage, when he uses sick leave allowance, Mr. Smith may be required to show a doctor's note
   (A) even if his absence is for only 1 day.
   (B) only if his absence is for more than 2 days.
   (C) only if his absence is for more than 3 days.
   (D) only if his absence is for 3 days or more.

56. By far the greatest number of calls to 911 are calls intended for the police department. Which of the following emergency calls should be directed to someone other than the police department?

  (A) A call reporting a man going up the fire escape at a neighboring building

  (B) A call reporting a group of young people burning an American flag in the park

  (C) A call reporting youths breaking car windows

  (D) A call reporting a customer who appears to have suffered a heart attack in a department store

57. Off-duty police officer Howard Kenzie notices an apparently unsupervised small boy wandering aimlessly on East 18th Street between Avenue P and Kings Highway. He asks the child his name and is told "Jimmy." The child, who appears to be no more than three years old, has curly blond hair and is wearing striped pants and a white T-shirt with Bugs Bunny on the front. The youngster cannot tell his last name or where he lives. Officer Kenzie calls the police dispatcher from the nearest call box and asks the dispatcher to check with the local precinct, and possibly other precincts as well, to see if a child matching this description has been reported missing. Which of the following statements expresses this information to the precincts *most clearly* and *accurately*?

  (A) Jimmy is all alone on East 18th Street between Avenue P and Kings Highway. Has anyone missed him?

  (B) A small blond boy wearing striped pants and a Bugs Bunny T-shirt and identifying himself as "Jimmy" is wandering on East 18th Street between Avenue P and Kings Highway. Has he been reported missing?

  (C) Police Officer Howard Kenzie, who is not on duty, has little Jimmy on East 18th Street between Avenue P and Kings Highway in striped pants. He is blond.

  (D) An off-duty little boy named Jimmy is with Police Officer Howard Kenzie at a call box near East 18th Street and Kings Highway. He likes Bugs Bunny and wears striped pants.

58. Operator Steve Goldman received a call from someone who says there is a man standing at a bank teller window with a gun pointed at the cashier. Operator Goldman's first course of action should be to

  (A) ask the caller the name of the bank.

  (B) ask if an ambulance is needed.

  (C) ask the caller the address of the bank.

  (D) None of the above.

59. Operator Goldman's next step should be to

  (A) send several police cars to the location, because the bank robber is still in the bank.

  (B) advise his supervisor, because a bank robbery is a newsworthy event.

  (C) get the description of the bank robber.

  (D) get the name of the bank.

60. After Operator Goldman gets the description of the bank robber, he will

  (A) find out if anyone is injured.

  (B) find out if any weapon was used. If so, get a description of the weapon, etc.

  (C) find out how the bank robber got away.

  (D) None of the above.

61. An emergency operator must be able to size up calls very quickly, refer true emergencies to the proper departmental dispatchers, and rapidly dispose of nonemergency calls with referrals or suggestions. Sometimes, however, the best course is for the emergency operator to consult the supervisor. Which one of the following calls should the operator turn to his or her supervisor?

(A) A call complaining of rudeness by another operator

(B) A call complaining that there is no hot water in the building

(C) A call reporting that a helicopter has just crashed into the river

(D) A call reporting an explosion in a toy factory

ANSWER QUESTION 62 ON THE BASIS OF THE FOLLOWING INFORMATION.

In the event of a maritime accident, the emergency operator must follow this procedure:

1. Determine the precise location of the accident.

2. Ask for an estimate of the number of victims involved.

3. Ask if there is fire.

4. Notify police boats, fireboats, and helicopters.

5. Request name, location, and telephone number from which call is being made.

6. Request that the caller remain by that telephone in case there are problems in locating victims.

62. A pleasure craft has just collided with a garbage scow traveling down the river. Sarah Small, who was looking out her office window at the time, dials 911. Emergency operator Brian Isco asks Ms. Small which river, and with what street it is in line. He then learns from Ms. Small that the boat has capsized, tossing about five people into the water and that neither vessel is on fire at this time. Operator Isco instantly alerts police boats, fireboats, and police helicopter services. He then asks Ms. Small for her name, home address, and home telephone number. Operator Isco has acted

(A) correctly; he did everything required in the proper order.

(B) incorrectly; there was no fire; so he should not have sent fire boats.

(C) incorrectly; he should have asked Sarah Small for her office address and telephone number.

(D) incorrectly; he should have told Ms. Small to stay right where she was.

63. Operator James Monroe takes a call from a woman who has just been raped. Here are the details:

> **Location:** 583 Cooper Terrace, elevator
>
> **Time:** 2:15 p.m.
>
> **Occurrence:** Rape and robbery
>
> **Weapon:** Knife
>
> **Perpetrator:** White male, approx. 25 yrs. old, slight build, medium height, wearing blue jeans and red T-shirt
>
> **Items stolen:** Pocketbook, pearl ring, cameo brooch
>
> **Victim:** Bella Luciano, age 67, of 583 Cooper Terrace

Operator Monroe is preparing a bulletin for police officers. Which of the following expresses the information *most clearly* and *accurately*?

(A) A 25-year-old white male raped 67-year-old Bella Luciano in the elevator with a knife. He robbed her, too.

(B) At 2:15 p.m. a man raped Bella Luciano in the elevator of 583 Cooper Terrace and robbed her of her pocketbook, pearl ring, and cameo brooch.

(C) A pocketbook, pearl ring, and cameo brooch were stolen at knifepoint from Bella Luciano when a man raped her in the elevator. He was 67 years old, medium sized, and wearing blue jeans and a red T-shirt.

(D) A white male, approximately 25 years of age, slightly built and of medium height, wearing blue jeans and a red T-shirt, robbed and raped at knifepoint Bella Luciano, age 67, in the elevator of 583 Cooper Terrace at 2:15 p.m. Items stolen were a pocketbook, pearl ring, and cameo brooch.

ANSWER QUESTION 64 ON THE BASIS OF THE FOLLOWING INFORMATION.

The main role of the emergency operator is to receive information and to pass it on to the appropriate services or dispatchers. Occasionally, the operator should take it upon himself or herself to give emergency instructions. If it appears to the operator that a caller might be in danger by remaining at the location from which the call is being made, the operator should do the following:

1. Ask for the name of the caller and the address of the emergency.

2. Tell the caller to leave the premises at once and to call from the nearest available telephone at another location.

3. Dispatch the police at once.

4. Alert all other emergency operators to expect the call back.

   a. Inform other operators as to the nature of the situation and what has been done so far.

   b. Ask to have the call transferred to you if your line is not occupied when the caller calls back.

5. Get additional information to complete call information report 518B when caller calls back.

64. Operator Sirhan Amin receives a call from a woman who says that she is certain that she locked the front door when she left to take her husband to the airport for a business trip three hours earlier, and she has just returned to a wide-open door. Operator Amin takes down the woman's name and address and tells her to get out immediately in case there are burglars in the house and to call from the home of the nearest neighbor or street phone.

Operator Amin then dispatches police to the woman's home and begins to tell other emergency operators about the situation. While Amin is briefing the operators, he receives a call from a man whose kitchen curtains have blown into the flames on his gas range. Just as Amin is taking down location information from the man with the kitchen fire, the first woman calls back. Operator Shirley Hyacinth receives the call. Operator Hyacinth should

(A) interrupt Sirhan Amin to tell him that his caller is back on the line.

(B) ask the woman more questions about the appearance of the house, possible activity, pets inside, etc.

(C) ask the woman to hold, because operator Amin is busy but will be available soon.

(D) tell the woman that the police are on the way.

65. A park should be a restful, safe place, but sometimes emergency situations may arise. On this balmy Sunday afternoon, the emergency call box is constantly busy. To which of the following emergencies should the dispatcher **not** send an ambulance?

(A) A jogger has fallen unconscious on the running path.

(B) A man is systematically stopping cyclists, robbing them with a heavy stick in hand, then releasing them.

(C) A child went sailing off an actively swinging swing and cannot get up.

(D) A teenager was hit in the eye by a baseball and says he cannot see with that eye.

ANSWER QUESTIONS 66–70 ON THE BASIS OF THE INFORMATION IN THE FOLLOWING PASSAGE AND ON THE INFORMATION IN THE QUESTIONS THEMSELVES. EACH QUESTION STANDS BY ITSELF UNLESS OTHERWISE STATED.

The city is divided into six police precincts roughly gridded:

4	5	6
1	2	3

The circumstances of each precinct are different, so each has a unique allotment of personnel and equipment.

The first precinct encompasses the business district. The daytime needs in the first tend to be limited to traffic control; however, burglary and assault on pedestrians are nighttime problems. Twenty-four patrol cars serve this precinct along with 5 motorcycles and, of course, foot patrols.

The second precinct includes municipal, state, and federal buildings. Daytime pedestrian traffic is heavy here, and there are frequent demonstrations and protests of various sorts. The precinct is served by 10 patrol cars, 8 motorcycles, 6 horses for mounted police, a bomb squad, 2 patrol wagons for transporting suspects and for transferring prisoners, and 6 specially trained sharpshooters.

The third precinct is a well-to-do apartment house district in which each building has some sort of security of its own. This precinct is served by 16 patrol cars, along with a full complement of detectives, investigators, and foot patrols.

The fourth precinct is a congested apartment house district. There is heavy unemployment here, with consequent loitering, criminal activity, and drug use and trade. Though the precinct is geographically small, its population and police needs are high. The precinct has 40 patrol cars and many officers assigned to foot patrol. The fourth precinct is also the home base of the narcotics squad.

The fifth precinct contains the city's warehouses and docks. It is also the center of the red-light district. Much of the crime here is at night in the form of hijacking and large-scale burglary. This precinct boasts a canine squad, undercover agents, and 2 patrol wagons, along with 14 patrol cars.

The sixth precinct consists mainly of one- and two-family dwellings and neighborhood stores. The police needs of this precinct are best served by 30 patrol cars and 2 motorcycles. The police maintenance garage is located in the sixth precinct. It can service up to 25 vehicles at one time but is seldom full.

It is the dispatcher's job to send the closest-available appropriate vehicles or services to wherever they are needed, without leaving any precinct unprotected.

66. The President of the United States has come to the city. He entered through the first precinct and is en route to the federal buildings. His motorcade is being escorted by 8 motorcycles and 30 patrol cars. Sharpshooters are stationed strategically on area roofs. The mounted police are all in the federal area for crowd control. The patrol cars should have been drawn from the precincts as follows:

    (A) 22 from the first; 8 from the second.

    (B) 10 from the first; 5 from the second; 3 from the third; 2 from the fourth; 5 from the fifth; 5 from the sixth.

    (C) 12 from the first; 5 from the second; 2 from the third; 6 from the fourth; 5 from the fifth.

    (D) 5 from each of the six precincts.

67. Under the scenario of question 66, the dispatcher suddenly receives a call reporting a heavily armed bank robbery in progress in the first precinct. The foot patrols in the area request immediate reinforcement and cover from 8 cars. (Some of these could be drawn from the President's escort, if necessary.) The best array of cars for the dispatcher to send in order to supply 8 cars quickly and to not expose other areas unduly is

    (A) 4 from the first, 4 from the second.

    (B) 8 from the first.

    (C) 8 from the fourth.

    (D) 8 from the sixth.

68. It is 10 p.m. A nine-year-old girl seated in a car in the fourth precinct has just been caught in a drug-related crossfire and has been shot and killed. The neighbors have chased down the perpetrators and are beating them severely. The violence is rapidly escalating as angry, frustrated residents of the neighborhood break windows, overturn cars, and start fires. Fourteen cars from the fourth precinct have already converged on the scene, but much more help is needed. The dispatcher should send

    (A) more cars from the fourth, motorcycles from the first and second, and cars and paddy wagons from the second.

    (B) cars from the third and sharpshooters and motorcycles from the first.

    (C) cars from the sixth, a paddy wagon from the fifth, and the mounted police.

    (D) the canine unit, the bomb squad, and cars and motorcycles from the first.

69. A police officer in the sixth precinct suspects that drugs are entering a neighborhood grocery on his post and major drug dealing is going on in the store. This is not an emergency situation, but the dispatcher should arrange assistance for the sixth precinct from units in the

    (A) second and fourth precincts.

    (B) first and second precincts.

    (C) second and fifth precincts.

    (D) fourth and fifth precincts.

70. A citizen has called to report finding two burglars inside his premises at 8:30 p.m. This call is least likely to originate from the

    (A) first precinct.

    (B) second precinct.

    (C) third precinct.

    (D) fourth precinct.

71. At 5:17 p.m. on May 3, Operator Krikor Mardikian takes a call that warns that a bomb has been placed under a third-row seat at the Savoy Theater on Main Street. The theater is showing an R-rated movie of which the caller disapproves. The caller tells Operator Mardikian that the bomb should go off within 1-1/2 hours. Krikor Mardikian must notify the police, bomb squad, and theater management. Which of the following bulletins expresses the information *most clearly* and *accurately*?

(A) It is May 3 at 5:17 p.m. The bomb at the Savoy Theater will go off at 6:47 p.m.

(B) The bomb in the third row of the Savoy Theater on Main Street will go off in an hour and a half.

(C) Report has been received of a bomb under a third-row seat in the Savoy Theater on Main Street. It is 5:17 p.m.

(D) At 5:17 p.m. a bomb with a 1-1/2-hour fuse was reported to have been placed under a third-row seat of the Savoy Theater on Main Street.

ANSWER QUESTION 72 ON THE BASIS OF THE FOLLOWING INFORMATION.

In the event of a major disaster, the emergency operator should take the following steps in this order:

1. Determine the precise location of the disaster.

2. Estimate the numbers of victims involved.

3. Notify and alert the following services citywide:

   a. firefighters

   b. emergency medical services (ambulances)

   c. police

   d. hospitals

4. Request state police assistance in keeping access routes open for emergency vehicles.

72. 911 Operator Kimberly Kane receives a horrifying report that a large passenger train has just derailed in a residential area. Operator Kane learns the basic location of the wreckage and realizes that hundreds will be affected, including passengers and residents of the neighborhood. Kane immediately sends out the alert for all available fire companies to rush to the scene and also sounds the alarm for emergency ambulances. The next step Operator Kane must take is to

(A) notify police in the precinct in which the wreckage is strewn.

(B) notify police citywide.

(C) contact state police.

(D) alert hospitals to prepare for trauma victims.

ANSWER QUESTIONS 73–78 BASED ON THE INFORMATION PROVIDED BELOW.

CRIME DEFINITIONS

Criminal mischief	Intentionally damages another's property
Burglary	Enters or remains unlawfully in a dwelling with intent to commit a crime
Assault	Causes injury to another person or persons
Robbery	Forcible stealing of another's property
Harassment	Strikes, shoves, kicks, or subjects another to physical contact but without causing injury
Larceny	Deprives another of property by wrongfully taking, obtaining, or withholding it from the other party (no physical force involved)
Aggravated harassment	To harass or annoy another by means of a tele-communications device
Theft of service	To avoid payment for services
Illegal eviction	When a person evicts or attempts to evict without a warrant

73. Mary Newman calls 911 and states her husband just slapped her, but that she is not injured. Under the crime definitions, this is considered

    (A) criminal mischief.

    (B) larceny.

    (C) harassment.

    (D) assault.

74. Mr. Jim Jones reports that he just came home from work and found that his apartment was broken into. Under the crime definitions, this is considered

    (A) robbery.

    (B) burglary.

    (C) larceny.

    (D) illegal eviction.

75. The school nurse calls 911 and states that a group of kids are spray painting the side of the school building. Under the crime definitions, this is considered

    (A) aggravated harassment.

    (B) theft of service.

    (C) larceny.

    (D) criminal mischief.

76. An elderly women states that her pocketbook was taken from her at gunpoint. Under the crime definitions, this is considered

    (A) robbery.

    (B) assault.

    (C) larceny.

    (D) theft of service.

77. The gas station owner advises that he just filled up a car with a tank of gas and the driver left without paying. Under the crime definitions, this is considered

    (A) larceny.

    (B) theft of service.

    (C) harassment.

    (D) aggravated harassment.

78. Mrs. Francois is receiving numerous phone calls from her estranged husband. He is threatening to kill her. Under the crime definitions, this is considered

    (A) aggravated harassment.

    (B) harassment.

    (C) criminal mischief.

    (D) assault.

79. Operator Irene Tortino receives a call from a woman who complains bitterly of obscene phone calls. Operator Tortino takes down the following information:

Complaint: Unsolicited phone calls with heavy breathing and obscene questions and suggestions

Complainant: Dorothy Hultz of 17-12 Highland Way

Phone number being called: 555-6686

Caller: Unknown male with husky voice, no particular accent

Target of calls: Any female answering phone

Time of day calls take place: Between 7 and 9 p.m.

Operator Tortino recommends to Ms. Hultz that she instruct all household members to hang up immediately when they receive these calls. Then Ms. Tortino prepares an information report for the police department and telephone company. Which of the following expresses the information *most clearly* and *accurately*?

(A) An unidentified male with a husky voice has been making obscene phone calls to 555-6686, the home of Dorothy Hultz at 17-12 Highland Way between 7 and 9 p.m.

(B) Dorothy Hultz gets obscene calls from a husky man at 555-6686 at 17-12 Highland Way.

(C) A husky voice breathes hard and is obscene between 7 and 9 p.m., says Dorothy Hultz.

(D) Between 7 and 9 p.m., any female receives a husky voice at 555-6686 from 17-12 Highland Way by Dorothy Hultz.

ANSWER QUESTION 80 ON THE BASIS OF THE FOLLOWING INFORMATION.

911 operators are given the following instructions with regard to telephoned complaints about lack of heat.

1. If the outside temperature is above 30 degrees Fahrenheit (°F), give the caller the telephone number of the Buildings Department.

2. If the outside temperature is below 30°F, ask the following:

a. name of caller

b. address of premises without heat

c. number of units in building

d. number of people in unit and their ages

e. if there are any special health problems among occupants

f. if occupants have enough blankets

3. If any occupant of the unit is over the age of 65 or under the age of 18 months, or if there is severe illness in the household, notify the Health Department.

4. Ask the name of the landlord and the address to which rent is paid.

5. Notify the Buildings Department and the mayor's emergency heat force.

80. The outside temperature is 24°F when Operator Aliza Chatzky receives a call from a woman complaining that there is no heat in the apartment, that there has been no heat for more than a week, and that furthermore some windows are broken. Operator Chatzky learns the woman's name and the address of the building. The building has 24 apartments, none of which has heat. There are 8 people living in this apartment, all between the ages of 4 and 55. The woman's 8-year-old daughter is running a fever of 105 degrees. The family has piled all of its blankets on the little girl because she has chills. Aliza Chatzky next asks the name of the landlord. Operator Chatzky's action is

(A) incorrect, because no one in the apartment is under the age of 18 months or over the age of 65 years.

(B) incorrect, because the 8-year-old girl is sick.

(C) correct, because there are plenty of blankets.

(D) correct, because the mayor's emergency heat force will need to know the name of the landlord in order to compel him or her to provide heat.

practice test

ANSWER KEY AND EXPLANATIONS

1. C	17. C	33. C	49. B	65. B
2. A	18. A	34. C	50. D	66. B
3. C	19. B	35. B	51. C	67. C
4. D	20. D	36. A	52. B	68. A
5. A	21. D	37. C	53. C	69. D
6. D	22. C	38. A	54. B	70. C
7. C	23. B	39. B	55. A	71. D
8. D	24. C	40. D	56. D	72. B
9. C	25. D	41. C	57. B	73. C
10. D	26. B	42. B	58. C	74. B
11. D	27. C	43. D	59. D	75. D
12. B	28. C	44. C	60. B	76. A
13. C	29. C	45. B	61. A	77. B
14. C	30. B	46. A	62. C	78. A
15. A	31. B	47. C	63. D	79. A
16. D	32. A	48. C	64. B	80. B

1. **The correct answer is (C).** Small children may disobey, but they are mobile on their own or can be scooped up easily. Kindergartens are generally adequately staffed to deal with quick evacuation. Nursing home residents, on the other hand, often are disabled or even bedridden. The staff is unlikely to be able to remove all residents unaided. Many rescue workers are needed right away.

2. **The correct answer is (A).** The ambulance services and the children's hospital are for people, not pets. You should refer her to the local animal hospital.

3. **The correct answer is (C).** This statement tells what happened, where, and when. It gives a brief description of the suspect and identifies the witness. Choices (A) and (B) neglect to mention the fire; choice (D) omits the height of the suspect, an important fact, and does not identify the relationship of the witness for later questioning, if necessary.

4. **The correct answer is (D).** This statement gives the precise location, what took place, and a direction in which the suspect might be traced. Since the statement says that the event just occurred, the time is irrelevant. The recipient of the message knows to move quickly. Choice (A) does not give enough details to be of use; choice (B) makes a disjointed statement; choice (C) makes a flat statement that is not necessarily true. The purse-snatcher may have exited by another route.

5. **The correct answer is (A).** The white female is armed with a sawed-off shotgun.

6. **The correct answer is (D).** The white female has long brown hair.

7. **The correct answer is (C).** The police officers observed the suspects running. The Hispanic male ran with a slight limp.

8. **The correct answer is (D).** The white male was bearded and carried a white duffel bag. The Hispanic male carried the blue duffel bag.

9. **The correct answer is (C).** The female wore blue sneakers.

10. **The correct answer is (D).** The black male carried the toolbox.

11. **The correct answer is (D).** Because someone caused injury to this person, it is considered an assault.

12. **The correct answer is (B).** The superintendent was attempting to evict the person without a warrant by tampering with the lock.

13. **The correct answer is (C).** The kids were wrongfully taking property and no force was used.

14. **The correct answer is (C).** Regardless of the reason they didn't pay, because they avoided payment for their meal, this would be considered a theft of service.

15. **The correct answer is (A).** The water leak should be reported and repaired, but it does not constitute an emergency. The caller should be referred to the Buildings Department. An occupied elevator that is stuck between floors represents a clear emergency situation. The man cracking the whip could injure people. A gas odor may indicate an imminent explosion. The fire department and/or utility company should be summoned on an emergency basis.

16. **The correct answer is (D).** This statement gives all the relevant information in logical order. Choice (A) omits the location. Choices (B) and (C) are garbled messages.

17. **The correct answer is (C).** He gave only 1 hour notice, and therefore he was wrong.

18. **The correct answer is (A).** He will be docked, because he failed to follow the late procedure.

19. **The correct answer is (B).** He is in training and therefore must also notify the training center.

20. **The correct answer is (D).** Lateness is not tolerated.

21. **The correct answer is (D).** In the first year, you are allowed 25 vacation days. After 1 year of service, you receive 27 days. This answer was not a choice.

22. **The correct answer is (C).** Henry Hansen has followed procedures correctly to step 5. Since the caller does not know the victim, it would be pointless to ask about motive or ask for suggestions as to whom to call for assistance with this particular victim. The next step is to call out the rescue squad.

23. **The correct answer is (B).** This statement includes date, time, place, problem, and action taken. Choices (A) and (C) make assumptions that are not necessarily true. Choice (D) is incomplete.

24. **The correct answer is (C).** Look for the points of agreement. Three callers agree that the man is white, three agree that he is youthful, and all agree that he is wearing a hat and sneakers. It certainly appears that caller (D) simply reversed colors and descriptions. Choice (C) contains all points on which there is agreement.

25. **The correct answer is (D).** The narrative has brought dispatcher Melendez up to step 3. It is his respon-

sibility to locate the nearest squad car and dispatch it to the site.

26. **The correct answer is (B).** This choice combines two steps of the procedure, but since these two steps do indeed follow in rapid succession in this order, the choice is correct.

27. **The correct answer is (C).** While not complete in every detail, this report is quite adequate to direct police to the scene and to tell them what they are looking for. Choice (A) does not even say that the woman is dead, and does not give adequate directions. Choice (B) is inadequate only in that it does not identify the train station. Choice (D) gives no location at all.

28. **The correct answer is (C).** A panhandler at the bus stop presents no emergency. First priority should be given to the dangling wire; it might be a live electric wire.

29. **The correct answer is (C).** Tim Weitz has correctly followed all steps through step 6. Since there is no fire, he must skip over step 7 and ask about the cab. If the cab is only dented, there is no need for a tow truck. The bicycle, even if totally destroyed, does not require a tow truck.

30. **The correct answer is (B).** Jenny Wong must write the address as given and pass it to another operator with the code 202. The code gives notice of the urgency of the matter to the other operator. Wong must maintain contact with the caller to distract her from carrying out her threat.

31. **The correct answer is (B).** Patsy "Boots" Brescia has no arrest record. Fick and Ahern have previous convictions, so they obviously have been previously arrested. Jackson is under arrest right now.

32. **The correct answer is (A).** Patrick Ahern is wanted for kidnapping in California and, if apprehended, may be extradited to California. No mention is made of any other gang member's being wanted by another state.

33. **The correct answer is (C).** Fred Fick's list of convictions does not include robbery.

34. **The correct answer is (C).** A person who stands 6 feet, 2 inches, yet weighs only 145 pounds, is tall and thin.

35. **The correct answer is (B).** If Patrick Ahern is known to be extremely dangerous when under the influence of drugs, then he must be a user.

36. **The correct answer is (A).** Brescia is a conservative dresser with a swarthy complexion. Fick is the one with a knife scar. We were not told how Brescia got his nickname.

37. **The correct answer is (C).** According to the information provided, the address or location is the first thing to ask.

38. **The correct answer is (A).** According to the information provided, your next course of action is to find out how long the alarm has been ringing.

39. **The correct answer is (B).** According to the information provided, the last thing you need to know is the name and address of the caller.

40. **The correct answer is (D).** Rules are rules. Even though Marisol Gonzalez may have been perfectly able to handle this caller and perfectly correct in her choice of referral, she was not permitted to carry through with this call.

41. **The correct answer is (C).** Even though this report neglects the fact that the car had out-of-state plates, it is clearly the most complete and accurate. Choice (D) identifies the witness

by name and address but does not give the location of the accident.

42. **The correct answer is (B).** A boarded-up building *should* be empty, but squatters often take advantage of such shelter. There is a real possibility that someone may be trapped inside. The question at step 5 is a very important one and must not be overlooked.

43. **The correct answer is (D).** Choose the answer through elimination. Color is not the determinant; people's descriptions of colors vary. However, Ford and Mercury are built by the same company, and three witnesses agree that it was one of these two makes, so eliminate the Buick in choice (B). Three witnesses agree that it was a 2-door car, so eliminate choice (C). You are left with choices (A) and (D). The plate numbers are similar. Two witnesses identified the plate as being from New Jersey, so Mullins should go with choice (D).

44. **The correct answer is (C).** With important information in hand, the operator must transmit all details to police and emergency medical services. The police or ambulance crew will take over notifying the receiving hospital of unique circumstances.

45. **The correct answer is (B).** It is important that the right name be connected with the right address, the location of the occurrence be reported accurately, and the dog be described as completely as possible.

46. **The correct answer is (A).** To be useful, the information must be organized, complete, and correct.

47. **The correct answer is (C).** An open question such as "What do they look like?" satisfies the requirement of 3a and helps the operator determine if this is a dangerous delusion. If the caller reports that there are 8 little green men, each 2 feet high and waving a flag, there need be less concern than if the caller "sees" 15 creatures that look like gorillas and are carrying machine guns.

48. **The correct answer is (C).** Operators should be aware that not all calls to 911 represent an emergency. Police are not elevator repairmen. If the elevator is not working in an hour, the police still can't help. The superintendent or landlord is responsible for repairs to the building. A professional operator does not hang up on a caller, regardless of the nature of the call.

49. **The correct answer is (B).** Choice (D) is also accurate, but choice (B) is clearer and more easily interpreted. Choices (A) and (C) are garbled.

50. **The correct answer is (D).** You, or the operator next to you, should not be giving out this type of information because this does not involve 911. A parking hotline is set up to give you this information.

51. **The correct answer is (C).** See the second sentence.

52. **The correct answer is (B).** From 8 to 15 years of service, the annual leave is 25 days.

53. **The correct answer is (C).** The sixteenth year, in which leave is earned at the rate of 2-1/4 days per month, comes after fifteen full years.

54. **The correct answer is (B).** See the first sentence of the second paragraph.

55. **The correct answer is (A).** See the last sentence.

56. **The correct answer is (D).** This is a situation for emergency medical services, paramedics, or ambulances. While police might easily be called to

this scene as well, you must consider the question in light of the other answer choices. All others are strictly police concerns.

57. The correct answer is (B). This statement gives a full description of the child and the location at which he was found. None of the others is so complete.

58. The correct answer is (C). According to procedure, the first question to ask is the location of the bank.

59. The correct answer is (D). The bank name is the second thing you should ask for, according to the procedure.

60. The correct answer is (B). According to procedure, after obtaining a description of the bank robber, you then should ask for a description of the weapon(s).

61. The correct answer is (A). The complaint about another operator can only be handled by the supervisor. The hot water call is a nonemergency referral to the buildings department or the health department. Police and emergency squads should be rushed to the scene of the helicopter crash, and the fire department should be dispatched to the toy factory.

62. The correct answer is (C). Sarah Small is calling from her office, and step 5 requires the operator to obtain location and telephone number from which the call is being made. There is no stated qualification that fireboats need not be alerted if there is no fire. Fire could break out at any time. However, it is important for the operator to be able to tell the fireboats that there is no fire right now, so that they can determine which boats and haw many to send.

63. The correct answer is (D). This report is correct and complete. Choice (A) gives neither description nor address; choice (B) misses describing the perpetrator; and choice (C) describes the man incorrectly and omits the location.

64. The correct answer is (B). Since Sirhan Amin is handling another emergency call, the conditions of step 4b lead directly to step 5. Operator Hyacinth must now obtain additional information about the caller and the premises involved. It would be entirely reasonable for her to tell the caller that the police are on the way, but that is not the next step on the mandated order of procedure.

65. The correct answer is (B). The armed robber is only threatening—not hurting—his victims, so they do not require an ambulance. A police car should be sent to intercept the robber. The unconscious jogger clearly requires an ambulance. The child who was fallen from the swing may have sustained a back injury that should be handled only by a trained ambulance crew, not by a police car. Similarly, the eye injury might be a detached retina, so the teenager should be moved with care.

66. The correct answer is (B). This arrangement allows for the best distribution. The activity is taking place in the first and second precincts, so they can spare the greatest number of cars from regular patrol. Those cars could rapidly be redirected if necessary. Choice (A) takes too many cars from regular patrol; choice (C) takes too many from the fourth, which cannot spare them, and none at all from the sixth, which can; Choice (D) makes no sense. The bulk of the protection should be supplied from within the precincts involved.

67. **The correct answer is (C).** This question takes some thinking. Since speed is of the essence and the sixth precinct is far away, eliminate choice (D). Many of the cars from the first and second are guarding the president. Pulling them from the motorcade would take time; sending so many of the remaining cars to one spot would underprotect the remainder of the precincts. The fourth is close by. While the fourth will have difficulty sparing 8 cars, it did start with 40 before the president came to town, so presumably will not be left with no police protection.

68. **The correct answer is (A).** The problem is in the fourth precinct, which is a geographically small area. More cars from the fourth can help to quell the riot. There are no motorcycles in the fourth; however, motorcycles move quickly in narrow areas, so they should be called in. Generally, a riot culminates with a roundup of rioters. Paddy wagons will be needed. Sharpshooters, dogs, and the bomb squad would be inappropriate for a riot. Mounted police are very helpful in crowd control, but they must be planned for well in advance. Mounted police are for parades and rock concerts, not for riots.

69. **The correct answer is (D).** The sixth precinct could use help from the Narcotics Unit, which is based in the fourth, and from the Canine Unit (for sniffing drugs), which is based in the fifth.

70. **The correct answer is (C).** Buildings in the third precinct have doormen and other security. Burglars are least likely to have gained access here.

71. **The correct answer is (D).** There is not much information to report, but it must be totally accurate and complete. Choice (A) makes an unwarranted assumption. We know only how long the timer was set for, not when it was set. Choice (B) makes a similar leap. Choice (C) does not impart the urgency required.

72. **The correct answer is (B).** This disaster requires massive response. The local police precinct cannot handle it alone. Following the prescribed order of calls, Kimberly Kane must next call out the police citywide, then alert hospitals, then bring in the state police for further assistance.

73. **The correct answer is (C).** This is harassment, since no injury was sustained.

74. **The correct answer is (B).** When someone enters a building with the intent to commit a crime, it is a burglary.

75. **The correct answer is (D).** If there is intent to damage another's property, it would be considered criminal mischief.

76. **The correct answer is (A).** Because her property was taken from her by force, it would be considered a robbery.

77. **The correct answer is (B).** The driver avoided payment for services, and thus, it was a theft of service.

78. **The correct answer is (A).** He is harassing her by means of a telecommunications device and, according to the definitions, this is aggravated harassment.

79. **The correct answer is (A).** Choice (B) leaves out the critical time of day; choice (C) omits phone number and address; choice (D) is garbled.

80. **The correct answer is (B).** A fever of 105 degrees constitutes illness. The health department should be notified.

ANSWER SHEET PRACTICE TEST 2

Part One

1. Ⓐ Ⓑ Ⓒ Ⓓ Ⓔ	31. Ⓐ Ⓑ Ⓒ Ⓓ Ⓔ	61. Ⓐ Ⓑ Ⓒ Ⓓ Ⓔ	91. Ⓐ Ⓑ Ⓒ Ⓓ Ⓔ
2. Ⓐ Ⓑ Ⓒ Ⓓ Ⓔ	32. Ⓐ Ⓑ Ⓒ Ⓓ Ⓔ	62. Ⓐ Ⓑ Ⓒ Ⓓ Ⓔ	92. Ⓐ Ⓑ Ⓒ Ⓓ Ⓔ
3. Ⓐ Ⓑ Ⓒ Ⓓ Ⓔ	33. Ⓐ Ⓑ Ⓒ Ⓓ Ⓔ	63. Ⓐ Ⓑ Ⓒ Ⓓ Ⓔ	93. Ⓐ Ⓑ Ⓒ Ⓓ Ⓔ
4. Ⓐ Ⓑ Ⓒ Ⓓ Ⓔ	34. Ⓐ Ⓑ Ⓒ Ⓓ Ⓔ	64. Ⓐ Ⓑ Ⓒ Ⓓ Ⓔ	94. Ⓐ Ⓑ Ⓒ Ⓓ Ⓔ
5. Ⓐ Ⓑ Ⓒ Ⓓ Ⓔ	35. Ⓐ Ⓑ Ⓒ Ⓓ Ⓔ	65. Ⓐ Ⓑ Ⓒ Ⓓ Ⓔ	95. Ⓐ Ⓑ Ⓒ Ⓓ Ⓔ
6. Ⓐ Ⓑ Ⓒ Ⓓ Ⓔ	36. Ⓐ Ⓑ Ⓒ Ⓓ Ⓔ	66. Ⓐ Ⓑ Ⓒ Ⓓ Ⓔ	96. Ⓐ Ⓑ Ⓒ Ⓓ Ⓔ
7. Ⓐ Ⓑ Ⓒ Ⓓ Ⓔ	37. Ⓐ Ⓑ Ⓒ Ⓓ Ⓔ	67. Ⓐ Ⓑ Ⓒ Ⓓ Ⓔ	97. Ⓐ Ⓑ Ⓒ Ⓓ Ⓔ
8. Ⓐ Ⓑ Ⓒ Ⓓ Ⓔ	38. Ⓐ Ⓑ Ⓒ Ⓓ Ⓔ	68. Ⓐ Ⓑ Ⓒ Ⓓ Ⓔ	98. Ⓐ Ⓑ Ⓒ Ⓓ Ⓔ
9. Ⓐ Ⓑ Ⓒ Ⓓ Ⓔ	39. Ⓐ Ⓑ Ⓒ Ⓓ Ⓔ	69. Ⓐ Ⓑ Ⓒ Ⓓ Ⓔ	99. Ⓐ Ⓑ Ⓒ Ⓓ Ⓔ
10. Ⓐ Ⓑ Ⓒ Ⓓ Ⓔ	40. Ⓐ Ⓑ Ⓒ Ⓓ Ⓔ	70. Ⓐ Ⓑ Ⓒ Ⓓ Ⓔ	100. Ⓐ Ⓑ Ⓒ Ⓓ Ⓔ
11. Ⓐ Ⓑ Ⓒ Ⓓ Ⓔ	41. Ⓐ Ⓑ Ⓒ Ⓓ Ⓔ	71. Ⓐ Ⓑ Ⓒ Ⓓ Ⓔ	101. Ⓐ Ⓑ Ⓒ Ⓓ Ⓔ
12. Ⓐ Ⓑ Ⓒ Ⓓ Ⓔ	42. Ⓐ Ⓑ Ⓒ Ⓓ Ⓔ	72. Ⓐ Ⓑ Ⓒ Ⓓ Ⓔ	102. Ⓐ Ⓑ Ⓒ Ⓓ Ⓔ
13. Ⓐ Ⓑ Ⓒ Ⓓ Ⓔ	43. Ⓐ Ⓑ Ⓒ Ⓓ Ⓔ	73. Ⓐ Ⓑ Ⓒ Ⓓ Ⓔ	103. Ⓐ Ⓑ Ⓒ Ⓓ Ⓔ
14. Ⓐ Ⓑ Ⓒ Ⓓ Ⓔ	44. Ⓐ Ⓑ Ⓒ Ⓓ Ⓔ	74. Ⓐ Ⓑ Ⓒ Ⓓ Ⓔ	104. Ⓐ Ⓑ Ⓒ Ⓓ Ⓔ
15. Ⓐ Ⓑ Ⓒ Ⓓ Ⓔ	45. Ⓐ Ⓑ Ⓒ Ⓓ Ⓔ	75. Ⓐ Ⓑ Ⓒ Ⓓ Ⓔ	105. Ⓐ Ⓑ Ⓒ Ⓓ Ⓔ
16. Ⓐ Ⓑ Ⓒ Ⓓ Ⓔ	46. Ⓐ Ⓑ Ⓒ Ⓓ Ⓔ	76. Ⓐ Ⓑ Ⓒ Ⓓ Ⓔ	106. Ⓐ Ⓑ Ⓒ Ⓓ Ⓔ
17. Ⓐ Ⓑ Ⓒ Ⓓ Ⓔ	47. Ⓐ Ⓑ Ⓒ Ⓓ Ⓔ	77. Ⓐ Ⓑ Ⓒ Ⓓ Ⓔ	107. Ⓐ Ⓑ Ⓒ Ⓓ Ⓔ
18. Ⓐ Ⓑ Ⓒ Ⓓ Ⓔ	48. Ⓐ Ⓑ Ⓒ Ⓓ Ⓔ	78. Ⓐ Ⓑ Ⓒ Ⓓ Ⓔ	108. Ⓐ Ⓑ Ⓒ Ⓓ Ⓔ
19. Ⓐ Ⓑ Ⓒ Ⓓ Ⓔ	49. Ⓐ Ⓑ Ⓒ Ⓓ Ⓔ	79. Ⓐ Ⓑ Ⓒ Ⓓ Ⓔ	109. Ⓐ Ⓑ Ⓒ Ⓓ Ⓔ
20. Ⓐ Ⓑ Ⓒ Ⓓ Ⓔ	50. Ⓐ Ⓑ Ⓒ Ⓓ Ⓔ	80. Ⓐ Ⓑ Ⓒ Ⓓ Ⓔ	110. Ⓐ Ⓑ Ⓒ Ⓓ Ⓔ
21. Ⓐ Ⓑ Ⓒ Ⓓ Ⓔ	51. Ⓐ Ⓑ Ⓒ Ⓓ Ⓔ	81. Ⓐ Ⓑ Ⓒ Ⓓ Ⓔ	111. Ⓐ Ⓑ Ⓒ Ⓓ Ⓔ
22. Ⓐ Ⓑ Ⓒ Ⓓ Ⓔ	52. Ⓐ Ⓑ Ⓒ Ⓓ Ⓔ	82. Ⓐ Ⓑ Ⓒ Ⓓ Ⓔ	112. Ⓐ Ⓑ Ⓒ Ⓓ Ⓔ
23. Ⓐ Ⓑ Ⓒ Ⓓ Ⓔ	53. Ⓐ Ⓑ Ⓒ Ⓓ Ⓔ	83. Ⓐ Ⓑ Ⓒ Ⓓ Ⓔ	113. Ⓐ Ⓑ Ⓒ Ⓓ Ⓔ
24. Ⓐ Ⓑ Ⓒ Ⓓ Ⓔ	54. Ⓐ Ⓑ Ⓒ Ⓓ Ⓔ	84. Ⓐ Ⓑ Ⓒ Ⓓ Ⓔ	114. Ⓐ Ⓑ Ⓒ Ⓓ Ⓔ
25. Ⓐ Ⓑ Ⓒ Ⓓ Ⓔ	55. Ⓐ Ⓑ Ⓒ Ⓓ Ⓔ	85. Ⓐ Ⓑ Ⓒ Ⓓ Ⓔ	115. Ⓐ Ⓑ Ⓒ Ⓓ Ⓔ
26. Ⓐ Ⓑ Ⓒ Ⓓ Ⓔ	56. Ⓐ Ⓑ Ⓒ Ⓓ Ⓔ	86. Ⓐ Ⓑ Ⓒ Ⓓ Ⓔ	116. Ⓐ Ⓑ Ⓒ Ⓓ Ⓔ
27. Ⓐ Ⓑ Ⓒ Ⓓ Ⓔ	57. Ⓐ Ⓑ Ⓒ Ⓓ Ⓔ	87. Ⓐ Ⓑ Ⓒ Ⓓ Ⓔ	117. Ⓐ Ⓑ Ⓒ Ⓓ Ⓔ
28. Ⓐ Ⓑ Ⓒ Ⓓ Ⓔ	58. Ⓐ Ⓑ Ⓒ Ⓓ Ⓔ	88. Ⓐ Ⓑ Ⓒ Ⓓ Ⓔ	118. Ⓐ Ⓑ Ⓒ Ⓓ Ⓔ
29. Ⓐ Ⓑ Ⓒ Ⓓ Ⓔ	59. Ⓐ Ⓑ Ⓒ Ⓓ Ⓔ	89. Ⓐ Ⓑ Ⓒ Ⓓ Ⓔ	119. Ⓐ Ⓑ Ⓒ Ⓓ Ⓔ
30. Ⓐ Ⓑ Ⓒ Ⓓ Ⓔ	60. Ⓐ Ⓑ Ⓒ Ⓓ Ⓔ	90. Ⓐ Ⓑ Ⓒ Ⓓ Ⓔ	120. Ⓐ Ⓑ Ⓒ Ⓓ Ⓔ

ANSWER SHEET PRACTICE TEST 2

Part Two

1. Ⓐ Ⓑ Ⓒ Ⓓ Ⓔ	24. Ⓐ Ⓑ Ⓒ Ⓓ Ⓔ	47. Ⓐ Ⓑ Ⓒ Ⓓ Ⓔ	70. Ⓐ Ⓑ Ⓒ Ⓓ Ⓔ
2. Ⓐ Ⓑ Ⓒ Ⓓ Ⓔ	25. Ⓐ Ⓑ Ⓒ Ⓓ Ⓔ	48. Ⓐ Ⓑ Ⓒ Ⓓ Ⓔ	71. Ⓐ Ⓑ Ⓒ Ⓓ Ⓔ
3. Ⓐ Ⓑ Ⓒ Ⓓ Ⓔ	26. Ⓐ Ⓑ Ⓒ Ⓓ Ⓔ	49. Ⓐ Ⓑ Ⓒ Ⓓ Ⓔ	72. Ⓐ Ⓑ Ⓒ Ⓓ Ⓔ
4. Ⓐ Ⓑ Ⓒ Ⓓ Ⓔ	27. Ⓐ Ⓑ Ⓒ Ⓓ Ⓔ	50. Ⓐ Ⓑ Ⓒ Ⓓ Ⓔ	73. Ⓐ Ⓑ Ⓒ Ⓓ Ⓔ
5. Ⓐ Ⓑ Ⓒ Ⓓ Ⓔ	28. Ⓐ Ⓑ Ⓒ Ⓓ Ⓔ	51. Ⓐ Ⓑ Ⓒ Ⓓ Ⓔ	74. Ⓐ Ⓑ Ⓒ Ⓓ Ⓔ
6. Ⓐ Ⓑ Ⓒ Ⓓ Ⓔ	29. Ⓐ Ⓑ Ⓒ Ⓓ Ⓔ	52. Ⓐ Ⓑ Ⓒ Ⓓ Ⓔ	75. Ⓐ Ⓑ Ⓒ Ⓓ Ⓔ
7. Ⓐ Ⓑ Ⓒ Ⓓ Ⓔ	30. Ⓐ Ⓑ Ⓒ Ⓓ Ⓔ	53. Ⓐ Ⓑ Ⓒ Ⓓ Ⓔ	76. Ⓐ Ⓑ Ⓒ Ⓓ Ⓔ
8. Ⓐ Ⓑ Ⓒ Ⓓ Ⓔ	31. Ⓐ Ⓑ Ⓒ Ⓓ Ⓔ	54. Ⓐ Ⓑ Ⓒ Ⓓ Ⓔ	77. Ⓐ Ⓑ Ⓒ Ⓓ Ⓔ
9. Ⓐ Ⓑ Ⓒ Ⓓ Ⓔ	32. Ⓐ Ⓑ Ⓒ Ⓓ Ⓔ	55. Ⓐ Ⓑ Ⓒ Ⓓ Ⓔ	78. Ⓐ Ⓑ Ⓒ Ⓓ Ⓔ
10. Ⓐ Ⓑ Ⓒ Ⓓ Ⓔ	33. Ⓐ Ⓑ Ⓒ Ⓓ Ⓔ	56. Ⓐ Ⓑ Ⓒ Ⓓ Ⓔ	79. Ⓐ Ⓑ Ⓒ Ⓓ Ⓔ
11. Ⓐ Ⓑ Ⓒ Ⓓ Ⓔ	34. Ⓐ Ⓑ Ⓒ Ⓓ Ⓔ	57. Ⓐ Ⓑ Ⓒ Ⓓ Ⓔ	80. Ⓐ Ⓑ Ⓒ Ⓓ Ⓔ
12. Ⓐ Ⓑ Ⓒ Ⓓ Ⓔ	35. Ⓐ Ⓑ Ⓒ Ⓓ Ⓔ	58. Ⓐ Ⓑ Ⓒ Ⓓ Ⓔ	81. Ⓐ Ⓑ Ⓒ Ⓓ Ⓔ
13. Ⓐ Ⓑ Ⓒ Ⓓ Ⓔ	36. Ⓐ Ⓑ Ⓒ Ⓓ Ⓔ	59. Ⓐ Ⓑ Ⓒ Ⓓ Ⓔ	82. Ⓐ Ⓑ Ⓒ Ⓓ Ⓔ
14. Ⓐ Ⓑ Ⓒ Ⓓ Ⓔ	37. Ⓐ Ⓑ Ⓒ Ⓓ Ⓔ	60. Ⓐ Ⓑ Ⓒ Ⓓ Ⓔ	83. Ⓐ Ⓑ Ⓒ Ⓓ Ⓔ
15. Ⓐ Ⓑ Ⓒ Ⓓ Ⓔ	38. Ⓐ Ⓑ Ⓒ Ⓓ Ⓔ	61. Ⓐ Ⓑ Ⓒ Ⓓ Ⓔ	84. Ⓐ Ⓑ Ⓒ Ⓓ Ⓔ
16. Ⓐ Ⓑ Ⓒ Ⓓ Ⓔ	39. Ⓐ Ⓑ Ⓒ Ⓓ Ⓔ	62. Ⓐ Ⓑ Ⓒ Ⓓ Ⓔ	85. Ⓐ Ⓑ Ⓒ Ⓓ Ⓔ
17. Ⓐ Ⓑ Ⓒ Ⓓ Ⓔ	40. Ⓐ Ⓑ Ⓒ Ⓓ Ⓔ	63. Ⓐ Ⓑ Ⓒ Ⓓ Ⓔ	86. Ⓐ Ⓑ Ⓒ Ⓓ Ⓔ
18. Ⓐ Ⓑ Ⓒ Ⓓ Ⓔ	41. Ⓐ Ⓑ Ⓒ Ⓓ Ⓔ	64. Ⓐ Ⓑ Ⓒ Ⓓ Ⓔ	87. Ⓐ Ⓑ Ⓒ Ⓓ Ⓔ
19. Ⓐ Ⓑ Ⓒ Ⓓ Ⓔ	42. Ⓐ Ⓑ Ⓒ Ⓓ Ⓔ	65. Ⓐ Ⓑ Ⓒ Ⓓ Ⓔ	88. Ⓐ Ⓑ Ⓒ Ⓓ Ⓔ
20. Ⓐ Ⓑ Ⓒ Ⓓ Ⓔ	43. Ⓐ Ⓑ Ⓒ Ⓓ Ⓔ	66. Ⓐ Ⓑ Ⓒ Ⓓ Ⓔ	89. Ⓐ Ⓑ Ⓒ Ⓓ Ⓔ
21. Ⓐ Ⓑ Ⓒ Ⓓ Ⓔ	44. Ⓐ Ⓑ Ⓒ Ⓓ Ⓔ	67. Ⓐ Ⓑ Ⓒ Ⓓ Ⓔ	90. Ⓐ Ⓑ Ⓒ Ⓓ Ⓔ
22. Ⓐ Ⓑ Ⓒ Ⓓ Ⓔ	45. Ⓐ Ⓑ Ⓒ Ⓓ Ⓔ	68. Ⓐ Ⓑ Ⓒ Ⓓ Ⓔ	
23. Ⓐ Ⓑ Ⓒ Ⓓ Ⓔ	46. Ⓐ Ⓑ Ⓒ Ⓓ Ⓔ	69. Ⓐ Ⓑ Ⓒ Ⓓ Ⓔ	

FOLLOWING ORAL DIRECTIONS: WORKSHEET

25 Minutes

Directions: While listening carefully to each set of instructions, mark each item on this worksheet as directed. Then complete each question by marking the answer sheet as directed. For each answer, you will darken the answer for a number-letter combination. Should you fall behind and miss an instruction, don't be alarmed. Let that one go and listen for the next one. When you start to darken a space number, if you find that you have already darkened another space for that number, either erase the first mark and darken the space for the new combination or let the first mark stay and do not darken a space for the new combination. Write with a pencil that has a clean eraser. When you finish, you should have no more than one space darkened for each number.

1.   59   35   62   58   8

2.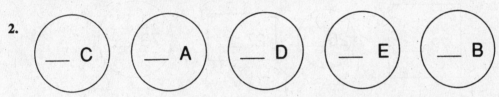

3.   15 _____   20 _____

4.
| 83 __ | 37 __ | 36 __ | CURE DAMP BEAR |

5.   A   C   B   A   B   D   C   E   D

6.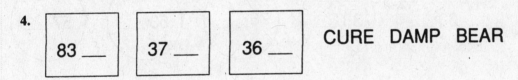

7.   51 _____   69 _____   50 _____

8.

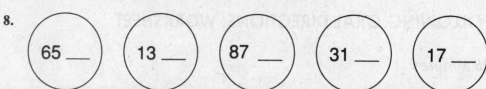

65 ___   13 ___   87 ___   31 ___   17 ___

9.

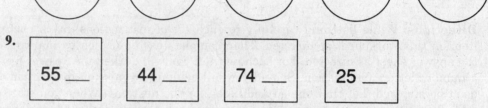

55 ___   44 ___   74 ___   25 ___

10.   40   85   17   87   52   55   80   45   75

11.

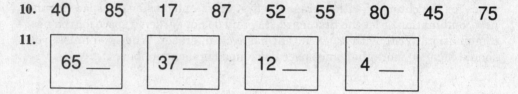

65 ___   37 ___   12 ___   4 ___

12.   X O O O X O O X X O X O X

13.

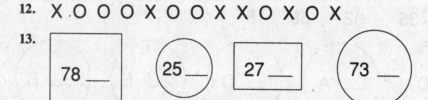

78 ___   25 ___   27 ___   73 ___

14.   88   2   69   84   34

15.

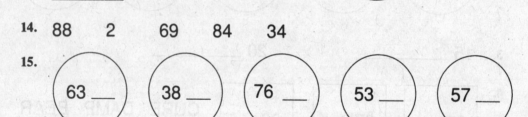

63 ___   38 ___   76 ___   53 ___   57 ___

16.

| 435 ___ B | 466 ___ C | 474 ___ E | 467 ___ A | 489 ___ D |

17.   79 _____   39 _____

18.

| ___ C | ___ E | ___ A | ___ D | ___ B |

Practice Test 2

Part One

120 Questions • 150 minutes

Directions: Choose the best answer to each question and darken its letter on your answer sheet.

1. FLEXIBLE means most nearly
   (A) breakable.
   (B) flammable.
   (C) pliable.
   (D) weak.

2. OPTION means most nearly
   (A) use.
   (B) choice.
   (C) value.
   (D) blame.

3. To VERIFY means most nearly to
   (A) examine.
   (B) explain.
   (C) confirm.
   (D) guarantee.

4. INDOLENT means most nearly
   (A) moderate.
   (B) hopeless.
   (C) selfish.
   (D) lazy.

5. RESPIRATION means most nearly
   (A) recovery.
   (B) breathing.
   (C) pulsation.
   (D) sweating.

Directions: Find the correct spelling of the word, and darken the proper answer space. If no suggested spelling is correct, darken space (E).

6. (A) corregated
   (B) corrigated
   (C) corrugated
   (D) corriegated
   (E) none of these

7. (A) accumalation
   (B) accumulation
   (C) accumullation
   (D) accumilation
   (E) none of these

8. (A) consumation
   (B) consumeation
   (C) consummation
   (D) consummacion
   (E) none of these

9. (A) retorical
   (B) rhetorrical
   (C) rehtoricle
   (D) retoricle
   (E) none of these

10. (A) hieght
    (B) height
    (C) heighth
    (D) hieghth
    (E) none of these

Directions: Compare the names or numbers and darken on your answer sheet the letter

(A) if ALL THREE names or numbers are exactly ALIKE.

(B) if only the FIRST and SECOND names or numbers are exactly ALIKE.

(C) if only the FIRST and THIRD names or numbers are exactly ALIKE.

(D) if only the SECOND and THIRD names or numbers are exactly ALIKE.

(E) if ALL THREE names or numbers are DIFFERENT.

11.	Robert F. Taft	Robert F. Taft	Robert P. Taft
12.	Eduardo Ingles	Eduardo Inglese	Eduardo Inglese
13.	Roger T. DeAngelis	Roger T. D'Angelis	Roger T. DeAngeles
14.	7692138	7692138	7692138
15.	2633342	2633432	2363342

Directions: Choose the best answer to each question, and darken its letter on your answer sheet.

16. VIGILANT means most nearly
    (A) sensible.
    (B) watchful.
    (C) suspicious.
    (D) restless.
    (E) unhappy.

17. VEGETATION means most nearly
    (A) food.
    (B) plant life.
    (C) moisture.
    (D) bird life.
    (E) mixture.

18. MARSHY means most nearly
    (A) swampy.
    (B) sandy.
    (C) wooded.
    (D) rocky.
    (E) soft.

19. INCIDENTAL means most nearly
    (A) independent.
    (B) needless.
    (C) infrequent.
    (D) casual.
    (E) happening.

20. PREFACE means most nearly
    (A) title page.
    (B) introduction.
    (C) table of contents.
    (D) appendix.
    (E) justification.

Directions: Find the correct spelling of the word, and darken the proper answer space. If no suggesting spelling is correct, darken space (E).

21. (A) faciliatate
    (B) facilitate
    (C) faceilitate
    (D) fasilitate
    (E) none of these

22. (A) proletarian
    (B) prolatarian
    (C) proleterian
    (D) prolaterian
    (E) none of these

23. (A) occasionally
    (B) occassionally
    (C) ocasionally

    (D) occasionaly
    (E) none of these

24. (A) esential
    (B) essential
    (C) essencial
    (D) essensial
    (E) none of these

25. (A) ommision
    (B) omission
    (C) ommission
    (D) omitsion
    (E) none of these

Directions: Compare the names or numbers and darken:

(A) if ALL THREE names or numbers are exactly ALIKE.

(B) if only the FIRST and SECOND names or numbers are exactly ALIKE.

(C) if only the FIRST and THIRD names or numbers are exactly ALIKE.

(D) if only the SECOND and THIRD names or numbers are exactly ALIKE.

(E) if ALL THREE names or numbers are DIFFERENT.

26.	Yoshihito Saito	Yoshito Saito	Yoshihito Saito
27.	Helmut V. Lochner	Helmut V. Lockner	Helmut W. Lochner
28.	2454803　　2548403	2454803	
29.	9670243　　9670423	9670423	
30.	2789350　　2789350	2798350	

Directions: Read the paragraph and the five suggested answers to the question. Choose the answer that is best supported by the paragraph, and darken the proper space on the answer sheet.

31. Through advertising, manufacturers exercise a high degree of control over consumers' desires. However, the manufacturer assumes enormous risks in attempting to predict what consumers will want, and in producing goods in quantity and distributing them in advance of final selection by the consumers.

The paragraph best supports the statement that manufacturers

(A) can eliminate the risk of overproduction by advertising.

(B) distribute goods directly to the consumers.

(C) must depend upon the final consumers for the success of their undertakings.

(D) can predict with great accuracy the success of any product they put on the market.

(E) can produce whatever consumers want, whenever they want.

32. Economy once in a while is just not enough. I expect to find it at every level of responsibility, from cabinet member to the newest and youngest recruit. Controlling waste is something like bailing out a boat; you have to keep at it. I have no intention of easing up on my insistence on getting a dollar's worth of value for each dollar we spend.

The paragraph best supports the statement that

(A) we need not be concerned about items that cost less than a dollar.

(B) it is advisable to buy the cheaper of two items.

(C) the responsibility of economy is greater at high levels than at low levels.

(D) economy is a continual responsibility.

(E) bailing out a boat is economical.

33. What constitutes skill in any line of work is not always easy to determine; economy of time must be carefully distinguished from economy of energy, as the quickest method may require the greatest expenditure of muscular effort, and it may not be essential or at all desirable.

The paragraph best supports the statement that

(A) the most efficiently executed task is not always the one done in the shortest time.

(B) energy and time cannot both be conserved in performing a single task.

(C) a task is well done when it is performed in the shortest time.

(D) skill in performing a task should not be acquired at the expense of time.

(E) more effort and time put into a task will guarantee success.

34. It is a common assumption that city directories are prepared and published by the cities concerned. However, the directory business is as much a private business as is the publishing of dictionaries and encyclopedias. The companies financing the publication make their profits through the sales of the directories themselves and through the advertising in them.

The paragraph best supports the statement that

(A) the publication of a city directory is a commercial enterprise.

(B) the size of a city directory limits the space devoted to advertising.

(C) many city directories are published by dictionary and encyclopedia concerns.

(D) city directories are sold at cost to local residents and business people.

(E) city directories are published by nonprofit organizations.

35. It is difficult to distinguish between bookkeeping and accounting. In attempts to do so, bookkeeping is called the art, and accounting the science, of recording business transactions. Bookkeeping gives the history of the business in a systematic manner and accounting classifies, analyzes, and interprets the facts thus recorded.

The paragraph best supports the statement that

(A) accounting is less systematic than bookkeeping.

(B) accounting and bookkeeping are closely related.

(C) bookkeeping and accounting cannot be distinguished from one another.

(D) bookkeeping has been superseded by accounting.

(E) science is more important than art, especially in business.

36. "White collar" is a term used to describe one of the largest groups of workers in American industry and trade. It distinguishes those who work with the pencil and the mind from those who depend on their hands and the machine. It suggests occupations in which physical exertion and handling of materials are not primary features of the job.

The paragraph best supports the statement that "white collar" workers are

(A) not so strong physically as those who work with their hands.

(B) those who supervise workers handling materials.

(C) all whose work is entirely indoors.

(D) not likely to use heavy machines so much as are other groups of workers.

(E) a rapidly expanding minority in American labor.

37. Any business not provided with capable substitutes to fill all-important positions is a weak business. Therefore, a supervisor should train each worker not only to perform his or her own particular duties but also to do those of two or three positions.

The paragraph best supports the statement that

(A) dependence on substitutes is a sign of a weak organization.

(B) training will improve the strongest organization.

(C) the supervisor should be the most expert at any particular job under him or her.

(D) vacancies in vital positions should be provided for in advance.

(E) a weak business should hire more substitutes.

38. Some fire-resistant buildings, although wholly constructed of materials that will not burn, may be completely gutted by the spread of fire through their contents by way of hallways and other openings. They may even suffer serious structural damage by the collapse of metal beams and columns.

The paragraph best supports the statement that some fire-resistant buildings

(A) can be damaged seriously by fire.

(B) have specially constructed halls and doors.

(C) afford less protection to their contents than would ordinary buildings.

(D) will burn readily.

(E) are not structurally sound.

39. According to Congressman Johnson, "Too much of our taxpayers' money is spent on the rehabilitation of drug addicts. This is no way to solve the problem. Most of the people who spend time in rehabilitation centers go right back to taking narcotics after they leave. Instead of wasting money on rehabilitation, we should be using it to get rid of the drug peddlers."

The paragraph best supports the statement that Congressman Johnson implies that the way to solve the problem of drug addiction is to

(A) create more rehabilitation centers.

(B) do away with rehabilitation centers.

(C) put drug addicts in jail.

(D) tax drug peddlers.

(E) eliminate the source of the drugs.

40. When gas is leaking, any spark or sudden flame can ignite it. This can create a "flashback," which burns off the gas in a quick puff of smoke and flame. But the real danger is in a large leak that can cause an explosion.

The paragraph best supports the statement that the real danger from leaking gas is a(n)

(A) flashback.

(B) puff of smoke and flame.

(C) explosion.

(D) spark.

(E) ignition.

41. The indiscriminate or continual use of any drug without medical supervision is dangerous. Even drugs considered harmless may result in chronic poisoning if used for a period of years. Prescriptions should not be refilled without consulting your doctor. A given amount was prescribed in order to limit your use of the drug to a certain time. Never use a drug prescribed for someone else just because your symptoms appear similar. There may be differences, apparent to an expert but hidden from you, that indicate an entirely different ailment requiring different medication.

The paragraph best supports the statement that

(A) the use of drugs is very dangerous.

(B) if a physician prescribes a drug, it is safe to refill the prescription.

(C) people with similar symptoms are usually suffering from the same ailment.

(D) a drug considered harmless may be dangerous if taken over a long period of time without supervision.

(E) doctors always limit the use of prescription drugs to a definite period of time.

42. Civilization started to move ahead more rapidly when people freed themselves of the shackles that restricted their search for the truth.

The statement best supports the idea that the progress of civilization

(A) came as a result of people's dislike for obstacles.

(B) did not begin until restrictions on learning were removed.

(C) has been aided by people's efforts to find the truth.

(D) is based on continually increasing efforts.

(E) was enhanced when slavery was abolished.

43. Federal investigators must direct their whole effort toward success in their work. If they wish to succeed in each investigation, their work will be by no means easy, smooth, or peaceful; on the contrary, they will have to devote themselves completely and continuously to a task that requires all their ability.

The paragraph best supports the statement that an investigator's success depends most upon

(A) ambition to advance rapidly in the service.

(B) persistence in the face of difficulty.

(C) training and experience.

(D) willingness to obey orders without delay.

(E) superior ability.

44. Since the government can spend only what it obtains from the people and this amount is ultimately limited by their capacity and willingness to pay taxes, it is very important that the people be given full information about the work of the government.

The paragraph best supports the statement that

(A) governmental employees should be trained not only in their own work, but also in how to perform the duties of other employees in their agency.

(B) taxation by the government rests upon the consent of the people.

(C) the release of full information on the work of the government will increase the efficiency of governmental operations.

(D) the work of the government, in recent years has been restricted because of reduced tax collections.

(E) the foundation of our government is abhorrence of the principle of taxation without representation.

45. Foreign-born adults hold on to the habits, preferences, and loyalties of their homelands. Their speech, if they learn English at all, reflects the accent and idiom of their land of origin. Children, on the other hand, acquire English without a trace of accent and, through their playmates and school life, learn to prefer American clothing and mannerisms to the customs and dress of their parents.

The paragraph best supports the statement that

(A) American customs are more complicated that the customs of other countries.

(B) immigrant children do not respect their parents.

(C) it is nearly impossible for foreigners to adopt American ways.

(D) foreign-born adults seldom learn English.

(E) foreign-born children become Americanized more quickly than their parents.

Directions: Choose the answer to each question, and darken its letter on your answer sheet.

46. ANNOUNCEMENT means most nearly

(A) a person who announces.

(B) yearly grant.

(C) irritate.

(D) newscaster.

(E) public notice.

47. PREVENT means most nearly

(A) allow.

(B) suggest.

(C) hinder.

(D) urge.

(E) annoy.

48. NOTIFY means most nearly
   (A) intention.
   (B) inform.
   (C) image.
   (D) visible.
   (E) trusting.

49. IRRITATING means most nearly
   (A) nervous.
   (B) unsuitable.
   (C) annoying.
   (D) noisy.
   (E) expanding.

50. CONCISELY means most nearly
   (A) accurately.
   (B) briefly.
   (C) full.
   (D) officially.
   (E) quickly.

Directions: Choose the word in each group of four that is spelled correctly, and darken its letter on your answer sheet. If no word is spelled correctly, darken (E).

51. (A) hoyste
   (B) inteference
   (C) spaciul
   (D) winsome
   (E) none of these

52. (A) suficient
   (B) wheather
   (C) actueally
   (D) minimum
   (E) none of these

53. (A) volentary
   (B) syllabus
   (C) embodeying
   (D) pertanent
   (E) none of these

54. (A) ordineraly
   (B) comunity
   (C) enfasis
   (D) advant
   (E) none of these

55. (A) terriffic
   (B) expedient
   (C) eigth
   (D) inocence
   (E) none of these

practice test

Directions: Compare the names or numbers and darken on your answer sheet the letter

(A) if ALL THREE names or numbers are exactly ALIKE.

(B) if only the FIRST and SECOND names or numbers are exactly ALIKE.

(C) if only the FIRST and THIRD names or numbers are exactly ALIKE.

(D) if only the SECOND and THIRD names or numbers are exactly ALIKE.

(E) if ALL THREE names or numbers are DIFFERENT.

56. 1357901   1357910   1358910

57. ARX5B36   ARX5B36   AR5XB36

58. Frederic Mollicone   Frederick Mollicone   Frederic Mollicone

59. David C. Routzon   David E. Routzon   David C. Routzron

60. Arthur R. Stanick   Arthur R. Stanic   Arthur R. Stanich

Directions: Choose the best answer to each question, and darken its letter on your answer sheet.

61. SHORE means most nearly
    (A) gulf.
    (B) coast.
    (C) inlet.
    (D) beach.
    (E) edge.

62. AIM means most nearly
    (A) bulls-eye.
    (B) goal.
    (C) duty.
    (D) promise.
    (E) trajectory.

63. ACUTE means most nearly
    (A) dull.
    (B) slight.
    (C) alarming.
    (D) sharp.
    (E) charming.

64. COMPEL means most nearly
    (A) tempt.
    (B) persuade.
    (C) force.
    (D) disable.
    (E) rate.

65. AROMA means most nearly
    (A) flavor.
    (B) warmth.
    (C) fragrance.
    (D) steam.
    (E) texture.

Directions: Choose the word in each group of four that is spelled correctly and darken its letter on your answer sheet. If no word is spelled correctly, darken (E).

66. (A) unconsiously
    (B) pamflet
    (C) asess
    (D) adjacent
    (E) none of these

67. (A) mortgages
    (B) infalible
    (C) eradecated
    (D) sourse
    (E) none of these

68. (A) predescessor
    (B) obsolete
    (C) unimpared
    (D) sporadicaly
    (E) none of these

69. (A) impenitrable
    (B) recognisable
    (C) paresite
    (D) buisness
    (E) none of these

70. (A) accross
    (B) manefold
    (C) anxieties
    (D) expence
    (E) none of these

Directions: Compare the names or numbers and darken on your answer sheet the letter

(A) if ALL THREE names or numbers are exactly ALIKE.

(B) if only the FIRST and SECOND names or numbers are exactly ALIKE.

(C) if only the FIRST and THIRD names or numbers are exactly ALIKE.

(D) if only the SECOND and THIRD names or numbers are exactly ALIKE.

(E) if ALL THREE names or numbers are DIFFERENT.

71.	Desean Louis Green	DeSean Lewis Greene	Desean Louis Green
72.	Fernando Silva, Jr.	Fernando Silva, Jr.	Fernand Silva, Jr.
73.	PT090901	PT090901	PT1090901
74.	2789327	2879327	2789327
75.	5927681	5927861	5927681

Directions: For questions 76–80, carefully read the rules for use of the community room and the information about the applications that were received on July 1. On the basis of the rules and the facts, determine the disposition of each application. Darken the letter of the answer you choose.

RULES FOR USE OF COMMUNITY ROOM (CR)

Note: Assume that, in order to be granted use of the CR, a tenant group ("TG") must comply fully with all the rules.

Rule 1. The head of the TG must submit a signed application in writing at least 20 days before the date requested.

Rule 2. The application must state the number of persons expected to attend and the general nature, date, and time of the requested use.

Rule 3. Included as part of the application must be a money order in the amount of $25, payable to the housing authority, to help defray the expense of cleanup after the use of the CR.

Rule 4. No TG may have use of the community room for more than six consecutive hours. No use will be permitted between 11 p.m. and 8 a.m.

Rule 5. Provided an application is otherwise acceptable, priority will be granted where applications conflict in the following order: senior citizen TGs, youth TGs, civic TGs, social TGs, athletic TGs.

The following applications were received on July 1:

1. A civic TG's head has sent a signed application, accompanied by a money order for $25, payable to the housing authority, requesting the CR for a political discussion to be attended by 100 people on August 12 from 7 p.m. to 10 p.m.

2. A youth TG's head has sent a signed application, accompanied by his personal check for $25, payable to the housing authority, requesting the CR for a film showing to be attended by 70 people on August 12 from 7:30 p.m. to 11:30 p.m.

3. A senior citizen TG's head has sent a signed application, accompanied by a money order for $25, payable to the housing authority, requesting the CR for a cake sale to be attended by 80 people on July 18 from 2 p.m. to 8:30 p.m.

4. An athletic TG's head has sent a signed application, accompanied by a money order for $25, payable to the housing authority, requesting the CR for a weight-lifting contest to be attended by 50 people on July 31 from 4 p.m. to 7 p.m.

5. A social TG's head has sent a signed application, accompanied by a money order for $25, payable to the housing authority, requesting the CR for a singles' party to be attended by 60 people on July 31 from 2 p.m. to 5 p.m.

76. The first application should be
    (A) granted.
    (B) denied: it does not comply with Rules 1 and 5.
    (C) denied: it does not comply with Rules 2 and 4.
    (D) denied: it does not comply with Rule 3.
    (E) denied: it does not comply with Rules 1 and 4.

77. The second application should be
    (A) granted.
    (B) denied: it does not comply with Rules 1 and 2.
    (C) denied: it does not comply with Rules 3 and 4.
    (D) denied: it does not comply with Rule 5.
    (E) denied: it does not comply with Rule 3.

78. The third application should be
    (A) granted.
    (B) denied: it does not comply with Rules 1 and 4.
    (C) denied: it does not comply with Rules 2 and 5.
    (D) denied: it does not comply with Rule 3.

    (E) denied: it does not comply with Rules 2 and 4.

79. The fourth application should be
    (A) granted.
    (B) denied: it does not comply with Rules 1 and 3.
    (C) denied: it does not comply with Rules 2 and 4.
    (D) denied: it does not comply with Rule 5.
    (E) denied: it does not comply with Rule 2.

80. The fifth application should be
    (A) granted.
    (B) denied: it does not comply with Rule 1.
    (C) denied: it does not comply with Rules 2 and 5.
    (D) denied: it does not comply with Rules 3 and 4.
    (E) denied: it does not comply with Rules 1 and 2.

Directions: For questions 81–83, read the rules governing clinic appointments, and make the decisions required by the questions that follow. Darken the letter of each answer you choose.

RULES GOVERNING CLINIC APPOINTMENTS

1. No more than eight appointments should be scheduled for each three-hour clinic session for each dentist who will be on duty.

2. A new patient's first appointment should allow time for a complete examination by the dentist.

3. Appointments should not be made less than four days apart for any patient without the consent of the dentist.

4. Appointments should be made in person or over the telephone whenever possible, so that the patient may give his or her consent while the appointment is being made. If a request for an appointment is made in any other manner, it must contain a statement of the date(s) and term(s) acceptable to the patient in order to be approved. No patient shall be given an appointment to which he or she does not consent.

5. A card stating the place, date, and time of the appointment shall be given to or mailed to the patient on the same day on which the appointment is made.

6. If a patient fails to keep three appointments in a row, his or her case is to be terminated, and no further appointments are to be made for him or her unless a new authorization is received.

81. A patient calls to request an appointment at a clinic session for which 8 patients are scheduled for each dentist who will be on duty. As the appointments receptionist you should

   (A) give the patient the appointment since he or she has already consented to it.

   (B) tell the patient that he or she cannot be given an appointment at that clinic session.

   (C) give the patient an appointment at another session without his or her consent.

   (D) tell the patient to come in without an appointment and hope for a cancellation.

   (E) ask for authorization to make an appointment for the patient.

82. A patient requests that he be given appointments on three successive days. You must deny this request if

   (A) the schedule for each of those days is already partly filled.

   (B) the dentist has treated the patient only once previously.

   (C) the patient has requested the appointments by mail.

   (D) this is a new patient.

   (E) the dentist does not give his or her consent to the appointments.

83. A patient has failed to keep three successive appointments. You should

   (A) send her a card stating the place, date, and time of the next appointment.

   (B) not give her another appointment without a new authorization.

   (C) give her an emergency appointment.

   (D) not give her another appointment unless she appears in person to make the appointment.

   (E) insist upon payment in advance.

practice test

Directions: Read the following rules governing pharmacists, and answer questions 84–90 as if you were a pharmacist. Darken the letter of your answer choice.

1. No person shall compound or dispense any drug or a prescription in which any drug is stated in a code name or a name not generally recognized in the pharmaceutical profession; nor shall any ingredient be substituted for another in any prescription.

2. Drugs compounded or dispensed on a written prescription shall bear a label containing the name and place of business of the dispenser, the serial number and date of compounding such prescription, the direction for use, and the name of the practitioner. In the case of barbiturates, the label shall contain in addition the name and address of the patient, and—if such a drug was prescribed for an animal—a statement showing the species of the animal.

3. In addition to any other records required to be kept by this article or by any other law, every prescription when filled shall be kept on file by the pharmacist for at least two (2) years and shall be open to inspection by a representative of the Department of Health or such other agency as is authorized by law. Every prescription for a barbiturate shall be endorsed with the name of the compounder of the prescription and, if refilled, the name of the person compounding the prescription at the time of the refilling, together with the date thereof.

84. In labeling a drug dispensed on a written prescription, you must include
   (A) a description of the ingredients.
   (B) a statement of the amount of each ingredient.
   (C) the name of the practitioner.
   (D) the name, address, and telephone number of the pharmacy.
   (E) the age of the patient.

85. A regulation that you must keep in mind is that
   (A) you must not keep prescriptions on file for a period longer than two years.
   (B) if you do not have in stock an ingredient named in a prescription, you may use an equivalent ingredient.
   (C) when filling a prescription for a barbiturate, you should sign your name on the label.

   (D) you must write the directions for use on the label when filling the prescription for a barbiturate.
   (E) code names for drugs must not be disclosed to the public.

86. If you are refilling a prescription for a barbiturate, you should write on the prescription
   (A) the name and address of the pharmacy, the date of the refilling, and the species of the animal.
   (B) the date of the original filling of the prescription, the name of the person who filled it, and the doctor's name.
   (C) the directions for use and the name and address of both doctor and patient.
   (D) the date of inspection by the Department of Health.
   (E) your name and the date.

87. A patient hands you a prescription for an unfamiliar drug. You should
(A) call the Department of Health.
(B) type onto the label the serial number, date of compounding, directions for use, and doctor's name.
(C) substitute a well-known product.
(D) refuse to fill it.
(E) write down the name and address of the patient.

88. The prescription handed you orders barbiturates for a dog. The information you type onto the label must include
(A) the directions for use, your name, and the date.
(B) the name, address, and serial number of the dog.
(C) the doctor's name, directions for use, and designation that the patient is a dog.
(D) the names of the doctor, dog, owner, and pharmacist.
(E) the name of the pharmacist, the date of refilling, and the description of dog by breed.

89. If the drug is not a barbiturate, you need not
(A) sign the prescription.
(B) put directions for use on the label.
(C) assign a serial number to the prescription.
(D) fill it precisely as written.
(E) keep the prescription on file.

90. Every prescription label must include
(A) the name of the substance, the date, and the name of the doctor.
(B) the name and address of the pharmacy, the date, and the directions for use.
(C) the name and address of the pharmacist, the serial number of the prescription, and the name of the doctor.
(D) the name and address of the patient, the date, and the directions for use.
(E) the list of ingredients, the name and address of the pharmacy, the date, and the name of the patient.

Directions: Choose the best answer to each question, and darken its letter on your answer sheet.

91. To ACCENTUATE means most nearly to
(A) modify.
(B) hasten.
(C) sustain.
(D) intensify.

92. BANAL means most nearly
(A) commonplace.
(B) tranquil.
(C) original.
(D) indifferent.

93. INCORRIGIBLE means most nearly
    (A) intolerable.
    (B) retarded.
    (C) irreformable.
    (D) brazen.

94. NOTORIOUS means most nearly
    (A) convicted.
    (B) dangerous.
    (C) well-known.
    (D) escaped.
    (E) decorated.

95. CREVICE means most nearly
    (A) plant.
    (B) uneven spot.
    (C) crack.
    (D) puddle.
    (E) shellfish.

Directions: In each group of words, one word may be spelled incorrectly. Choose the word that is spelled incorrectly, and darken its letter on your answer sheet. If no word is spelled incorrectly, darken (E).

96. (A) executive
    (B) rainbow
    (C) irigation
    (D) multiply
    (E) none of these

97. (A) acquarium
    (B) aerial
    (C) livery
    (D) declaration
    (E) none of these

98. (A) final
    (B) foundation
    (C) hardships
    (D) deoderant
    (E) none of these

99. (A) salary
    (B) weakly
    (C) swallow
    (D) wilderness
    (E) none of these

100. (A) seashore
     (B) picnicking
     (C) chopping
     (D) lipstick
     (E) none of these

Directions: Compare the names or numbers and darken on your answer sheet the letter

(A) if ALL THREE names or numbers are exactly ALIKE.

(B) if only the FIRST and SECOND names or numbers are exactly ALIKE.

(C) if only the FIRST and THIRD names or numbers are exactly ALIKE.

(D) if only the SECOND and THIRD names or numbers are exactly ALIKE.

(E) if ALL THREE names or numbers are DIFFERENT.

101.	Franklin D. Roosevelt	Franklyn D. Roosevelt	Franklin D. Roosevelt
102.	Lambent Forman, M.D.	Lambent Forman, M.D.	Lambent Forman, M.D.
103.	Joseph A. Gurreri	Joseph A. Gurreri	Joseph A. Gurreri
104.	4xy932958	4xy939258	4xy932758
105.	9631695	9636195	9631695

Directions: Choose the best answer to each question, and darken its letter on your answer sheet.

106. UNIFORM means most nearly
(A) increasing.
(B) unchanging.
(C) unusual.
(D) neat.
(E) ignorant.

107. UNITE means most nearly
(A) improve.
(B) serve.
(C) uphold.
(D) combine.
(E) open.

108. GRATITUDE means most nearly
(A) thankfulness.
(B) excitement.
(C) disappointment.
(D) sympathy.
(E) politeness.

109. EMBELLISH means most nearly
(A) exaggerate.
(B) play down.
(C) scrutinize.
(D) facilitate.
(E) sympathize.

110. ASSEMBLE means most nearly
(A) examine carefully.
(B) bring together.
(C) locate.
(D) fill.
(E) make.

Directions: In each group of words, one word may be spelled incorrectly. Choose the word that is spelled incorrectly, and darken its letter on your answer sheet. If no word is spelled incorrectly, darken (E).

111. (A) innate
     (B) cannoneer
     (C) passtime
     (D) auditorium
     (E) none of these

112. (A) hinderance
     (B) offered
     (C) embarrass
     (D) syllabus
     (E) none of these

113. (A) privilege
     (B) pavilion
     (C) underrate
     (D) questionnaire
     (E) none of these

114. (A) dilletante
     (B) liquefy
     (C) physiology
     (D) proscribe
     (E) none of these

115. (A) harass
     (B) vilify
     (C) similar
     (D) superceed
     (E) none of these

Directions: Compare the names or numbers and darken on your answer sheet the letter

   (A) if ALL THREE names or numbers are exactly ALIKE.

   (B) if only the FIRST and SECOND names or numbers are exactly ALIKE.

   (C) if only the FIRST and THIRD names or numbers are exactly ALIKE.

   (D) if only the SECOND and THIRD names or numbers are exactly ALIKE.

   (E) if ALL THREE names or numbers are DIFFERENT.

116.	Sylnette Lynch	Sylnette Lynch	Sylnette Lynch
117.	7370527	7375027	7370537
118.	Zion McKenzie, Jr.	Zion McKenzie, Sr.	Zion MacKenzie, Jr.
119.	2799379	2739779	2799379
120.	J. Randolph Rea	J. Randolph Rea	J. Randolphe Rea

End of Part One

If you finish before time is up, check over your work on this part only.

PART TWO

Total Time: *25 Minutes*

> **Directions:** When you are ready to try this part of the exam, give the following instructions to a friend and have the friend read them aloud to you at 80 words per minute. Do NOT read them to yourself. Your friend will need a watch with a second hand. Listen carefully and do exactly what your friend tells you to do with the worksheet and with the answer sheet. Your friend will tell you some things to do with each item on the worksheet. After each set of instructions, your friend will give you time to mark your answer by darkening a circle on the answer sheet. **Before proceeding further, tear out the worksheet on pages 223–224. Then hand this book to your friend.**

To the Reader: The directions are to be read at the rate of 80 words per minute. Do not read aloud the material that is in parentheses. Once you have begun the test itself, do not repeat any directions. The next three paragraphs consist of approximately 120 words. Read these three paragraphs aloud to the candidate in about one and one-half minutes.

On the job, you will have to listen to directions and then do what you have been told to do. In this test, I will read instructions to you. Try to understand them as I read them; I cannot repeat them. Once we begin, you may not ask any questions until the end of the test.

On the job you won't have to deal with pictures, numbers, and letters like those in the test, but you will have to listen to instructions and follow them. We are using this test to see how well you can follow instructions.

You are to mark your test booklet according to the instructions that I'll read to you. After each set of instructions, I'll give you time to record your answers on the separate answer sheet.

The actual test begins now.

Look at line 1 on your worksheet. (Pause slightly.) Draw a line under the largest number in the line. (Pause 2 seconds.) Now on your answer sheet, find the number under which you just drew a line and darken space "D" as in dog for that number. (Pause 5 seconds.)

Look at line 1 on your worksheet again. (Pause slightly.) Draw two lines under the smallest number in the line. (Pause 2 seconds.) Now on your answer sheet, find the number under which you just drew two lines and darken space "E." (Pause 5 seconds.)

Look at the circles in line 2 on your worksheet. (Pause slightly.) In the second circle, write the answer to this question: How much is 6 plus 4? (Pause 8 seconds.) In the third circle, write the answer to this question: Which of the following numbers is largest: 67, 48, 15, 73, or 61? (Pause 5 seconds.) In the fourth circle, write the answer to this question: How many months are there in a year? (Pause 2 seconds.) Now, on your answer sheet, darken the number-letter combinations that are in the circles in which you wrote. (Pause 10 seconds.)

Look at line 3 on your worksheet. (Pause slightly.) Write the letter "C" on the blank next to the right-hand number. (Pause 2 seconds.) Now on your answer sheet, find the space for the number beside which you wrote and darken space "C." (Pause 5 seconds.)

Now look at line 3 on your worksheet again. (Pause slightly.) Write the letter "B" as in baker on the blank next to the left-hand number. (Pause 2 seconds.) Now on your answer sheet, find the space for the number beside which you just wrote and darken space "B" as in baker. (Pause 5 seconds.)

Look at the boxes and words in line 4 on your worksheet. (Pause slightly.) Write the first letter of the second word in the third box. (Pause 2 seconds.) Write the last letter of the first word in the second box. (Pause 2 seconds.) Write the first letter of the third word in the first box. (Pause 2 seconds.) Now on your answer sheet, darken the space for the number-letter combinations that are in the three boxes in which you just wrote. (Pause 10 seconds.)

Look at the letters on line 5 on your worksheet. (Pause slightly.) Draw a line under the fifth letter on the line. (Pause 2 seconds.) Now on your answer sheet, find the number 56 (pause 2 seconds) and darken the space for the letter under which you drew two lines. (Pause 5 seconds.)

Look again at the letters on line 5 on your worksheet. (Pause slightly.) Draw two lines under the fourth letter in the line. (Pause 2 seconds.) Now on your answer sheet, find the number 66 (pause 2 seconds) and darken the space for the letter under which you drew two lines. (Pause 5 seconds.)

Look at the drawings on line 6 on your worksheet. (Pause slightly.) The four boxes indicate the number of buildings in four different office parks. In the box for the office park with the fewest number of buildings, write an "A." (Pause 2 seconds.) Now on your answer sheet, darken the space for the number-letter combination that is in the box in which you just wrote. (Pause 5 seconds.)

Now look at line 7 on your worksheet. (Pause slightly.) If fall comes before summer, write the letter "B" as in baker on the line next to the middle number. (Pause slightly.) Otherwise, write an "E" on the blank next to the left-hand number. (Pause 5 seconds.) Now on your answer sheet, darken the space for the number-letter combination that you have just written. (Pause 5 seconds.)

Now look at line 8 on your worksheet. (Pause slightly.) Write a "D" as in dog in the circle with the lowest number. (Pause 2 seconds.) Now on your answer sheet, darken the space for the number-letter combination that is in the circle in which you just wrote. (Pause 5 seconds.)

Look at the drawings on line 9 on your worksheet. The four boxes are planes for carrying mail. (Pause slightly.) The plane with the highest number is to be loaded first. Write an "E" in the box with the highest number. (Pause 2 seconds.) Now on your answer sheet, darken the space for the number-letter combination that is in the box in which you just wrote. (Pause 5 seconds.)

Look at line 10 on your worksheet. (Pause slightly.) Draw a line under every number that is more than 35 but less than 55. (Pause 12 seconds.) Now on your answer sheet, for each number under which you drew a line, darken space "A." (Pause 25 seconds.)

Now look again at line 10 on your worksheet. (Pause slightly.) Draw two lines under every number that is more than 55 and less than 80. (Pause 12 seconds.) Now on your answer sheet for each number under which you drew two lines, darken space "C." (Pause 25 seconds.)

Look at line 11 on your worksheet. (Pause slightly.) Write an "E" in the last box. (Pause 2 seconds.) Now on your answer sheet, find the number in that box and darken space "E" for that number. (Pause 5 seconds.)

Look at line 12 on your worksheet. (Pause slightly.) Draw a line under every "X" in the line. (Pause 5 seconds.) Count the number of lines that you have drawn, add 3, and write that number at the end of the line. (Pause 5 seconds.) Now on your answer sheet, find that number and darken space "E" for that number. (Pause 5 seconds.)

Look at line 13 on your worksheet. (Pause slightly.) If the number in the right-hand box is larger than the number in the left-hand circle, add 4 to the number in the left-hand circle, and change the number in the circle to this number. (Pause 8 seconds.) Then write "C" next to the new number. (Pause slightly.) Otherwise, write "A" next to the number in the smaller box. (Pause 3 seconds.) Now on your answer sheet, darken the space for the number-letter combination that is in the box or circle in which you just wrote. (Pause 5 seconds.)

Look at line 14 on your worksheet. (Pause slightly.) Draw a line under the middle number on the line. (Pause 2 seconds.) Now on your answer sheet, find the number under which you just drew the line and darken space "D" as in dog for that number. (Pause 5 seconds.)

Look at line 15 on your worksheet. (Pause slightly.) Write a "B" as in baker in the third circle. (Pause 2 seconds.) Now on your answer sheet, find the number in that circle and darken space "B" as in baker for that number. (Pause 5 seconds.)

Now look at line 15 again. (Pause slightly.) Write a "C" in the last circle. (Pause 2 seconds.) Now on your answer sheet, find the number in that circle and darken space "C" for that number. (Pause 5 seconds.)

Look at the drawings on line 16 on your worksheet. The number in each box is the number of employees in an office. (Pause slightly.) In the box for the office with the smallest number of employees, write on the line the last two figures of the number of employees. (Pause 5 seconds.) Now on your answer sheet, darken the space for the number-letter combination that is in the space in which you just wrote. (Pause 5 seconds.)

Now look at line 17 on your worksheet. (Pause slightly.) Write an "A" on the line next to the right-hand number. (Pause 2 seconds.) Now on your answer sheet, find the space for the number next to which you just wrote and darken space "A." (Pause 5 seconds.)

Look at line 18 on your worksheet. (Pause slightly.) In the fourth box, write the answer to this question: How many feet are in a yard? (Pause 2 seconds.) Now on your answer sheet, darken the space for the number-letter combination that is in the space in which you just wrote. (Pause 5 seconds.)

Look at line 18 again. (Pause slightly.) In the second box, write the number 32. (Pause 2 seconds.) Now on your answer sheet, find the number-letter combination that is in the space in which you just wrote. (Pause 5 seconds.)

END OF EXAMINATION

ANSWER KEY AND EXPLANATIONS

Part One

1. C	25. B	49. C	73. B	97. A
2. B	26. C	50. B	74. C	98. D
3. C	27. E	51. D	75. C	99. E
4. D	28. C	52. D	76. A	100. E
5. B	29. D	53. B	77. C	101. C
6. C	30. B	54. E	78. B	102. A
7. B	31. C	55. B	79. D	103. A
8. C	32. D	56. E	80. A	104. E
9. E	33. A	57. B	81. B	105. C
10. B	34. A	58. C	82. E	106. B
11. B	35. B	59. E	83. B	107. D
12. D	36. D	60. E	84. C	108. A
13. E	37. D	61. B	85. D	109. A
14. A	38. A	62. B	86. E	110. B
15. E	39. E	63. D	87. D	111. C
16. B	40. C	64. C	88. C	112. A
17. B	41. D	65. C	89. A	113. E
18. A	42. C	66. D	90. B	114. A
19. D	43. B	67. A	91. D	115. D
20. B	44. B	68. B	92. A	116. A
21. B	45. E	69. E	93. C	117. E
22. A	46. E	70. C	94. C	118. E
23. A	47. C	71. C	95. C	119. C
24. B	48. B	72. B	96. C	120. B

Part One

1. **The correct answer is (C).** Flexible means *adjustable* or *pliable*. An office that offers flexible hours may operate from 6 a.m. to 10 p.m.

2. **The correct answer is (B).** An option is a *choice*. When you cast your vote, you are exercising your option.

3. **The correct answer is (C).** To verify is to *check the accuracy of* or to *confirm*. A notary stamp verifies that the signature on the document is the signature of the person named.

4. **The correct answer is (D).** Indolent means *idle* or *lazy*. An indolent person is not likely to become a productive employee.

5. **The correct answer is (B).** Respiration is *breathing*. Respiration is the process by which animals inhale and exhale air.

6. **The correct answer is (C).** The correct spelling is *corrugated*.

7. **The correct answer is (B).** The correct spelling is *accumulation*.

8. **The correct answer is (C).** The correct spelling is *consummation*.

9. **The correct answer is (E).** The correct spelling is *rhetorical*.

10. **The correct answer is (B).** The correct spelling is *height*. This word is one of the few exceptions to the rule: "*I* before *e* except after *c* or when sounded like *ay*." If you do not know the exceptions to the rule, you must memorize them.

11. **The correct answer is (B).** The first two names are exactly alike, but the third name has a different middle initial.

12. **The correct answer is (D).** "Inglese" of the second and third names is different from "Ingles" of the first name.

13. **The correct answer is (E).** Look carefully at the last names: DeAngelis; D'Angelis; DeAngeles.

14. **The correct answer is (A).**

15. **The correct answer is (E).** The first number ends in 342, the second in 432. The first two numbers begin with 263, the third with 236.

16. **The correct answer is (B).** Vigilant means *alert* or *watchful*. A worker must remain vigilant to avoid accidents on the job.

17. **The correct answer is (B).** The term vegetation includes all *plant life*. The jungle is characterized by lush vegetation.

18. **The correct answer is (A).** Marshy means *boggy* or *swampy*. The marshy area around the inlet is a breeding ground for mosquitoes.

19. **The correct answer is (D).** Incidental means *happening in connection with something else* or *casual*. Having the windshield washed is incidental to filling the gas tank and checking the oil.

20. **The correct answer is (B).** A preface is an *introduction*. The preface of the book was very interesting.

21. **The correct answer is (B).** The correct spelling is *facilitate*.

22. **The correct answer is (A).** The correct spelling is *proletarian*.

23. **The correct answer is (A).** The correct spelling is *occasionally*.

24. **The correct answer is (B).** The correct spelling is *essential*.

25. The correct answer is (B). The word *omission is* based upon the word *omit,* which contains only one *"m."* The accent in *omit* falls upon the second syllable, so the final consonant is doubled in adding *-ion.*

26. The correct answer is (C). The "Yoshito" of the second name is different from the first and third name. It is missing the middle "ih" of "Yoshihito."

27. The correct answer is (E). The "Lockner" of the second name is different from the "Lochner" of the first and third names. The middle initial "W" of the third name is different from the middle initial "V" of the first and second names.

28. The correct answer is (C). The "254" of the beginning of the second number is different from the "245" opening of the first and third numbers.

29. The correct answer is (D). The "243" ending of the first number is different from the "423" ending of the second and third numbers.

30. The correct answer is (B). The "2798" opening of the third number is different from the "2789" opening of the first and second numbers.

31. The correct answer is (C). Since manufacturers are assuming risks in attempting to predict what consumers will want, their success depends on the ultimate purchases made by the consumers.

32. The correct answer is (D). See the first sentence.

33. The correct answer is (A). Time and effort cannot be equated. Efficiency must be measured in terms of results.

34. The correct answer is (A). The business of publishing city directories is a private business operated for profit. As such, it is a commercial enterprise.

35. The correct answer is (B). The first sentence of the paragraph makes this statement.

36. The correct answer is (D). The answer suggested by the paragraph is that "white collar" workers work with their pencils and their minds, rather than with their hands and machines.

37. The correct answer is (D). The point of this paragraph is that a business should be prepared to fill unexpected vacancies with pretrained staff members.

38. The correct answer is (A). The paragraph presents the problems of fire in fire-resistant buildings. It suggests that the contents of the buildings may burn even though the structural materials themselves do not, and the ensuing fire may even cause the collapse of the buildings. The paragraph does not compare the problem of fire in fire-resistant buildings with that of fire in ordinary buildings.

39. The correct answer is (E). When Congressman Johnson suggests that money be spent to "get rid of the drug peddlers," he is suggesting eliminating the source of the drugs.

40. The correct answer is (C). The last sentence makes this statement.

41. The correct answer is (D). See the second sentence. Choice (E) may appear to say the same thing, but it is a categorical statement that is not supported by the paragraph in an unqualified way.

42. The correct answer is (C). The search for truth has speeded the progress of civilization. Choice (B) is incorrect in its statement that "civilization did not begin until ...." Civilization moved ahead slowly even before restrictions on learning were removed.

43. **The correct answer is (B).** In saying that investigators must devote themselves completely though the work may not be easy, smooth, or peaceful, the paragraph is saying that they must be persistent in the face of difficulty.

44. **The correct answer is (B).** According to the paragraph, the government can spend only what it obtains from the people. The government obtains money from the people by taxation. If the people are unwilling to pay taxes, the government has no source of funds.

45. **The correct answer is (E).** Foreign-born adults hold on to their old ways, children adapt to the language, clothing, and mannerisms of their playmates. In other words, the children become Americanized more quickly than their parents.

46. **The correct answer is (E).** An announcement is a *public notice*. Everyone heard the announcement about the circus coming to town.

47. **The correct answer is (C).** To prevent is to *keep from happening* or to *hinder*. Prevent bedroom fires by not smoking in bed.

48. **The correct answer is (B).** To notify is *to inform*. They planned to notify the employees of the upcoming pay raise.

49. **The correct answer is (C).** To irritate is to *incite impatience* or *displeasure*, to *exasperate*, or to *annoy*.

50. **The correct answer is (B).** Concisely means *briefly*. The word that means "accurately" is "precisely."

51. **The correct answer is (D).** Correct spellings are
    (A) hoist
    (B) interference
    (C) spatial

52. **The correct answer is (D).** Other correct spellings are
    (A) sufficient
    (B) whether or weather
    (C) actually

53. **The correct answer is (B).** Other correct spellings are
    (A) voluntary
    (C) embodying
    (D) pertinent

54. **The correct answer is (E).** Correct spellings are
    (A) ordinarily
    (B) community
    (C) emphasis
    (D) advent

55. **The correct answer is (B).** Other correct spellings are
    (A) terrific
    (C) eighth
    (D) innocence

56. **The correct answer is (E).** The "901" ending of the first number is different from the "910" ending of the second and third numbers. The third choice begins with "1358" while the first and second begin with "1357."

57. **The correct answer is (B).** The third choice begins with AR5X, while the first and second begin with ARX5.

58. **The correct answer is (C).** "Frederick" of the second name is different from "Frederic" of the first and third names.

59. **The correct answer is (E).** The middle initial of the second name differs from that of the first and third names; the spelling of the last name in the third name differs from that of the first and second names.

60. **The correct answer is (E).** All three last names are different.

61. **The correct answer is (B).** The shore is the *land bordering a body of water*, in other words, the *coast*. The sailors reached the shore in a landing barge.

62. **The correct answer is (B).** An aim is an *intention* or a *goal*. To aim is to direct toward the goal. The aim of the enlistee was to join the navy.

63. **The correct answer is (D).** An acute pain is a *sharp* pain. When I lifted the rock, I felt an acute pain in my back.

64. **The correct answer is (C).** To compel is to *require,* to *coerce,* or to *force*. Compel is a much stronger word than persuade. The law compels all 18-year-old males to register.

65. **The correct answer is (C).** An aroma is a *pleasing smell* or *fragrance*. I love the aroma of fresh-brewed coffee.

66. **The correct answer is (D).** Other correct spellings are
(A) unconsciously
(B) pamphlet
(C) assess

67. **The correct answer is (A).** Other correct spellings are
(B) infallible
(C) eradicated
(D) source

68. **The correct answer is (B).** Other correct spellings are
(A) predecessor
(C) unimpaired
(D) sporadically

69. **The correct answer is (E).** Correct spellings are
(A) impenetrable
(B) recognizable
(C) parasite
(D) business

70. **The correct answer is (C).** Other correct spellings are
(A) across
(B) manifold
(D) expense

71. **The correct answer is (C).** The second name used a capital "S" in DeSean, Lewis is spelled differently, and an "e" is added to Greene.

72. **The correct answer is (B).** "Fernand" of the third name is different from "Fernando" of the first and second names.

73. **The correct answer is (B).** The first and second selections begin with PT190; the third begins with PT109.

74. **The correct answer is (C).** The "287" beginning of the second number is different from the "278" beginning of the first and third numbers.

75. **The correct answer is (C).** The "861" ending of the second number is not the same as the "681" ending of the first and third numbers.

76. **The correct answer is (A).** This application complies with all the rules. It is signed and submitted far more than 20 days before the date requested; includes the proper money order; states purpose, date, time, and expected number of people; and makes a request for permitted hours.

77. **The correct answer is (C).** The $25 must be submitted by money order; a personal check is not acceptable. The CR must be used only until 11 p.m.; 11:30 is too late.

78. **The correct answer is (B).** The rules require 20 days' notice; July 18th is not 20 days from July 1. A time stretch from 2 p.m. to 8:30 p.m. is 6-1/2 hours; this is in excess of the permitted 6 consecutive hours.

79. **The correct answer is (D).** The problem here lies not with the application itself but with a conflict in priorities. You must look not only at the rules but also at the other applications. Application 5 from a social TG asks for the CR during a period of time that overlaps with that of the athletic TG's request. Since social TG's have priority over athletic TG's, the fourth application must be denied.

80. **The correct answer is (A).** This request complies with all the rules.

81. **The correct answer is (B).** Rule 1 allows for no exceptions.

82. **The correct answer is (E).** Rule 3 requires that appointments must be at least four days apart unless the dentist consents otherwise. Appointments on three consecutive days must clearly be denied without the dentist's consent.

83. **The correct answer is (B).** Rule 6 is very clear on this point.

84. **The correct answer is (C).** Rule 2 requires that the name of the practitioner (doctor) appear on every prescription label. The telephone number of the pharmacy is not required, though it generally is preprinted on the labels along with name and address.

85. **The correct answer is (D).** The directions for use must appear on the label for all prescription drugs. The pharmacist's name must be recorded on the prescription for the barbiturate, not on the label. The requirement is that prescriptions must be kept on file for at least two years; there is no limit.

86. **The correct answer is (E).** You must write your own name and the date on the prescription when refilling the prescription for a barbiturate. The date of original filling and the name of that pharmacist should already be on the prescription.

87. **The correct answer is (D).** Rule 1 is clear on this point.

88. **The correct answer is (C).** The doctor's name and directions for use go on all prescription labels. The second part of Rule 2 requires that barbiturates prescribed for a dog must be labeled with that information.

89. **The correct answer is (A).** Only the prescription for barbiturates need be signed by the dispensing pharmacist. The other choices refer to rules that govern all prescriptions.

90. **The correct answer is (B).** Only this choice includes items that must appear on all labels.

91. **The correct answer is (D).** To accentuate is to *stress, emphasize,* or *intensify.* Life is more pleasant when those we deal with accentuate the positive.

92. **The correct answer is (A).** Banal means *insipid* or *commonplace.* His commentary was so banal that I had to stifle many yawns.

93. **The correct answer is (C).** One who is incorrigible *cannot be changed or corrected;* the person is *irreformable.* Incorrigible offenders should be sentenced to prison for life.

94. **The correct answer is (C).** Notorious means *well known,* generally in an unfavorable sense. The face on the poster was that of a notorious bank robber.

95. **The correct answer is (C).** A crevice is a *narrow opening* or *crack.* The climbers caught their axes in several crevices in the rocks.

96. **The correct answer is (C).** The correct spelling is *irrigation.*

97. **The correct answer is (A).** The correct spelling is *aquarium.*

98. **The correct answer is (D).** The correct spelling is *deodorant*.

99. **The correct answer is (E).**

100. **The correct answer is (E).**

101. **The correct answer is (C).** "Franklyn" of the second name is different from "Franklin" of the first and third names.

102. **The correct answer is (A).**

103. **The correct answer is (A).**

104. **The correct answer is (E).** The three numbers end 2958, 9258, and 2758.

105. **The correct answer is (C).** The first and third numbers end 1695; the second ends 6195.

106. **The correct answer is (B).** Uniform means *all the same, consistent,* or *unchanging*. The cyclist pedaled at a uniform rate.

107. **The correct answer is (D).** To unite is to *put together,* to *combine,* or to *join*. At their marriage, two people unite to create a family.

108. **The correct answer is (A).** Gratitude is the *state of being grateful* or *thankfulness*. In gratitude for his good health, he made a donation to his church.

109. **The correct answer is (A).** Embellish means *to exaggerate*. She embellished the truth when she told him how much money she earned.

110. **The correct answer is (B).** To assemble is to *congregate,* to *convene,* or to *bring together*. During a fire drill, we assemble the whole school on the front lawn.

111. **The correct answer is (C).** The correct spelling is *pastime*.

112. **The correct answer is (A).** The correct spelling is *hindrance*.

113. **The correct answer is (E).**

114. **The correct answer is (A).** The correct spelling is *dilettante*.

115. **The correct answer is (D).** The correct spelling is *supersede*.

116. **The correct answer is (A).**

117. **The correct answer is (E).** The three numbers end in 0527, 5027, and 0537.

118. **The correct answer is (E).** The second name is Sr., while the first and third names are Jr. The third surname begins with "Mac," while the first and second names begin with "Mc."

119. **The correct answer is (C).** The first and third numbers are identical; the second number differs in a number of digits.

120. **The correct answer is (B).** "Randolphe" in the third name is different from "Randolph" of the first and second names.

Part Two

1. Ⓐ Ⓑ Ⓒ Ⓓ Ⓔ	31. Ⓐ Ⓑ Ⓒ Ⓓ Ⓔ	61. Ⓐ Ⓑ Ⓒ Ⓓ Ⓔ
2. Ⓐ Ⓑ Ⓒ Ⓓ Ⓔ	32. Ⓐ Ⓑ Ⓒ Ⓓ ●	62. Ⓐ Ⓑ Ⓒ ● Ⓔ
3. Ⓐ Ⓑ Ⓒ ● Ⓔ	33. Ⓐ Ⓑ Ⓒ Ⓓ Ⓔ	63. Ⓐ Ⓑ Ⓒ Ⓓ Ⓔ
4. Ⓐ Ⓑ Ⓒ Ⓓ ●	34. Ⓐ Ⓑ Ⓒ Ⓓ Ⓔ	64. Ⓐ Ⓑ Ⓒ Ⓓ Ⓔ
5. Ⓐ Ⓑ Ⓒ Ⓓ Ⓔ	35. Ⓐ ● Ⓒ Ⓓ Ⓔ	65. Ⓐ Ⓑ Ⓒ Ⓓ Ⓔ
6. Ⓐ Ⓑ Ⓒ Ⓓ Ⓔ	36. Ⓐ Ⓑ Ⓒ ● Ⓔ	66. ● Ⓑ Ⓒ Ⓓ Ⓔ
7. Ⓐ Ⓑ Ⓒ Ⓓ Ⓔ	37. Ⓐ Ⓑ Ⓒ Ⓓ ●	67. Ⓐ Ⓑ Ⓒ Ⓓ Ⓔ
8. Ⓐ Ⓑ Ⓒ Ⓓ ●	38. Ⓐ Ⓑ Ⓒ Ⓓ Ⓔ	68. Ⓐ Ⓑ Ⓒ Ⓓ Ⓔ
9. Ⓐ Ⓑ Ⓒ Ⓓ ●	39. ● Ⓑ Ⓒ Ⓓ Ⓔ	69. Ⓐ Ⓑ Ⓒ ● Ⓔ
10. ● Ⓑ Ⓒ Ⓓ Ⓔ	40. ● Ⓑ Ⓒ Ⓓ Ⓔ	70. Ⓐ Ⓑ Ⓒ Ⓓ Ⓔ
11. Ⓐ Ⓑ Ⓒ Ⓓ Ⓔ	41. Ⓐ Ⓑ Ⓒ Ⓓ Ⓔ	71. Ⓐ Ⓑ Ⓒ Ⓓ Ⓔ
12. Ⓐ Ⓑ Ⓒ Ⓓ ●	42. Ⓐ Ⓑ Ⓒ Ⓓ Ⓔ	72. Ⓐ Ⓑ Ⓒ Ⓓ Ⓔ
13. Ⓐ Ⓑ Ⓒ ● Ⓔ	43. Ⓐ Ⓑ Ⓒ Ⓓ Ⓔ	73. Ⓐ Ⓑ Ⓒ ● Ⓔ
14. Ⓐ Ⓑ Ⓒ Ⓓ Ⓔ	44. Ⓐ Ⓑ Ⓒ Ⓓ Ⓔ	74. Ⓐ Ⓑ Ⓒ Ⓓ ●
15. Ⓐ ● Ⓒ Ⓓ Ⓔ	45. ● Ⓑ Ⓒ Ⓓ Ⓔ	75. Ⓐ Ⓑ ● Ⓓ Ⓔ
16. Ⓐ Ⓑ Ⓒ Ⓓ Ⓔ	46. Ⓐ Ⓑ Ⓒ Ⓓ Ⓔ	76. Ⓐ ● Ⓒ Ⓓ Ⓔ
17. Ⓐ Ⓑ Ⓒ Ⓓ Ⓔ	47. Ⓐ Ⓑ Ⓒ Ⓓ Ⓔ	77. Ⓐ Ⓑ Ⓒ Ⓓ Ⓔ
18. Ⓐ Ⓑ Ⓒ Ⓓ Ⓔ	48. Ⓐ Ⓑ Ⓒ Ⓓ Ⓔ	78. Ⓐ Ⓑ Ⓒ Ⓓ Ⓔ
19. Ⓐ Ⓑ Ⓒ Ⓓ Ⓔ	49. Ⓐ Ⓑ Ⓒ Ⓓ Ⓔ	79. Ⓐ Ⓑ Ⓒ Ⓓ Ⓔ
20. Ⓐ Ⓑ ● Ⓓ Ⓔ	50. Ⓐ Ⓑ Ⓒ Ⓓ Ⓔ	80. Ⓐ Ⓑ Ⓒ Ⓓ Ⓔ
21. Ⓐ Ⓑ Ⓒ Ⓓ Ⓔ	51. Ⓐ Ⓑ Ⓒ Ⓓ ●	81. Ⓐ Ⓑ Ⓒ Ⓓ Ⓔ
22. ● Ⓑ Ⓒ Ⓓ Ⓔ	52. ● Ⓑ Ⓒ Ⓓ Ⓔ	82. Ⓐ Ⓑ Ⓒ Ⓓ Ⓔ
23. Ⓐ Ⓑ Ⓒ Ⓓ Ⓔ	53. Ⓐ Ⓑ Ⓒ Ⓓ Ⓔ	83. Ⓐ ● Ⓒ Ⓓ Ⓔ
24. Ⓐ Ⓑ Ⓒ Ⓓ Ⓔ	54. Ⓐ Ⓑ Ⓒ Ⓓ Ⓔ	84. Ⓐ Ⓑ Ⓒ Ⓓ Ⓔ
25. Ⓐ Ⓑ Ⓒ Ⓓ Ⓔ	55. Ⓐ Ⓑ Ⓒ Ⓓ Ⓔ	85. Ⓐ Ⓑ Ⓒ Ⓓ Ⓔ
26. Ⓐ Ⓑ Ⓒ Ⓓ Ⓔ	56. Ⓐ ● Ⓒ Ⓓ Ⓔ	86. Ⓐ Ⓑ Ⓒ Ⓓ Ⓔ
27. Ⓐ Ⓑ Ⓒ Ⓓ Ⓔ	57. Ⓐ Ⓑ ● Ⓓ Ⓔ	87. Ⓐ Ⓑ Ⓒ Ⓓ Ⓔ
28. Ⓐ Ⓑ Ⓒ Ⓓ Ⓔ	58. Ⓐ Ⓑ Ⓒ Ⓓ Ⓔ	88. Ⓐ Ⓑ Ⓒ Ⓓ Ⓔ
29. Ⓐ Ⓑ ● Ⓓ Ⓔ	59. Ⓐ Ⓑ Ⓒ Ⓓ Ⓔ	89. Ⓐ Ⓑ Ⓒ Ⓓ Ⓔ
30. Ⓐ Ⓑ Ⓒ Ⓓ Ⓔ	60. Ⓐ Ⓑ Ⓒ Ⓓ Ⓔ	

answers practice test 2

Part Two

1.   59   35   <u>62</u>   58   <u>8</u>

2.   (___ C)   (*10* A)   (*73* D)   (*12* E)   (___ B)

3.   15 ___*B*___   20 ___*C*___

4.   [83 *B*]   [37 *E*]   [36 *D*]   **CURE   DAMP   BEAR**

5.   A   C   B   <u>A</u>   <u>B</u>   D   C   E   D

6.   [48 ___]   [28 ___]   [22 *A*]   [43 ___]

7.   51 ___*E*___   69 _____   50 _____

8.   (65 ___)   (13 *D*)   (87 ___)   (31 ___)   (17 ___)

9.   [55 ___]   [44 ___]   [74 *E*]   [25 ___]

10.   <u>40</u>   85   17   87   <u>52</u>   55   80   <u>45</u>   <u>75</u>

11.   [65 ___]   [37 ___]   [12 ___]   [4 *E*]

12.   <u>X</u> O O O <u>X</u> O O <u>X</u> <u>X</u> O <u>X</u> O <u>X</u>   *9*

13.

| 78 ___ | 29 C / 25 | 27 ___ | 73 ___ |

14. 88   2   <u>69</u>   84   34

15.

63 ___   38 ___   76 _B_   53 ___   57 _C_

16.

| 435
 _35_ B | 466
 ___ C | 474
 ___ E | 467
 ___ A | 489
 ___ D |

17. 79 _____   39 ___ _A_ _____

18.

| ___ C | _32_ E | ___ A | _3_ D | ___ B |

APPENDIXES

Career Information Resources

Finding a job is very often a combination of luck, direction, and skill. Sometimes it seems as though you simply stumble upon an opening that seems perfect for you; other times you'll find that you need to conduct a great deal of research to find what you're interested in.

If you want to become a public safety dispatcher, you may not know where to look for the type of openings that will likely yield success. The best places to start your search for dispatcher opportunities are your local police and fire departments. The following tips will help you make the most of your time and effort as you seek information about public safety dispatcher/911 operator positions.

HOW TO GET A GOVERNMENT JOB

The procedure for seeking a government job varies little from one position to another or from one level of government to another. There are variations in details, of course, but certain steps are common to all. Let's review them here.

The Notice of Examination or Announcement

A Notice of Examination, often called an announcement, will be posted for each government position. Once you find what you're looking for, read it very carefully. Make a copy for yourself if you can; if not, take detailed notes and be sure you've made a note of every detail listed. Each Notice of Examination provides a brief job description, including the title of the job and a description of the basic duties and responsibilities of the position. Based on this description, you can decide whether you want to apply.

If the job appeals to you, concentrate on the following aspects of the Notice of Examination:

- **Education and experience requirements.** If you cannot meet these requirements, do not apply. Government service can be very competitive. The government receives thousands of job applications, and it will not waive requirements for you.

- **Age requirements.** Discrimination based on age is illegal. However, certain types of work demand a great deal of sustained physical effort. These positions carry an entry age limit. If you are already beyond that age, do not apply. If you are too young to qualify but are still interested, ask about the average time span between applying and hiring. It's possible that you may reach the minimum age by the time the position will be filled.

- **Citizenship requirements.** Many government jobs are open to anyone eligible to work in the United States, but all law enforcement jobs and most federal jobs are open only to U.S. citizens. If you are well along in the process of becoming a U.S. citizen and you expect to be naturalized soon, you should ask about your exact status with respect to the job.

- **Residency requirements.** If a Notice of Examination mentions a residency requirement, you must live within the prescribed limits or be willing to move

appendix A

to that area. If you are not willing to live in the area defined on the notice, do not bother to apply for the position.

- **Required forms.** The announcement of the position for which you are applying will specify the form of application you're required to submit. For most federal jobs, you may submit either a resume or the Optional Application for Federal Employment (OF-612, available online at www.opm.gov/forms/pdf_fill/of612.pdf). For other than federal jobs, the *Notice of Examination* may tell you where you must go or whom you need to contact to get the necessary paperwork. Make sure you get everything you need. The application might be a simple form that asks for nothing more than name, address, citizenship, and Social Security number, or it may be a more complex form, such as an Experience Paper. As the name implies, an Experience Paper requires extensive information about your education, job training and experience, and life experiences. Typically, an Experience Paper does not ask for identification by name, gender, or race; the only identifying mark is your Social Security number. This is done to avoid bias of any sort to enter into the weighting of responses. The Experience Paper generally follows a short form of application that requires your name. When the rating process is completed, the two forms are matched by Social Security number.

- **Filing date, place, and fee.** There is great variation in this area. Some openings allow you to file your application at any time; others state a specific filing period or deadline. For the latter, filing too early or too late disqualifies your application. Sometimes it is sufficient to have your application postmarked by the last day for filing, but more often, your application must be *received* by that date. If you are submitting your application by mail, allow five full business days for it to arrive on time. The address to which you send your application will be stated in the notice. Most applications may be filed by mail, but occasionally in-person filing is specified. Follow these directions precisely. Federal and postal positions require no filing fee, but most other government jobs charge a fee for processing applications—and these fees vary.

- **How to qualify.** This portion of the notice explains the basis by which a candidate will be chosen. There are two types of qualifying scores. Some scores are the result of the total of weighted education and experience factors. This is called an "unassembled exam" score because candidates for the position do not assemble in one place to take a qualifying test. Instead, the score is based on your responses on the application and supplementary forms. (Obviously, though, to receive full credit for your education, experience, and accomplishments, you must fill out these forms completely.) A Notice of Examination may state that a qualifying exam is necessary in addition to an unassembled, written, or performance test. Alternatively, the notice may inform you of a competitive exam that consists of a written, performance, or combined test. Depending on the notice, the competitive exam may be described in very general terms or in great detail; in some cases, a few sample questions are included. If the date of the assembled exam has been set, that date will appear on the notice. Make sure you write it down.

Once you have the proper application forms, photocopy them, then use the photocopies as your worksheet. This way, you can correct mistakes or make changes before you transfer your information to the original. Do your best to fit what you have to say into the space allowed. Do not exaggerate, but be sure to give yourself credit for responsibilities you have assumed, for cost-saving ideas you may have devised for a previous employer, or for any other accomplishments. Be clear and thorough in communicating what you have learned and what you can do.

When you are satisfied with your draft, copy the application onto the original form(s). Be sure to include any required documentation. However, do not send more "evidence" than is truly needed to support your claims of qualification. Your application must be complete according to the requirements of the announcement, but it should not be overwhelming. You want to command attention by conforming to requirements, not by overdoing it.

Check all forms for neatness and completeness, and sign wherever indicated. Attach the fee, if required. Then mail or personally file the application on time.

When the civil service commission or personnel office to which you submitted your application receives it, an official will date, stamp, log, and open your file. The office may acknowledge receipt with more forms, with sample exam questions, or with a simple notice of receipt. It's not uncommon, however, to hear nothing at all for months.

Eventually, you will receive a testing date or an interview appointment. Write or type these dates on your calendar so that you do not let them slip by. If you receive an admission ticket for an exam, put it in a safe place but keep it in sight so that you don't forget to take it with you to the exam. Begin studying and preparing immediately, if you have not already done so.

If you are called for an exam, arrive promptly and dress appropriately. Neatness is always appropriate; however, you need not "dress up" for a performance or written exam. If you will do manual work for your performance exam, wear clean work clothes. For a written exam, neat, casual clothing will do.

PUBLIC SAFETY DISPATCHER JOBS

The nation's public safety communications centers have been facing staffing shortages for more than a decade. These shortages are the direct result of an overall increase in number of positions, competition with the part of private-sector employment that offers similar but higher-paying jobs, and a large turnover rate for existing employees. As a result, nearly every communications center in the United States is seeking qualified candidates who may not have relevant experience but who can be trained to perform the job. Of course, having prior public contact or public safety experience makes you a more attractive candidate, but most agencies hire dispatchers at entry-level positions, for which only a high school diploma and a clean background check are required.

So where do you start your search for public safety dispatcher openings? Here are some tips:

1. **Find your local dispatch center.** Check a phone directory for the phone number of your local police department. (If your city or town is small, it may not have its own police department, so look for the nearest sheriff's department instead.)

2. **Speak with someone on the job.** Call the non-emergency phone number at the local police or sheriff's department and ask to speak with the dispatch or communications supervisor. (In some areas, this person may be a sergeant or lieutenant.) If he or she is unavailable, ask to speak with a senior dispatcher.

3. **Get all the details you need.** Once you have the appropriate person on the phone, explain politely that you're interested in becoming a dispatcher and would like information. Here are some "starter" questions:

    a. Are you presently hiring? If not, when do you expect to be doing so?

    b. What are the requirements in your department for becoming a dispatcher?

    c. Is a typing certificate required? If so, where can I get one? (Some agencies will accept typing certificates only from certain certifying companies.)

    d. Are training courses available for preparing to become a dispatcher? If so, where can I find them?

    e. Does your agency allow people who are interested in being dispatchers to observe workers on the job? If so, how can I arrange to do so?

JOB REQUIREMENTS FOR PUBLIC SAFETY DISPATCHERS

Many states hold dispatchers to the same hiring standards as law officers—and every city, county, and state has different policies. For this reason, try to be as flexible as you can about meeting specific requirements.

Any or all of the following may be required of applicants seeking public safety dispatcher positions:
- an exam (may be written, computerized, or oral)
- an interview (typically with a panel of officials)
- a medical exam
- a psychological exam
- a polygraph test
- a background investigation
- an interview with the communications manager, police chief, or sheriff

Public Safety Dispatcher Job Resources
- Job listings are posted on the Web sites of the following organizations: National Emergency Number Association (www.nena.org); Association of Public-Safety Communications Officials (www.apcointl.org); *9-1-1 Magazine* (www.9-1-1magazine. com); *DISPATCH Magazine On-line* (www.911dispatch.com); and Jobs in 911 (www. jobsin911.com).
- The *Occupational Outlook Handbook,* published by the Bureau of Labor Statistics (BLS), posts an annual analysis of job availability. This and other useful information can be viewed online at http://stats.bls.gov/oco (http://stats.bls.gov/oco/ocos138.htm for information specific to public safety dispatchers). For current pay rates, check the Bureau of Labor Statistics' Occupational Employment Statistics page at www. bls.gov/oes. Search on this page for the phrase "public safety dispatchers" to find the latest salary and job outlook information.
- Enter the search term "public safety dispatcher" into your favorite search engine to find hundreds of sites with information on agency job descriptions and job openings in the field.
- The O*NET OnLine Web site (http://online.onetcenter.org) has occupational information about dispatching, including an interesting list of skills, abilities, and other requirements, at online.onetcenter.org/link/summary/43-5031.00.
- *DISPATCH Magazine On-line* (www.911dispatch.com) provides facts and figures about public safety dispatchers as well as current job listings.
- The *Journal of Emergency Medical Services (JEMS)*, online at www.jems.com, lists current salary surveys that include call taker and radio dispatcher positions, as well as job listings.
- Check the Web site www.payscale.com for median pay information for public safety dispatchers.

Federal Positions

For federal jobs, start your search with the Office of Personnel Management (OPM). The OPM updates its list of job openings daily. Although it is not responsible for hiring employees, the OPM provides access to each hiring agency in the federal government. From the hiring agencies, you can acquire specific details about each open position. On the OPM Web site, www.opm.gov, click on "Job Seekers" under the heading "Browse by Audience."

You can also access thousands of federal job announcements directly by checking out the official job Web site of the U.S. Federal Government: www.usajobs.gov. The site allows you to search for positions by agency, location, occupation, keyword, title, series number, salary range, and many other specifications. You can find out how federal jobs get filled, learn more about federal hiring processes, and get tips on building your resume, interviewing successfully, and answering a posted position's Knowledge, Skills, and Abilities (KSA) requirements. If you create a free account on the Web site, you can post your resume online, apply for jobs electronically, and received automated job alerts for updated listings. USAJOBS also provides a wealth of information on special opportunities available to military veterans, students, disabled persons, and senior workers, as well as job opportunities with international organizations.

Another excellent source of job information is the *Federal Jobs Digest*, a biweekly newspaper that lists thousands of government jobs in the United States and in foreign countries. The newspaper's companion Web site, www.jobsfed.com, also features thousands of job listings at any one time. The site also offers searches by occupation and state and allows you to set up an "automated search" using location, salary range, occupation, and keywords.

You might also look under "U.S. Government" in the blue pages of your local telephone directory to find the nearest Office of Personnel Management or Federal Job Information Center. By calling this number you may receive automated information pertinent to your own area, or you may be directed to a center where you can get printed materials or conduct a search using a computer touch screen.

State Positions

Every state has its own official Web site. In most cases, you can reach these sites quickly by using either the naming convention www.state.__.us or www. __.gov, with the two-letter postal code of the state or the state name in place of the blank. For example, if you want to search for job openings with the state of Arizona, you type "www.state.az.us." If you're looking for job openings with the state of Oregon, you type "www.oregon.gov." Note that a few state Web sites, such as Florida's, deviate from this convention.

The following is a list of current Web addresses for each state's official site. Keep in mind that these addresses occasionally change and that this may have occurred after this book went to press.

- **Alabama:** www.state.al.us
- **Alaska:** www.state.ak.us
- **Arizona:** www.state.az.us
- **Arkansas:** www.state.ar.us
- **California:** www.state.ca.us
- **Colorado:** www.state.co.us
- **Connecticut:** www.state.ct.us
- **Delaware:** www.state.de.us
- **District of Columbia:** www.dc.gov
- **Florida:** www.myflorida.com
- **Georgia:** www.georgia.gov
- **Hawaii:** www.state.hi.us
- **Idaho:** www.state.id.us
- **Illinois:** www.state.il.us
- **Indiana:** www.state.in.us
- **Iowa:** www.iowa.gov
- **Kansas:** www.kansas.gov
- **Kentucky:** www.kentucky.gov
- **Louisiana:** www.state.la.us
- **Maine:** www.state.me.us
- **Maryland:** www.maryland.gov
- **Massachusetts:** www.state.ma.us
- **Michigan:** www.state.mi.us
- **Minnesota:** www.state.mn.us
- **Mississippi:** www.ms.gov
- **Missouri:** www.mo.gov
- **Montana:** www.mt.gov
- **Nebraska:** www.state.ne.us
- **Nevada:** www.nv.gov
- **New Hampshire:** www.state.nh.us
- **New Jersey:** www.state.nj.us
- **New Mexico:** www.state.nm.us
- **New York:** www.state.ny.us
- **North Carolina:** www.ncgov.com
- **North Dakota:** www.nd.gov
- **Ohio:** www.state.oh.us
- **Oklahoma:** www.state.ok.us
- **Oregon:** www.oregon.gov

- **Pennsylvania:** www.state.pa.us
- **Rhode Island:** www.state.ri.us
- **South Carolina:** www.sc.gov
- **South Dakota:** www.state.sd.us
- **Tennessee:** www.state.tn.us
- **Texas:** www.state.tx.us
- **Utah:** www.utah.gov
- **Vermont:** www.vermont.gov
- **Virginia:** www.state.va.us
- **Washington:** www.access.wa.gov
- **West Virginia:** www.wv.gov
- **Wisconsin:** www.wisconsin.gov
- **Wyoming:** www.state.wy.us

Local Positions

Browse your state's Web site for city and county job openings. If you live in a metropolitan area, your city may have its own Web site. Use a popular search engine such as Google. com, Yahoo! Search, or Ask.com to locate other job-related sites. Using search terms such as *jobs*, *employment*, *labor*, *business*, *help wanted*, and so on and then adding to the term your specific city or state will give you an extensive number of suggested sites. For example, you might enter *"public safety dispatcher" Miami* to find positions available in Miami, Florida.

Be sure to investigate whether your city has a civil service publication that lists upcoming job announcements. In New York City, for example, *The Chief-Leader* is the primary source for learning about the most recent openings for civil service positions. (You can access this publication at www.thechief-leader.com.) You can also find information about state and federal jobs in local newspapers (online and in print) in the Help Wanted section.

The Private Sector

Although public safety dispatcher/911 operator positions do exist in the private sector, you are less likely to find openings because the demand for such work is lower than that of government agencies. However, if you already have experience as a public safety dispatcher/911 operator and want a career change, or you are seeking a job that requires similar skills, your experience will be invaluable in a private-sector job search. After all, what employer wouldn't want to hire a person with experience in handling the day-to-day, moment-to-moment pressure that comes with being a public safety dispatcher?

If you're certain that you want to work in the private sector, consider some of these related jobs:

- **Private ambulance service dispatchers** perform duties that are very similar to those of public safety dispatchers and 911 operators. They relay requests for patient transports to Emergency Medical Technicians (EMTs), handle multiple phone lines, take and route messages, map directions, handle paperwork efficiently and accurately, and have a broad knowledge of medical forms, documents, and procedures. Some of these positions require that candidates have EMT or Emergency Medical Dispatch (EMD) certification.

- **Truck dispatchers** work for local and long-distance trucking companies. They coordinate the movement of trucks and freight between cities, direct pickup and delivery activities of drivers, receive customer requests for freight pickup and delivery, consolidate freight orders into truckloads for specific destinations, assign drivers and trucks, and draw up routes and pickup and delivery schedules.

- **Bus dispatchers** ensure that local and long-distance buses stay on schedule. They handle problems that may disrupt service, and they dispatch other buses or arrange for repairs to restore service and schedules.

- **Train dispatchers** ensure the timely and efficient movement of trains according to orders and schedules. They must be aware of track switch positions, track maintenance areas, and the location of other trains running on the track.

- **Taxicab dispatchers**, or "starters," dispatch taxis in response to requests for service, and they maintain logs on all road service calls.

- **Tow-truck dispatchers** take calls for emergency road service. They relay the nature of the problem to a nearby service station or a tow-truck service and see that the road service is completed.

- **Gas and water service dispatchers** monitor gas lines and water mains, and they send out service trucks and crews to handle emergencies.

All of these are real possibilities for individuals accustomed to communicating with others and managing high-pressure situations.

Employment agencies and job postings are the two most common ways of finding positions in the private sector. Find a local agency and make an appointment to speak with someone about the position you're seeking. Bring two or three copies of your resume with you. Remember that the employment counselor is the first interview of your job search, so dress appropriately and be sure you've prepared for the interview by studying the types of jobs in which you're interested.

Another widely used method of searching for a job is to check postings in print and online newspapers and on career search Web sites. In some cases, you'll be directed to an employment agency to apply for a position. In other cases, you'll be able to apply directly with the company offering the position, and it's likely that you'll be able to submit your resume electronically at the same time. Remember that your phone call, cover letter, and resume make an important first impression on those who do the hiring—so be sure that you communicate in a professional manner at all times.

The following list of career-oriented Web sites is just a sampling of the many job-search resources available online:

- www.careerbuilder.com
- www.simplyhired.com
- www.careerpath.com
- www.hotjobs.com
- www.jobsearchusa.org
- www.jobsonline.net
- www.lawenforcementjobs.com
- www.monster.com
- www.vault.com
- www.wetfeet.com

MASTERING THE INTERVIEW

If you do not need to take an exam and you are called directly to an interview for a public safety dispatcher position, what you wear is very important. Take special care to present a businesslike and professional appearance. A neat and modest dress, slacks and a blouse, or a skirted suit is fine for women; men should wear a suit or slacks, a jacket, and a dress shirt and tie.

If you are contacted for an interview, you are most likely under serious consideration for the position. This doesn't mean that no competition exists for the job—but you are clearly qualified, and your skills and background have appealed to someone in the hiring office. The purpose of the interview is probably to gather information about the following:

- **Your knowledge.** The interviewer wants to know what you know about the area in which you will work. You may be asked questions that probe your knowledge of the agency for which you are interviewing. Make sure you've done your "homework" and educate yourself about the functions and role of the agency.

- **Your judgment.** You may be faced with hypothetical situations (job-related or personal). The interviewer(s) may pose questions that begin with the phrase "What would you do if . . . ?" Think carefully before answering. Be decisive and diplomatic when you reply. There are no "right answers," and the interviewer is aware that you are being put on the spot. How well you handle this type of questioning will indicate how flexible and mature you are.

- **Your personality.** If you are offered the job, you will have to be trained and supervised, and you will be working closely with others. What is your general work attitude? How well do you fit in? The interviewer will make judgments in these areas based on general conversation with you and on your responses to specific lines of questioning. Be pleasant, polite, and open in your responses, but do not volunteer a great deal of extra information. Stick to the subjects introduced by the interviewer. Answer fully, but resist the temptation to ramble.

- **Your attitude toward work conditions.** This is a practical concern. If the job requires frequent travel for extended periods, how do you feel about travel? What is your family's attitude toward your being away from home frequently? The interviewer wants to assess whether you'll be unhappy enough about extensive travel to quit the job—in which case your training will have been a waste of time and money. The interviewer also wants to know how you will react to the prospect of working overtime or irregular shifts.

WHAT TO EXPECT ON THE MEDICAL EXAMINATION

A medical exam is self-explanatory. If there are eyesight or hearing requirements for the position, your eyesight and hearing must be checked against agency standards. If the job requires standing, lifting, or running, you must be medically able to perform all of these activities. Because all government employers afford some sort of health coverage, the hiring agency must be assured of the general health of each employee, or at least have full awareness of current or potential health problems. Drug testing is often included in the medical exam. This is legal if applied routinely and equally to all applicants, and if notice is given to applicants beforehand.

The Physical Examination

Physical performance testing is limited to applicants for physically demanding jobs. Police officers, firefighters, and correction officers, for example, must be able to run, climb, and carry, often under the pressure of personal danger and of the immediate situation. Mail handlers and sanitation workers must be able to lift and carry heavy loads, one after the other. Usually, the physical performance test is a qualifying test—either you can complete it successfully or you cannot. If speed is a crucial aspect of a job, the physical test may be competitively scored and entered into the rating the candidate earns for placement on the certification list.

The Psychological Interview

For a public safety dispatcher/911 operator position, you will undergo psychological interview. This interview differs from the general information interview or the final hiring and placement interview in that the aim is to evaluate your behavior under stress.

Not all applicants for government jobs are subjected to a psychological interview. It is typically limited to individuals who must carry a weapon, make quick decisions in dangerous situations, or who may find themselves under interrogation by hostile forces. This includes police officers, firefighters, CIA agents, and Drug Enforcement Agency agents, to name a few. This type of position requires that you perform your job without "cracking" emotionally under the strain. Although public safety dispatchers work in far safer conditions, the stressful environment associated with the job usually warrants a psychological interview or test for prospective candidates.

A REWARD FOR PATIENCE

The government hiring process can be lengthy. Officials sort through hundreds of applications to eliminate unqualified applicants. They must weigh education and experience factors of prospective applicants, administer and score exams, conduct interviews, evaluate medical exams and physical performance tests, and verify applicants' references. And after all of this, the government agency must have the funds to fill vacancies. Going through a government job-seeking process may take up to eighteen months from the time you apply until you are hired.

This is the main reason why you should carefully consider whether you want to leave a job that you already have before you receive a formal offer to work as a public safety dispatcher/911 operator. Likewise, don't abandon your search for a government job simply because you've grown tired of waiting to hear about a position. Do not become discouraged by the long process. When you do receive that job offer, the door will open to a good income, many benefits, and great job security.

Public Safety Dispatcher Glossary

ACD: Automatic Call Distributor.

ALI: Automatic Location Identification. In E-911 systems, the caller's billing address is displayed on a screen or console. If the phone number is included, it is called **ANI-ALI**.

ALS: Advanced Life Support.

ANI: Automatic Number Identification. In E-911 systems, the caller's telephone number is displayed on a screen or console. If the address is also included, it is called ANI-**ALI**.

ATF: Shortened acronym denoting the Bureau of Alcohol, Tobacco, Firearms and Explosives, a division of the U.S. Department of Justice. The Bureau's primary duty is to investigate illegal use and possession of federally controlled firearms, such as machine guns and explosives.

CAD: Computer Aided Dispatch, a computer system that enables public safety dispatchers to manage 911 calls. The system locates the addresses of 911 callers, maintains status on units available, relays information to officers, and provides various reports.

Call Check: An instant playback recorder used by dispatchers to verify information they receive during calls for assistance. There are two types of call checks: tape and digital memory.

CAP: Civil Air Patrol, also known as the U.S. Air Force Auxiliary. CAP consists of volunteers—some with their own aircraft—who assist in locating downed aircraft and rescuing occupants of the aircraft.

Comm Center: Communications Center.

Consolidated Comm Center: A Communications Center that includes fire, EMS, and/or police all together.

CPS: Child Protective Services, a division of **DSHS** charged with investigating the abuse of minors. CPS places children in foster homes when no parent or guardian is available to care for them.

CTCSS: Continuous Tone Coded Squelch System. Used in public safety radio communications to filter out other users when more than one group is using the same channel.

DEM: Department of Emergency Management or Division of Emergency Management. The part of a city, town, or county government that coordinates disaster planning and resources.

DES: Department of Emergency Services. The part of a city, town, or county government that coordinates disaster planning and resources.

DHS: U.S. Department of Homeland Security, an agency of the U.S. government charged with preventing and deterring terrorist attacks and protecting against and responding to threats and hazards to the nation.

DLS: Dispatch Life Support, the provision of life-supporting advice and directions by telephone to a layperson awaiting the arrival of emergency responders to an out-of-hospital emergency.

DOE: The U.S. Department of Energy, an agency of the U.S. Government charged with overseeing the operation of nuclear reactor facilities and securing radioactive and weapons-grade materials such as plutonium.

DOT: The U.S. Department of Transportation, an agency of the U.S. Government charged with ensuring safe and efficient transportation systems to meet national interests. Agencies that operate under DOT include the Federal Aviation Administration (**FAA**), the National Highway Traffic Safety Administration (**NHTSA**), and the Federal Highway Administration (**FHWA**). Each state also has its own department of transportation, which maintains interstate highways and marine highways. These agencies' responsibilities vary by state.

DSHS: Department of Social and Health Services (in some states called the Department of Health and Human Services or the Department of Public Health and Human Services). A state department responsible for public services such as emergency medical assistance, child protective service, welfare, radiation control, and public health.

EMD: Emergency Medical Dispatch, a practice in which dispatchers provide medical information and instructions by phone to civilians before first responders arrive at the scene of an accident or disaster.

EMS: Emergency Medical Services, a term used to describe a branch of emergency services dedicated to providing out-of-hospital acute medical care and/or transport to definitive care to patients who have an illness or injury that the patient or medical practitioner believes constitutes a medical emergency. EMS may also be known locally as a first aid squad, an emergency or rescue squad, an ambulance squad or corps, or a life squad.

EMT: Emergency Medical Technician. An EMT is an emergency responder trained to provide immediate care for sick or injured people and to transport them to medical facilities.

EMT-P: An **EMT** with paramedic certification.

EOC: Emergency Operations Center, a central command and control facility responsible for carrying out the principles of emergency preparedness and emergency management or disaster management functions at a strategic level in an emergency situation. The EOC ensures the continuity of operation of a company, political subdivision, or other organization.

FAA: Federal Aviation Administration, a division of the U.S. Department of Transportation (**DOT**) charged with providing the safest, most efficient aerospace system possible.

FBI: Federal Bureau of Investigation, a division of the U.S. Department of Justice responsible for investigating federal crimes. The FBI also operates the National Crime Information Center (**NCIC**), which maintains histories of criminals.

FEMA: Federal Emergency Management Agency. An agency of the U.S. Department of Homeland Security (**DHS**) that coordinates nationwide communications, resources, and training for disasters. FEMA also operates the National Fire Academy of the U.S. Fire Administration (**USFA**).

FHWA: The Federal Highway Administration, a division of the U.S. Department of Transportation (**DOT**) that carries out federal highway programs in partnership with state and local agencies to meet the nation's transportation needs.

FPS: Federal Protective Service. A police agency of the U.S. General Services Administration that provides law enforcement and security services to tenants and visitors of all non-military federally owned and leased facilities nationwide.

IACP: International Association of Chiefs of Police.

IAEM: International Association of Emergency Managers.

ICE: U.S. Immigration and Customs Enforcement, an agency of the **DHS.** ICE was established to protect national security and uphold public safety by targeting criminal networks and terrorist organizations seeking to exploit vulnerabilities in the U.S. immigration system, in financial networks, along the nation's borders, and at federal facilities.

IAFC: International Association of Fire Chiefs.

ICS: Incident Command Center.

Logging Recorder: A large reel-to-reel tape recorder with multiple channels used for recording time, date, telephone, and radio traffic. Most tapes for logging recorders can hold 24 hours of data.

MAST: Military Aid to Safety and Traffic. A function of the U.S. Army Aviation Unit, MAST provides helicopter evacuation of injured or sick persons in need of long-distance transportation to a medical facility.

MIS: Management Information System.

Monitor: To listen to a channel before transmitting in an effort to prevent co-channel interference. If receiver is **CTCSS**-equipped, the CTCSS should be disabled so that the user can hear other group exchanges on the channel.

NCIC: National Crime Information Center, a program conducted by the **FBI** consisting of a computerized index of criminal justice information. NCIC is available to federal, state, and local law enforcement and other criminal justice agencies at all times.

NHTSA: National Highway Traffic Safety Administration, a division of the U.S. Department of Transportation (**DOT**) charged with saving lives, preventing injuries, and reducing economic costs that result from road traffic accidents through education, research, the establishment of safety standards, and enforcement activity.

OES: Office of Emergency Services (in some places called the Office of Emergency Management or the Office of Emergency Shelter and Services). The office or department in a city, town, or county that coordinates disaster planning and resources.

Operation Secure. A nationwide communications network of high-frequency radio bands managed by **FEMA.** All state **EOC**s have these radios.

ORI: Originating or issuing agency.

POV: Privately owned vehicle.

PSAP: Public safety answering point; the location where 911 calls are received and dispatched.

REACT: Radio Emergency Action & Coordination Team. A nationwide group of volunteers who monitor citizen band radio channel 9 for emergency communications from motorists who need assistance.

TTD: Telecommunication Device for the Deaf, sometimes called **TTY** (telephone typewriter or teletypewriter), although TTY is also a term used for teletypes in general. An electronic device for text communication via a telephone line, used when one or more of the communicating parties has hearing or speech difficulties.

TTY: See **TTD.**

USFA: U.S. Fire Administration, an entity of the Department of Homeland Security's Federal Emergency Management Agency (**FEMA**). USFA's mission is to foster a solid foundation in prevention, preparedness, and response by providing national leadership to local fire and emergency services.

VoBB: See **VoIP.**

VoIP: Voice over Internet protocol. This is a general term for a family of transmission technologies that deliver voice communications over IP networks, such as the Internet or other packet-switched networks. Other terms that are synonymous with VoIP are IP telephony, Internet telephony, voice over broadband (**VoBB**), broadband telephony, and broadband phone.

400 Frequently Misspelled Words

This list consists of words that have proven troublesome for most test takers and that frequently appear on civil service exam spelling sections. Ask a family member or friend to read this list to you and allow you time to write each word. Then compare your written list with the printed one. Mark with an *X* the words you misspelled and the ones you spelled correctly but guessed on. Now make a list of all the words you marked with an *X*. For each of these words:

1. **Look** at the word carefully.
2. **Pronounce** each syllable clearly.
3. **Picture** the word in your mind.
4. **Write** the word correctly at least three times.

When you feel confident that you have mastered this list, have a friend test you again. Check to see which words you're still having problems spelling. Repeat the study process and see how many you've mastered.

If you are still having trouble with words you are likely to use often, add them to your "spelling devils" list.

A	amateur	audience	bulletin
aberration	amendment	August	bureau
abscess	American	author	burial
absence	ancestor	available	
abundance	ancient	awkward	**C**
accessible	anecdote		cabinet
accidental	annoyance	**B**	cafeteria
accommodate	Antarctic	bankruptcy	caffeine
accumulation	anticipate	barbarian	calendar
accurately	apparatus	barren	campaign
achievement	apparently	basically	capital
acknowledgment	arctic	beautiful	capitol
acquaint	argue	because	career
address	arraignment	beggar	ceiling
adjunct	arrange	begun	cemetery
affectionate	ascertain	beleaguered	changeable
aggravate	asparagus	besiege	character
aisle	assessment	bewilder	charlatan
alleged	assistance	bicycle	chauffeur
all right	attaché	breathe	chief

chimney	diary	fascinated	heathen
choose	dictatorship	February	heavily
college	difficult	feudal	height
column	dilapidated	fiend	heinous
committal	diphtheria	fierce	heretic
committee	disappearance	financier	heritage
community	disappoint	freight	heroes
competitor	disastrous	Friday	hieroglyphic
confectionery	disease	friend	hindrance
conscience	dismal	forehead	hippopotamus
conscious	dissatisfied	foreign	horrify
consequence	distinguished	foreword	humorous
conquer	doubt	forfeit	hundredth
consul	dying	forward	hygienic
continuous		furniture	hymn
correlation	**E**	further	hypocrisy
council	ecstasy		
counsel	eczema	**G**	**I**
courageous	eight	gaseous	imaginary
criticism	either	gelatin	immediate
crucial	embarrass	geography	imminent
crystallized	eminent	ghost	impartiality
culpable	emphasis	gingham	incongruous
currency	emphatically	glacier	incumbent
curtain	ephemeral	glandular	independent
customer	equipment	gnash	indict
	essential	gonorrhea	inimitable
D	exaggerate	government	instantaneous
dairy	exceed	grammar	integrity
deceit	except	grandeur	intercede
December	exercise	grievous	interference
decide	exhaust	guarantee	interruption
deferred	exhibition	guard	introduce
demur	exhortation	guess	irreparably
derogatory	existence	guidance	
descendant	explain		
desecrated	extension	**H**	**J**
desert	extraordinary	hallelujah	January
desperate	**F**	harassed	jealous
dessert	familiar	hearth	jeopardy
			jewelry

journal
judgment
judicial
justice
justification

K
kernel
kindergarten
kiln
kilometer
kilowatt
kitchen
knee
knot
knowledge

L
laboratory
labyrinth
lacquer
leisure
legible
length
lieutenant
lightning
liquidate
literature
loneliness
loose
lose
lovable

M
maintenance
maneuver
marriage
masquerade
materialize
mathematics

matinee
mechanical
medallion
medicine
medieval
memoir
mischievous
misspell
muscle

N
naturally
necessary
negligible
neither
nickel
niece
ninth
noticeable
nucleus

O
oasis
obligatory
obsolescence
occasion
official
omitted
ordinance
outrageous

P
pamphlet
panicky
parallel
paraphernalia
parliamentary
patient
peculiar
persuade

physician
picnicking
pneumonia
possession
precious
preferred
prejudice
presumptuous
privilege
propaganda
publicity
punctilious
pursuit

Q
quarrel
queue
quiescent
quiet
quite
quotient

R
receipt
recognize
reference
regrettable
rehearsal
relevant
religious
renaissance
repetitious
requirement
resilience
reservoir
resources
restaurant
resurrection
rhetorical

rhythm
ridiculous
routine

S
sacrilegious
scenery
schedule
scissors
secretary
separate
siege
seizure
sophomore
source
sovereign
specialized
specifically
statute
staunch
subversive
succeed
sufficient
surgeon
surgical
surely
stationary
stationery
symmetrical
sympathetic

T
temperamental
temperature
tendency
thorough
through
tomorrow
tragedy
transferred

transient

truculent

Tuesday

typical

U–Z

umbrella

unctuous

undoubtedly

unique

unusual

usage

usual

vacillate

vacuum

valuable

variety

vegetable

veil

vengeance

villain

Wednesday

weight

weird

whether

wholesome

wholly

wield

wouldn't

written

Xerox

xylophone

yacht

yield

zombie